Gene Tunney

Gene Tunney

The Golden Guy Who Licked Jack Dempsey Twice

JOHN JARRETT

ROBSON BOOKS

First published in Great Britain in 2003 by Robson Books,
The Chrysalis Building, Bramley Road, London, W10 6SP

A member of Chrysalis Books plc

All photographs from the author's personal collection except for the following:
Page one (Bottom right), page 4 (inset) and page 7 (inset), which are from the
Chicago Daily News Negatives Collection and reproduced by courtesy of the
Chicago Historical Society.

The author has made every reasonable effort to contact all copyright holders.
Any errors that may have occurred are inadvertent and anyone who for any reason has
not been contacted is invited to write to the publishers so that a full acknowledgement
may be made in subsequent editions of this work.

British Library Cataloguing in Publication Data
A catalogue record for this title is available from the British Library.

ISBN 1 86105 618 4

Typeset by SX Composing DTP, Rayleigh, Essex
Printed by Creative Print & Design (Wales), Ebbw Vale

This book is for Diane and Glenda,
Jeffrey and Derek. My four champions.

Contents

Introduction

The agent says to the artist, 'You just die, I'll do the rest.' It was a bit like that with Gene Tunney as he punched his way to the top of the boxing world. Even after he twice licked Jack Dempsey to become heavyweight champion of the world in that wild and whacky period known as the Roaring Twenties, the prima donna pencil-pushers of the press box couldn't see Tunney, not even with field glasses! Such giants of the sporting pages as Paul Gallico of the *New York Daily News* and Westbrook Pegler of the *Chicago Tribune* freely admitted they sat up nights thinking of ways to belittle the boxer who preferred books to broads and booze.

'There was simply no logic to the reactions which the strange, contradictory personality of Tunney aroused in us,' wrote Gallico. 'On the one hand we bitterly resented Kid Galahad, while on the other we insisted he behave like same. We hated him for not acting boorishly, the way we felt a prizefighter should, and we despised him equally when in another area he was accused of doing so. The poor man could not win.'

Winning was one thing that Gene Tunney was good at. He lost only one of his 83 professional fights, to Harry Greb, and beat Greb four times in subsequent bouts. He won the world title in a stunning upset over the famed and feared Manassa Mauler, Jack Dempsey, America's hero in that rip-roaring lawless decade. And he won the return fight, the Battle of the Long Count, which became a legend in ring annals. He won a million-dollar purse for that fight, something no other prizefighter had aspired to since they fought with bare knuckles on barges.

Gene Tunney kept on winning after the gloves were put away. He won the hand of a beautiful heiress in marriage and raised a fine family. He stepped into the business world to once again become a champion, shifting from the boxing ring to the boardroom, the 'Sock Exchange' to the Stock Exchange. The title of 'former heavyweight champion of the world' opened many doors for the man who started his working life as a clerk in a shipping office.

A sportswriter having lunch with Tunney in a New York restaurant wrote, 'You listened to him talking to a friend and the conversation was all about stock quotations, board meetings, union negotiations, politics, the future of American business. Spicing the table talk was mention of the theatre, the opera, literature, art, science. Tunney listened attentively when it was time to listen and spoke intelligently, even brilliantly, when he felt it was time for him to talk.

'I asked him, "Looking back on all the years, and considering everything you've accomplished, would you say that you felt that you were primarily a prizefighter, or do you feel that you're essentially a businessman?" There was no hesitation in his voice as he spoke. "I am a professional prizefighter. I am a professional prizefighter and I am very proud of it."'

Gene Tunney was a good prizefighter, too. They realised that fact when his ring days were over. Ace trainer Whitey Bimstein: 'Tunney was cool, calm, and collected. Nothing ever bothered him. He was the most underrated heavyweight champion in history and in my book Tunney could have licked them all from Sullivan to Marciano.'

Jack Dempsey: 'Don't let anybody tell you Tunney wasn't a great fighter. I should know. Let me say that Tunney may have defeated me at any time in our careers. On that rainy night in Philadelphia he needed no help. I had one consolation. I had lost to a great fighter, one of the greatest.'

This is his story.

1

The Boy

Growing up in Greenwich Village, Gene Tunney was just like any other kid in that section of New York City. 'Our family knew what poverty meant,' he would recall. 'We had our heartaches, our troubles, our worries, but the Tunneys never complained. We lived a normal life and made the best of things. We had to earn our daily bread before we ate it. There was no coddling, no special care nor affection, just that which every boy and girl living in ordinary surroundings would have.'

James Joseph Tunney was born on 25 May 1897 at 414 West 52nd Street in Manhattan, the second child for John and Mary Tunney. They would be blessed with seven children in all: John, who was tragically killed in a road accident, James Joseph and Tom, who became a detective; Rose, Margaret, Agnes and Mary Assumpta, who became a nun in the Dominican order.

The baby boy destined to become heavyweight boxing champion of the world was only five months old when the family moved to Greenwich Village to live above a grocery store on the corner of Perry and Washington Streets. John and Mary Tunney felt more at home there, in that predominantly Irish neighbourhood. Both were from the Ould Country.

Grandfather John Tunney was born in Killeaden, County Mayo, Ireland, about a mile from Kiltimagh on the road to Bohola. John married Bridget Gill and when they were evicted from his small farm they moved to Kiltimagh. John died at sixty, leaving Bridget with three sons and three daughters.

Finding life difficult with six mouths to feed, Bridget remarried, to Patrick McNicholas of Gouldboy, Kiltimagh, and when she died the entire family emigrated to America, settling in New York City.

John Joseph, the second oldest of the boys, was not keen to see the New World. He had lost his heart to a pretty colleen named Mary Lydon who lived in Gortgoriff, about a mile along the road from Kiltimagh. But when Mary promised to join him in America, John packed his bag and sailed for New York. Mary followed him and they were married not long after she arrived. John was not a big man but he was strong and sturdy, physically suited for his job as a stevedore on the nearby docks, which brought in a weekly average wage of $15. It put food on the table but there was nothing left for luxuries.

James Joseph was still a skinny kid when he acquired the name of Gene. 'To show you how young we were at the time,' he would say many years later, 'my younger brother John couldn't say Jim. When he said my name, it sounded like Gene, and that's what everyone began to call me. I have never been anything but Gene as far back as I can remember, and if somebody called me Jim, I wouldn't even turn around. I wouldn't know they were talking to me.'

Gene's father was a rabid fight fan, according to author Mel Heimer in his 1969 book, *The Long Count*. 'When he could make the time, he went down to Owney Geaghan's boxing club on the Bowery, where John L Sullivan had fought when he first came to New York City, and where John Tunney had even had a bout himself. He took on the house professional and wasn't disgraced in losing, but when he looked at himself in the mirror the next morning, he had two fine, lusty black eyes.'

Young Gene Tunney's interest in boxing was triggered at an early age, as he recalled in his 1933 autobiography, *A Man Must Fight*. 'The first paragraph I ever read I remember distinctly as being part of Bob Edgren's column in the *New York Evening World*. Edgren excited my curious and childish interest with his cartoons of fighters and fights. Long before I was able to read, these drawings had me spellbound. I wanted to learn to read just to know what Edgren was writing about these fascinating pictures. I laboured for days and days and, eventually, with the aid of the nuns at Saint Veronica's Parochial School in New York, who were unconscious of my ambition, I finally deciphered the first paragraph. Edgren became and remained, for many years, my oracle. I believed Edgren to be not only the editor of the "best sporting page in New York" as he advertised the page, but "a Daniel come to judgement."'

Inspired no doubt by his son's avid reading of the daily sports pages, John Tunney presented Gene with a set of boxing gloves on his tenth birthday, saying, 'You look the most likely.' The boy was over the moon, even if his brothers and several pals who were pressed into service as sparring partners by the budding champion did not share his enthusiasm. Gene went to bed that night with a terrific headache and next morning they all had swollen noses and bruised lips – 'proud badges of honour', as he recalled. The daily bouts carried on after school until the gloves literally fell apart. His first punch bag had an even shorter life, which was not surprising since it was no more than an inflated turkey crop that his mother had given him from the Thanksgiving Day bird!

'Though I was not a belligerent kid, I do not think I ever passed a good opportunity to fight,' Gene Tunney wrote in his autobiography, *A Man Must Fight.* (1933), 'One fight lasted three days. My opponent and I met for the first time in front of the White Star Line pier and hammered each other until a policeman chased us. We continued for the next two days, meeting at different places after school was out, each time being chased by a policeman. On the third day, the other youngster decided that he had had enough and quit just before the arm of the law arrived.'

Those early street scuffles were recalled in a 1965 piece in *The Ring*, Ted Carroll writing, 'Gene Tunney, street fighter! One finds it difficult to imagine the dignified, urbane business executive that former undefeated heavyweight champion Gene Tunney turned out to be, a one-time street fighter. But in his younger days on New York's old West Side, roughians, toughs, and bullies found Gene more than a match for them in sidewalk encounters. Tunney lived on the corner of Perry and Washington Streets in New York's Greenwich Village and attended Saint Veronica's Parochial School at Leroy and Washington Streets. The school was some distance away from Tunney's home. Gene had a daily trip of several blocks through "hostile" territory. This meant fighting his way past the tough "neighbours' children" on adjoining blocks who looked upon youngsters from another street as common enemies. Gene never picked a fight or looked for trouble but he bested the brawlers and hooligans who infested the waterfront section so thoroughly. He gained a reputation for never losing a street fight. This proved a factor in directing his footsteps towards professional boxing.'

In those formative years, however, all sports attracted young Tunney. He learned to swim in the Hudson River and to dive from the old barges and tramp steamers moored off the dock at the foot of West 10th Street. 'In those days it was my great boast that I could dive from any place I could climb to,' he would recall. 'Naturally that boast brought me into serious trouble. On one occasion I climbed to the uppermost deck of the old *Majestic* to do a soldier's dive. A soldier's dive used to be made by holding the hands firm to the sides, as a soldier stands to attention, with the head striking the water first. I must have got a slight concussion, for I had a frightful headache for three days.'

Listening to the religious teachings of his mother, and of Father Drain, Brother Anderson and Brother Osborne at Saint Veronica's, the boy curbed his street fighting and channelled his enthusiasm for competition on to the sports field, where he excelled at running, jumping, handball and basketball. At the annual meets of the parochial schools of New York at Clason Point Military Academy, under the jurisdiction of the Christian Brothers, Tunney competed in the running long jump and the 200-yards dash.

'My interest in athletics was great,' he'd say. 'First, because I adored sports and, secondly, because I had an ambition to be well developed physically. I yearned for a healthy, strong athletic body, which I thought a glorious thing. I avoided smoking, late hours, and what habits I thought injurious.'

Lofty ideals indeed for any young man in those days, yet they were recalled by one of Tunney's boyhood pals a few weeks after he shocked the world by taking the heavyweight title off Jack Dempsey in 1926. Gene Boyle told Ed Van Every, veteran boxing writer and sports editor of the *New York Evening World*, 'Although we were all a pretty wild set of young ruffians and as full of spirit as the Old Harry, and Tunney's strength of character and difference from the rest of the boys would have had most of the gang on his neck, yet, somehow, the abnormal cleanness of the boy's mind just seemed something that was a part of the boy and strange to say we never resented it or thought it the least out of place.

'Now, as I think it over, the thing is more puzzling than ever. In a way, Gene was as out of place as a fish in a park lane. All I know is that if some other boy had been such a stickler in the matter of language and deportment, he would have been in danger of getting his head punched. And don't think some of us wouldn't have taken a try at it, even though Gene may have been a bit huskier than most of us.'

'I don't ever recall', said Bill Shea, who lived on the same street as the young Tunney, 'that Gene as a boy ever had to do much fighting. Even the boys from some of the tough neighbourhood gangs made it a point to steer clear of picking on Gene or his friends. Gene never looked for trouble, but he was certainly ready for it when it came his way. He was always handy with his mitts, as Captain Foster of the firehouse near Gene's home will testify, for Gene had the gloves on often with the boys around the firehouse. He was always ready for a bit of sparring and a bit too good in that line for us. And yet I don't think any of us then pictured him as becoming a professional boxer.'

Tunney graduated from Saint Veronica's in 1911 and from LaSalle Academy in 1913 after a course in business training. The academy was a Catholic high school run by the Christian

Brothers of Ireland, and charged a tuition fee of $45 a year, which was a financial drain on his parents. So like a dutiful son, young Tunney got himself a job. He worked as a butcher boy in John McNamara's meat market for $2.50 a week, taking orders from customers in the morning, then going back after school to deliver them. 'I would estimate that at least three mornings a week the good brothers would rap me on the knuckles for being late at school,' he remembered.

Now it was time for a real job, with the Ocean Steamship Company. 'In writing the letter of application,' he recalled many years later, 'I closed with "and, dear sir, believe me to be your most obedient servant." The letter is still on file with the Ocean Steamship Company.'

Young Tunney started work as an office boy on $5 a week and at the end of his first year he was earning $11 a week as mail clerk. One of his first jobs was delivering bills of laden to various companies along Broadway. On his way back to the office one day he saw a window demonstration by a well-muscled gentleman using spring exercisers. Tunney was back there the following week, with two weeks' pocket money, to buy a pair of the exercisers for 89¢.

'Next to the boxing gloves I had received from my father,' he recorded in his autobiography, 'I got more use out of those spring exercisers than I did out of any other thing I have owned. I got up an hour earlier to do the course of exercises prescribed in the pamphlet that came with the apparatus. It was a glorious sensation to notice the straight muscle line gradually curve with development and see little knots of firm muscle where formerly there was but skin and bone.'

By this time boxing was beginning to take up more of Tunney's leisure time. A boy from the neighbourhood, Willie Ward, was a budding professional boxer, and he asked Tunney to spar with him in the back of Dave Bernstein's drugstore. Finding themselves cramped for space, they moved to a recreation centre at the corner of Charles Street and Greenwich Avenue. Ward found plenty of sparmates there so Tunney, by this time a member of the Villagers' Athletic Club, went back to his running, training by using the Fifth Avenue buses as pacers.

A few doors away from Tunney's home on Perry Street lived Jack Goodman, a lightweight who had been in with some good fighters yet his face was unmarked. The sportswriters referred to him as 'Handsome Jack, the Idol of the West Side'. Tunney would often wait outside his house and follow Goodman through the streets at a safe distance, copying his snappy short strides.

'Later, another lightweight boxer developed in our neighbourhood,' recalled Tunney, 'Tommy Maloney. Tommy was the kind they called "a good boy." Every Sunday morning he swaggered down through Washington Street to Christopher and up the centre aisle of Saint Veronica's Church with his mother. He never missed a step. Yet, for some reason, we looked upon Tommy as a usurper who was trying to steal the position of his superior. Eventually, Tommy and Jack met. Jack knocked out Tommy in two rounds. I know of one bonfire that burned that night!'

However, it was another professional fighter who really started young Tunney on the road to the world championship. Willie Green had racked up 168 fights against guys like Leach Cross, Battling Hurley and Frankie Madden in a five-year career before hanging up his gloves to become an actor, playing a boxer in a travelling stock company. At 26, Green was ten years older than Tunney, yet when the kid heard that Green was training for a comeback he went along to the gym and asked if he could spar with him. Tunney gladly agreed to go three three-minute rounds and no sooner had the opening bell sent them on their way than he knew he was in a real fight. Willie Green wasn't pulling his punches! He backed Tunney into a corner, smashed in a left hook and the back of Tunney's head hit the wall. As he rebounded, Green ripped a vicious right to the mouth and the kid tasted blood. He stuck out the three rounds but knew he had been taken advantage of.

'I learned by this experience that I was but a child in the hands of a professional,' he recalled in *A Man Must Fight*. 'I never knew that nine minutes could be such an eternity. After a shower and a half-mile walk home, I was still dazed when I got to bed. I slept soundly. The next morning my head was clear and, after going over in my mind the experience of the night before, I decided that I would never box a professional again. I had a good position, as positions went in those days, with all the opportunity for advancement that is possible in a steamship or railroad office. I hoped one day to be chief clerk and later advance to the position of port agent. It would be a long, hard road, but one that could be gradually traversed if I applied the necessary driving force. I had the ambition.'

However, a few weeks later, Tunney was in the gym with Willie Ward when Green came in and asked them to give him a workout. Reluctant at first, Tunney finally agreed and acquitted himself well, much to his own satisfaction. Shortly afterwards he boxed Green over three rounds, this time in public, at the Knights of Columbus Council Hall at 23rd Street and Second Avenue. On each occasion that they boxed, Tunney was conscious of the fact that Willie Green was trying to knock him out. He never did. In fact Green's respect for the youngster grew to such an extent that when he became boxing coach at the Greenwich Settlement House, he asked Tunney to box with him on his free night, Saturday. And for the best part of two years, every Saturday night, young Tunney boxed ten rounds with Willie Green, learning how to slip leads, counterpunch with either hand, feint, side-step and conserve his energy. A champion was in the making, and by the end of those two years Willie Green had had enough of Gene Tunney. He refused to box him any more!

By that time the Greenwich Village youngster had earned himself quite a reputation boxing in smokers around the city, for nothing more than a ham sandwich and a glass of ginger ale. Billy Jacobs, matchmaker at the Sharkey Athletic Club, had heard of this promising youngster and paid him a visit with a proposition. 'Gene,' he said, 'I will put you in a star bout. No fighter that I have ever known has been given a star bout for his first professional fight.' Tunney was flattered by the offer, but turned Jacobs down. He was still with the Steamship Company, and he was also receiving a wage as an athletic instructor at Public School 41.

'For all his instinctive liking for boxing,' wrote Ed Van Every in 1926, 'many of Gene's pals of his early manhood are positive he was rather slow in expressing any desire toward embracing a professional boxing career. He was quite often an attendant at the weekly bouts of the old Pioneer AC, then located on West 44th Street.'

One of Tunney's boyhood pals recalled, 'The first time I ever really heard Gene get excited over the possibilities of professional pugilism was when we attended the Willie Ritchie–Leach Cross bout at the old Madison Square Garden, where some years later he was to lose and regain his title of light-heavyweight champion of America. It was the first big fight Gene had ever seen, and he certainly did rave about what this pair showed in the boxing line. I don't think Gene was more than sixteen at the time. We sat up in the gallery and paid two dollars each for our seats. But soon after his interest seemed to die down and he didn't talk much about boxing, though he was always ready to put on the mitts at any time. It just seemed as though a pair of gloves had him fascinated.'

Old Billy Jacobs did not give up on Gene Tunney. He turned to Willie Green, who was well aware of the kid's fistic prowess, and asked him to talk to Tunney. He turned to Eddie O'Brien, a local saloonkeeper who had followed Tunney's sporting career. O'Brien was a member of the Avonia Athletic Club, which had turned out some good fighters – men like Tommy Maloney, Jack Goodman, Harry Schumaker and Kid Black – and it was O'Brien who finally persuaded Tunney to accept the offer of Billy Jacobs.

'Gene,' Eddie would say, 'you are the greatest fighter I ever seen. There ain't no fellows ever produced in this city ever had such an offer, and you can lick anybody they throw into the ring with you.'

2

The Boxer

Gene Tunney had his first professional fight on a hot and humid July evening in 1915. As Billy Jacobs had promised, it was a ten-rounds star bout with Bobby Dawson coming out of the other corner. When the Greenwich Village youngster arrived at the arena, accompanied by Willie Green and Eddie O'Brien, he found he was sharing a dressing room with another fighter, 'KO' Eggers, and as he changed into his trunks and boxing shoes, Eggers struck up a conversation.

'This Bobby Dawson is a tough fellow,' he said, 'but he's not clever. I boxed him four years ago and gave him an awful beating for ten rounds. You won't have any trouble with him. Just don't be afraid of him.'

Tunney had already lost sleep thinking about the fight, as he recalled in *A Man Must Fight*. 'When they finally induced me to accept the match, I lay awake most of the night anticipating injuries to be sustained and regretting my decision. The evening of the match came along all too soon, and I found myself in the dingy Sharkey Athletic Club. This club was nothing more than a loft with tiers of wooden benches to the ceiling in an old building on Lincoln Square. It was an absolute firetrap. How they got permission from the fire department to hold matches in it is still a mystery.'

When Bobby Dawson weighed in, he looked around for his opponent. 'He's in the dressing room,' advised Jacobs. 'Get him out here, then,' growled Dawson, whereupon Jacobs

10

shrugged his shoulders and proposed Dawson fetch Mr Tunney himself. Dawson promptly charged off to find the kid he knew was having his first fight. Pushing his way into the dressing room, he said, 'Where's Tunney?'

The man in question was sitting on a bench in the corner, with Green and O'Brien either side of him.

'Come on,' growled Dawson, 'I want to see what you weigh.'

'Where are the scales?' asked Tunney.

'Right out here,' replied Dawson.

Tunney stood up and made to follow Dawson out of the room. Dawson took one look at the lanky, blond, blue-eyed kid he was to fight and said, 'Aw, sit down. I don't care if you weigh a ton!'

Just turned eighteen and weighing around 140 pounds, Gene Tunney looked an easy mark for the experienced Bobby Dawson. At the opening bell, Dawson came from his corner like a bat out of hell, both fists flying in Tunney's direction. The kid stepped lively, using the basic boxing skills he had learned in those back-room sessions with Willie Green, the left shooting out and finding Dawson's oncoming face time and time again. After two or three rounds, Dawson stopped rushing and tried to catch Tunney unawares.

The newcomer was feeling the pace after half a dozen rounds. His gloves weighed a ton and his legs were trembling. But he was ahead, and in the corner Willie Green and Eddie O'Brien told him to keep doing what he was doing. Towards the end of the seventh round, as Dawson came in, Tunney landed a wild right uppercut and Dawson dropped to the canvas with a thud. As the referee tolled off nine seconds, the bell rang ending the round. It was also the end of the fight. They got Dawson back to his corner but he didn't come out for round eight and Gene Tunney had won his first professional fight. His purse was $18. He gave Green six bucks, and was left with twelve when O'Brien refused to take his share.

'Although Eddie accompanied me and worked in my corner in all my early matches,' said Tunney, 'he never accepted a penny.' Next day Tunney treated his pals to a dinner at Rockaway Beach.

'Among those not present at my first professional fight was my father,' recalled Tunney. 'Although he had admired Corbett, Fitzsimmons, and some of the other old champions, he did not relish the notion of me being a professional boxer. He never came to see me box, though he lived until after my second match with Harry Greb, in 1923. When I asked him why he did not come, he said, "Do you think I would be happy seeing you bleeding?"

'I said, "No, but I didn't get a scratch." His reply was, "But how was I to know that beforehand? You take your mother's and my advice and do not do this thing any more. Just consider yourself lucky in getting away without a scratch this time. This kind of luck won't continue, if you make further attempts." Yet, in later days, I know that he was very proud to think that his son was climbing successfully.'

From that first bout against Bobby Dawson until he entered the US Marines almost three years later, he recalled nine fights, although he does make mention, in *A Man Must Fight,* of 'those matches which were not important enough to be entered in the boxing records.' In most editions of *The Ring Record Book,* compiled by *The Ring* founder and publisher Nat Fleischer, twelve fights are recorded for this period, while yet another record shows fifteen contests. Boxing in New York State at the time was governed by the Frawley Law, which permitted boxing without decisions, so unless a bout ended within the scheduled distance it was recorded as a No-Decision contest. Of the nine bouts recalled by Tunney, six were won via the short route, while three were of the No-Decision variety. The Fleischer record shows seven inside wins, one on a foul, four ending in No Decision. The fifteen-fight listing breaks down as six No-Decision bouts, while nine were won inside the scheduled distance.

Two of those early bouts, against Billy Rowe and George Lahey, took place at the Fairmont Athletic Club. One of New York's better-known fight clubs, the Fairmont was located in the Mott Haven section of the Bronx, on East 137th Street near Third Avenue. It was operated by Billy Gibson, a wealthy and politically prominent citizen who also ran the Criterion Restaurant, a popular watering hole in the Bronx. Gibson was a shrewd judge of boxing and staged well-matched bouts for his patrons. 'That's why I sell out the joint every Friday night,' he would say.

Gene Tunney brought his own cheering section with him when he boxed Rowe. One of his pals had just bought a new truck and they rolled up to the Fairmont with cheesecloth banners bearing Tunney's name. Billy Rowe was actually managed by Lou Brix who would become attached to the Tunney camp in later years. Billy Gibson would become Tunney's manager in later years but he couldn't be bothered to watch Tunney's bout that night, despite the pleas of Billy Jacobs that young Tunney was something special. 'I wouldn't walk twenty-five feet to see him,' Gibson told Jacobs. 'I watched him in training. He's nothing but a ham. He can't fight.'

The week before he fought Tunney, Billy Rowe had broken three ribs of his opponent at the Fairmont and in that first round someone yelled, 'C'mon, Billy, break a coupl'a more ribs!' Tunney blocked his vicious body swings by dropping his elbow and when his matchwinner failed to land, Rowe became somewhat discouraged. Tunney had his jab working overtime and looked like a winner when the six rounds ended.

'If Gibson saw me that night,' recalled Tunney, 'I know I made no impression on him, for later, when I became associated with him, he said, "No, I don't ever remember seeing you at the Fairmont Club." But why should the then "Mayor of the Bronx" remember a preliminary boxer?'

Tunney had drawn a good crowd of supporters for his fight with Rowe, and Tom McArdle, the matchmaker who would take over that position at Madison Square Garden, asked Jacobs to bring him back again. The opponent was George Lahey, a tall, rugged, hard-hitting middleweight from the Bronx. In the very first round a long right swing crashed against Tunney's nose and the blood ran for the rest of the fight. At the end of round three, Billy Joh, the resident referee at the club, walked to Tunney's corner to inspect the injury. Tunney jumped off his stool and said, 'Mr Joh, please don't stop the fight. The blood is nothing, I will knock him out before the fight is over.' Billy Joh looked at Tunney bloody nose, then walked back to the neutral corner. He didn't stop the fight and Tunney didn't knock Lahey out, although he tried hard enough.

Leaving the club that night, Tunney asked for a return bout with his Bronx rival, but before he hooked up with Lahey again Jacobs accepted a match at the new Polo Athletic Club at 129th Street and Park Avenue, where Pop Kirk was making the fights. Tunney's opponent was 'KO' Jaffee, a tough guy who soaked up punishment without ever looking like hitting the canvas.

'Often I think of that hot July night in 1916,' recalled Tunney in his autobiography, 'when I pummelled KO Jaffee about the ring for ten rounds to the delight of my many friends who had come up from Greenwich Village and from the offices of the Ocean Steamship Company. Some of the Greenwich Village boys had never been so far away from home before. During the entire contest Jaffee landed but one blow.

'Contemplating this later, I began to believe that I must be quite a boxer, but could not be persuaded entirely to leave the peaceful pursuits of rate clerk at the Ocean Steamship Company to follow the dubious profession of boxing. For seventeen dollars a week I classified freight, figured out the cheapest rates and railroad routes, and kept an eye on the changes in rates and classifications of the Interstate Commerce Commission. At the time I thought mine a most desirable and lucrative position.'

One of Tunney's pals, who sometimes worked his corner, recalled a wild night for Ed Van Every of the *New York Evening World*. 'I think the one bout around that time that made the most talk was an engagement with a powerful Italian boy known as the Battling Barber of Hoboken. His name was something like Genrimo and he brought over a great following which included his entire family. There was sure some tall rooting that night. Someone was in the Battling Barber's corner, I think it was his father, with his fist wrapped around the rung of a chair. Every time Gene knocked his foe down, the fellow with the chair rung threatened to break the weapon over Genrimo's head if he didn't get up. He was up and down quite a few times.'

There is a record of Tunney boxing a Battling Genrimo and scoring a knockout in the third round, but there is no record of Genrimo's father taking a chair rung to his unconscious offspring on the one occasion that he didn't get up against Gene Tunney!

Billy Jacobs was hiring Miner's Eighth Avenue Theater one night a week to stage boxing and he asked Tunney to appear there. The ring was on the stage and Tunney's friends had to agree to sell a certain number of tickets, with Tunney getting a percentage. He still yearned for a return bout with George Lahey and told Jacobs to arrange a fight against the Bronx middleweight. Canny old Jacobs countered with an offer of two fights, one of which would be against Lahey. Tunney agreed.

Training for those fights, Tunney had some excellent sparring with a friend of his, John Gaddi, the national amateur heavyweight champion, and he was in great shape when he faced George Lahey in their rematch. In the third round a solid right to the jaw finished Mr Lahey for the evening. His second match at Miner's saw him in with Young Guarini of Hoboken. As Tunney recalled, 'Guarini learned in the first round that he had overmatched himself, and proceeded to try losing on a foul. I did not know about aluminium cups in those days and took the most awful pummelling around the groin for three rounds. Finally Guarini went down, where he remained for ten seconds. He "retired."'

Tunney took a rest from boxing and kept fit playing basketball. He should have stayed with boxing. He injured his left elbow in a club game and waited too long before seeing a doctor. The pain had increased and his arm was visibly shrinking, but the doctor Tunney consulted mistakenly placed his arm in a plaster cast for six weeks. When the cast came off, his left arm had shrunk even more.

By this time war was raging in Europe and on 6 April 1917

the US Congress declared that a state of war existed between America and Germany. Within a few weeks young Gene Tunney had presented himself at the US Marines' recruiting station on East 23rd Street. He had been intrigued by a pamphlet that proclaimed 'A Marine is a two-fisted fighting man!' But this budding marine only had one fighting fist and the doctors turned him down, much to his disappointment.

Determined to get into uniform, Tunney visited a different doctor who prescribed exercise and sunshine. He gave up his job at the Ocean Steamship Company and took a summer job as a lifeguard at Keansburg, over in New Jersey. After a while there was some improvement in his arm and he even started sparring with a pal in his spare time. But he incurred a further injury and was back home in New York with no money, no job, and a useless left arm. Two months of mechano-therapy at Belle Vue Hospital did very little for his arm and even less for his morale.

One day Tunney bumped into Eddie O'Brien who, upon hearing his tale of woe, offered to loan him some money. Tunney refused the offer, having no means of repaying his friend, but he did say that if he could get a fight it would certainly help ease his financial situation. At that time the Frawley Law, which allowed boxing without decisions, had been repealed by the governor, but membership clubs still existed that were able to stage fights.

'You can get a fight,' said O'Brien.

'But even if I get one,' said Tunney, 'what can I do with only one arm?'

'You can lick any of those bums with one hand,' replied the faithful O'Brien. Tunney was encouraged by his friend's confidence and agreed. A few days later, O'Brien reported back to say that Pop Kirk had agreed to give Tunney a bout at the New Polo AC, against a big Italian coal-heaver named Young Joe Borelli. Training was out of the question – even skipping rope caused a strain on the arm. Tunney settled for a run around Washington Square every morning and some light shadow-boxing. Borelli had some fifty pounds on Tunney but that was all he did have. A southpaw, he was an easy mark for Tunney's good arm, the right. Tunney feinted with his left a few times and halfway through the second round a right to the jaw sat Borelli on his ample backside and he took the full count. Tunney's share of the purse came to $26.

A week later O'Brien took Tunney to see Charlie Doesserick at the Pioneer Club. He was looking for an opponent to box Hughey Weir on his next show and offered Tunney $40 for a six-round bout. His training still somewhat restricted, Tunney ran in the mornings and did more shadow-boxing. He found Weir no more of a problem than Borelli had been. Both boys weighed 158 pounds and in the third round, as Weir rushed in, a right hand landed flush on his jaw and he was all through for the evening.

Eddie O'Brien again proved a good friend to the young fighter. He got Gene a job with the J G White Engineering Corporation for $25 a week. Tunney worked at the Erie Pier in Jersey City, checking aeroplane parts to be shipped to France. Still hoping to go to France himself, in a marine uniform, Tunney accepted the advice of a workmate and went to see Dr Frederick de Kraft.

Dr Kraft specialised in giving electrical treatment for ailments such as neuritis and rheumatism, and after examining Tunney, he diagnosed traumatic neuritis, which could be cured with time and patience. For three nights a week Tunney visited the doctor for diathermic treatment, at a cost of $2 a visit. It took the best part of six months but the doctor finally pronounced the young man fighting fit, ironically cured by a German doctor so that he could join the Allied forces in their fight against Kraft's native land.

On 2 May 1918, James Joseph (Gene) Tunney enlisted and was passed physically fit for service in the US Marine Corps. A couple of days before he was to leave for basic training at Parris Island off the Carolina coast, Tunney went over to Jersey City to see if he could get a fight at Jack Jennings's Armoury Athletic Club. The matchmaker was Frank 'Doc' Bagley, who would later become Tunney's manager. He offered Tunney a bout with Danny Lynch, but when Lynch failed to show, the New Yorker found himself in with Young Guarini, a former victim. Guarini was less bother second time around. A stiff left jab sat him down in the first round and when he got up it was too late. Bagley had promised Tunney $30 for the fight. As Tunney recalled the incident, Bagley handed him the $20 bill and held the ten in his other hand while he searched his pocket for change.

'I always take thirty per cent from my boys,' said Bagley. 'Even Willie Jackson, who boxes the star bout tonight, cuts me in for thirty per cent. But since you are going off to war tomorrow, I will only take twenty-five per cent. Have you got any change?' 'No, I haven't,' replied Tunney.

'How are we going to break this ten dollar bill?' asked Bagley, still fumbling in his pockets.

'Well, Doc,' Tunney finally said, 'you keep it all.' They would meet again.

3

The Marine

'I was twenty-one when I enlisted,' Tunney told Dan Daniel in a 1971 interview for *The Ring* magazine. 'I had been talking about it at home. Finally I made up my mind after a sleepless night. I got up early, packed a bag, said goodbye to my mother as if I were going to work, and went up to the enlistment booth of the Marines at 23rd Street and Madison Square, not far from the old Garden. I had some time to wait for the train for the Paris Island training grounds of the Marines, in South Carolina. I sat down on a Madison Square bench and fed the squirrels and pigeons. Suddenly my mother stood before me, asking, "And where do you think you are going?" A neighbour had spotted me leaving with a bag and had told my mother. She had hunted me down. I told my mom there was no use arguing about my enlistment. I had taken the oath. She cried a little, went home, and I walked up to Penn Station on my long road to France.'

To young Gene Tunney it seemed that journey south from New York City took forever. Eventually the train steamed into a small town in South Carolina where, along with a crowd of other recruits, he was escorted to another train, this time with a tough-looking marine sergeant calling the shots. A few hours later the train stopped and the sergeant yelled, 'Everybody out, and make it snappy!'

As one guy remembered it, 'There were Marines everywhere. I wondered what place it was and one of the Marines said Port

Royal. What a place! I looked around and saw a few old houses and a barge. No ocean liners. I could not believe my eyes. Then a government tug came alongside and our tough sergeant marched us on two by two. We were bound for Paris Island, one hour's sail from Port Royal.'

Paris (it was spelled with just one 'r' in 1918) Island was a tract of land five and a half miles long covering some six thousand acres, half of it marshland. Bordered on the north by Archer's Creek, on the east by the Beaufort River, and on the south and west by Port Royal Sound and Broad River, its highest point was less than twenty feet above high tide. It was home to sand fleas, mosquitos, coral snakes, rattlesnakes, water moccasins, cottonmouths, and alligators, its surrounding waters the domain of sharks and the odd barracuda. In winter, cold wet fogs prevailed, broken by long days of desultory rain and even sleet; in summer there was constant high humidity, with temperatures in excess of 100 degrees not uncommon. Then there were the hurricanes. So much for the vacation brochure!

Writing in *The Ring* magazine many years later, Jersey Jones recalled, 'You remember the first time you saw Gene Tunney. It was during the summer of 1918, when America was gearing up for the all-out drive to end World War I. The locale was the Quarantine Camp of the United States Marines' boot training base at Paris Island. The Quarantine Camp was where they unloaded the new recruits to await final check-up and assignment to drill companies. Those summer days were blisteringly hot on that sandy tract off the marshy coast of South Carolina. But the evenings usually were cool, and the main diversion of the embryo leathernecks was the nightly boxing. It was informal stuff. There was no regular ring with posts and ropes. Action was on the sandy ground, with the onlookers spreading out in a wide circle around the battle pit. Anybody who felt like donning the gloves for a round or two could volunteer.

'This evening, Toughey Murray, a rugged, experienced featherweight out of Beaver Falls, Pennsylvania, was boxing a tall, skinny guy whose name you didn't pay much attention to when it was announced. They sparred two rounds and the lanky stranger looked very good. Though slow, and somewhat awkward in comparison with the lighter, nimbler Murray, he obviously was no novice. He handled himself as though he'd had some experience with the gloves. With a straight-up John L Sullivan stance, he showed a neat left jab, a snappy right, and a pretty fair defence. You were curious about him. You learned he was from New York, had been a stenographer in the offices of a steamship company, and had done some fighting on the side. His name, he said, was Tunney, James Joseph, but "everybody up home" called him Gene.'

The new recruits were put through their paces; up at the crack of dawn, cold showers, marching drills, scaling fifteen-foot walls, days on the rifle range. They were vaccinated and given four typhoid inoculations. Then there was the boxing and wrestling, which was compulsory. With the gloves on, the lanky kid from New York could not disguise his ability, and by the time training was completed he had quite a reputation in his own outfit. To his dismay, Tunney did not stay with his own company, being transferred to Quantico, Virginia, where he was assigned to the 11th Marine Regiment. A few days later he was on board the troopship *De Kalb* en route for Brest, France, where they docked on 13 October 1918.

Shortly after arriving in France, Tunney attended a boxing tournament at the YMCA hut in Romorantin, where he was stationed doing guard duty. In a match advertised as a contest for the middleweight championship of the camp, Joe Bedelli was to meet Kid McCoy. The latter failed to show up so Captain Greene announced that Bedelli was the new champion and that he was willing to box anyone in the place, regardless of weight. Tunney's pals egged him on to take up the challenge and when his sergeant promised he would be excused guard duty the following day, he made his way to the ring. Tunney, stripped to the waist and still wearing hobnail boots, soon had Bedelli's measure and he quit after two rounds.

Tunney's commanding officer, puffed up with pride, arranged a bout for the heavyweight championship of the camp between Tunney and Hank Wuerl, a professional fighter who had been champion of Montana before joining the colours. Using his pals as sparring partners, Tunney trained for three days before climbing into the ring with Wuerl. In 1926, when Tunney was training for his first fight with Jack Dempsey, one of his old marine buddies visited his training camp at Stroudsburg and recalled that service bout for Ed Van Every, veteran boxing writer for the *New York Evening World*.

'His opponent was a chap called Woerl, or something like that. Gene was told to go in training and he didn't know much about what this called for, neither did we. I know we decided on roadwork and it is a wonder we didn't run his legs off the way we had him jogging around the country. Along with this some bright mind remembered that Jim Corbett prescribed rope skipping. We prepared a rope with tape-covered ends for handles for Gene and we had him doing that skipping stuff until his fingers were rubbed raw.

'Well, the night of the fight, Gene's opponent, who was a wise sort of party, insisted on calling Gene up to the referee so they would both get his instructions right, but in reality to get Tunney's goat. "What do I do after I've knocked him down?" Woerl wanted to know. "That's a lot of noise," growled Gene, and he sure was fighting mad. I guess Gene learned something about keeping his temper and boxing in that fight. What that guy did to Tunney at the start with a straight left was plenty. But Gene kept trying and swinging and after a while I could notice that his right was missing his man by fewer and fewer inches, and after a while it didn't miss and that was that.'

'Though I was the post champion,' Tunney recalled, 'I was to see that no favouritism would be shown. For one who enlisted in an organisation inspired by the slogan "First to Fight!" doing guard duty around empty balloon sheds and aeroplane hangers two hours on and four off, twenty-four on and twenty-four off, was a terrible let-down. Of all the tasks I have been called upon to perform during my life, guarding empty balloon sheds has been the most boring.'

Tunney realised he had the solution to his problem in his

own two hands and went to see his commanding officer with a view to doing more boxing. He was surprised at the captain's response. 'Why, Private Tunney, I do not believe you ought to think of boxing any more. You have the spirit all right, but you get hit so much. Why do you let your opponent beat you up that way? Can't you do anything about avoiding such punishment?' Somewhat taken aback, Gene pointed out that he could not train and do guard duty at the same time. The officer shrugged and said he would speak to the top sergeant. 'By making it possible for me to train and devote most of my time to boxing,' said Gene, 'Captain Barthe permitted me to lay the firm foundation of my professional career.'

Boxing was very popular among the Allied forces in France, with regular tournaments being staged between service posts, and Gene Tunney soon began to make a name for himself once he was able to devote more time to training. His leatherneck buddies cheered like mad when he knocked out a sergeant, Howard Morrow, in three rounds. Morrow had been a professional fighter back home, as was Tunney's next opponent, Tommy Gavegan, a hard-hitting middleweight contender from Cleveland. Tunney boxed a draw with Gavegan, but he had entered the ring wearing a pair of football boots with the studs removed. After slipping all over the ring, his second pulled them off and Tunney boxed the other three rounds in his stocking feet.

Johnny Newton had been army middleweight champion on the Mexican border before being sent to France and he came into the ring like a champion, waving to his pals around the ring. 'The well-secured ring shook to its foundations when Johnny did his warming-up stuff,' recalled Tunney, adding, 'It did the same in the sixth round when Johnny tumbled to the canvas for the count.'

A friend of Gene's went up to Paris on a few days leave and Tunney asked him to see if he could get him a fight in the capital. A few days later a telegram from the Director of Athletics at the Knights of Columbus arrived at Romorantin requesting that Private Gene Tunney proceed to Paris to box a

French middleweight named 'KO' Marchand on 13 January 1919. On the day of the fight, Tunney and his two seconds went sightseeing around Paris and were late arriving at the theatre in Rue Saint-Martin. Matchmaker Billy Roche, thinking Tunney was not coming, arranged for Marchand to box another American soldier named Izzy Green.

'I appealed to Billy,' remembered Tunney in *A Man Must Fight*. 'I told him I was from the West Side of New York and that I had seen him referee at Madison Square Garden many times. I advised him that if I didn't fight somebody in Paris, my company commander would punish me when I got back to camp. Billy listened, then said he would ask Marchand to fight me instead of Green.'

Marchand appeared in Tunney's dressing room to check out the opposition, then nodded his head after taking a look at the lanky marine. The Frenchman had boxed in America before the war and was now belting out doughboys every week in the rings around Paris, so when Tunney knocked him out in the second round, the servicemen packing the hall were standing on their seats shouting and screaming, and next day the Fighting Marine was the talk of Paris.

A couple of weeks later Tunney was back in Paris to fight another Frenchman, but when he got to the Salle Wagram, where the fight was to be held, he learned that his opponent would be an American MP, Sergeant Bob Martin. Tunney had heard of Martin and didn't know quite what to expect when he got into the ring. He was surprised at how easy a target he found Martin, and was starting to enjoy the fight in the second round when a terrific right hand crashed into his jaw, sending him reeling back across the ring. He managed to duck a following left but took another right haymaker on the top of his head.

'This one felt as though a crossbeam over the ring had snapped and fallen on me,' Tunney would recall. 'The time for smiling was gone. With every ounce of energy I had I hurled myself at this big guy and hit him from all angles. He finally put his head between his knees to keep out of harm's way. I got the decision and with it the winner's prize, a dollar razor. When he stepped on the scales that night, Martin weighed 193 pounds, I weighed 168. Bob, in congratulating me, said, "You hit me the hardest punches tonight that I have ever been hit." I could have told him the same thing. As a matter of fact, no one punch ever hurt me so much as the belt he hit me in the second round.' Jimmy Bronson had organised the matches between the American troops and the French professionals in Paris and was putting together a team of boxers to visit Italy. Tunney was hoping to be included in the team but it was already made up by the time of his victory over Martin.

Before Tunney returned to Romorantin, he called at the Knights of Columbus office to get some altar linen for his camp priest. It was there that he met Billy McCabe. Secretary and Athletics Director of the organisation in France, McCabe was later described by Ed Van Every as 'a rather placid and affable Irish gentleman', and he took an instant liking to the young marine private who called on him that day in 1919. He had been following Tunney's developing fistic career for some time and counselled him, 'Live as a man, as the same clean boy you are now, and you'll see the day that you'll become the heavyweight champion of the world.'

McCabe believed every word he spoke and Tunney knew that he believed it, admitting years later that those words acted as his inspiration. 'We remained friends until the day he died,' Tunney would say of the man he first met in the French capital. 'He was associated with me after I won the world's heavyweight championship. Billy was a great person.'

When Tunney's commanding officer entered him in the American Expeditionary Forces (AEF) boxing tournament, Tunney was not too happy as there were some two and a half million Americans in France, with a good many seasoned professional fighters among them. But it was either fight or return to guard duty and those empty balloon sheds. Private Tunney elected to fight. Or rather, box.

'My slant always put emphasis on the mental side of prize fighting,' Tunney recalled in a 1940 article for the *Saturday Evening Post*. 'I had been told that championship was a state of

mind. I was told it, in a way, by Bob Fitzsimmons. Not that I'd
ever known Fitzsimmons. But I did know Eddie Behan, and
that was almost the same thing. Eddie was a Knights of
Columbus athletics director with the Army in France and was
grooming me for the AEF championship. Eddie knew boxing
completely. Above all, he knew Fitzsimmons. He had trained
the freckled wonder, sparred with him, had lived close to
Fitzsimmons for years.

'We had our hangout after fights in a warehouse in Paris, a
huge dingy place full of packing cases, and on the packing cases
we'd sit and talk Fitzsimmons. "Fitz would alter his stature,
change his height," Behan told me, and explained Fitzsimmons
would fight round after round from a crouch, doubled over.
He'd seem small of stature, and establish that in his opponent's
mind. Then abruptly he'd change his style and stand at full
height. His opponent would feel himself suddenly confronted
by a giant, a giant hitting savagely. Behan gave me the inside
story of how Fitz won the championship. For fourteen rounds
he lashed out at Corbett with an overhand right swing, and
missed. You couldn't hit the swift, elusive Corbett with that
kind of punch, and Fitzsimmons knew it. Yet for months of
training he had practised that overhand right, a punch he never
expected to land . . . Fitz wanted Corbett to raise his guard, and
with those rights whizzing high at his head, Corbett did hold his
guard higher and higher, never realising he was doing it.

'Then, in the fourteenth round, Fitzsimmons had the
champion's guard just where he wanted it. He launched
another ineffectual right, which Corbett blocked as he had
blocked them all. Fitzsimmons shifted with a left into Corbett's
midriff, the much-talked-of solar plexus blow. It laid Corbett
out on the ring floor, gasping, his body paralysed from the
hips down.'

Inspired by Behan's stories, Tunney sailed through the
opening rounds of the AEF tournament, boxing in the
light-heavyweight class, though little more than a heavy-
middleweight. When the winners of the various sectors came
together in Tours, he won his first matches by knockout and in

the final came up against a huge American Indian named Lewis. Wearing ten-ounce gloves, Tunney landed a hard right to the jaw and Lewis dropped in a heap. He didn't get up. Tunney had won his way through to the finals in Paris, but at a cost. The impact of that knockout punch broke the knuckle of his middle finger and when the glove was removed his right hand was already swelling up. The knuckle he broke that night would bother him for the next four years. It needed rest but there wasn't time. He had to report to Saint Nazaire for two weeks' training, so his hand was put in a splint and his training was confined to roadwork. He should have pulled out of the tournament, but he felt he could win the championship and for Gene Tunney there was no going back at that point.

The finals were held at the Cirque de Paris and his first opponent was a guy called 'KO' Sullivan. His real name was Peter Miroche and he was from Shenandoah, in the Pennsylvania coal regions. A tough, slugging southpaw, he had already mixed it with top fighters like Battling Levinksy and Jack Dillon back home. Tunney knew the best way to beat a southpaw was with a right hand, but he didn't have one that night in Paris. He did have a good left hand, however, and over ten rounds it was good enough to beat Sullivan and put Tunney into the final against Ted Jamieson, who had been amateur champion of America before getting into uniform.

From Milwaukee, Jamieson was a good fighter who would later fight the great Harry Greb; in fact he became one of only seven men to deck the Pittsburgh Windmill. Gene Tunney knew he would have to use his right if he were to beat Jamieson and win the title, so he did, to the best of his ability, allied to that solid left jab. In the tenth and final round a left hook to the jaw put Jamieson on the canvas. He beat the count but he couldn't beat Tunney that April night in 1919 and the lad from Greenwich Village was crowned AEF light-heavyweight champion by referee Jimmy Bronson, watched by high-ranking officers and dignitaries including General Pershing, General Foch and Prince Albert of Belgium.

The tournament winners were assigned to General HQ in

Paris and travelled all over to service posts giving exhibitions. Tunney boxed with Bob Martin, but his right hand was still giving him trouble, and when they returned to Paris he decided not to enter the Inter-Allied Games. His superior officers were disappointed but Gene Tunney had made up his mind. He was going to be a professional boxer when he returned home and he would need two good hands if he were to attain his goal.

Tunney had met a fellow marine called McReynolds, who had been a newspaperman in Joplin, Missouri, before enlisting. The sports news from home was all about a sensational young heavyweight called Dempsey who was to fight Jess Willard for the world title. McReynolds had seen Dempsey fight a few times at Jimmy Bronson's club in Joplin and in St Louis, and Tunney wanted to know all about this fellow Dempsey. As McReynolds described the man they were already calling the Manassa Mauler, Tunney began thinking out loud.

'Mike Gibbons, the clever boxer, defeated the great Jack Dillon, the fighter, by a decision. The question is, will Gene Tunney, the clever boxer, ever defeat Jack Dempsey, the rugged fighter?'

McReynolds smiled and said, 'Well, Gene, you are young, you are fast, you are clever, you can take it. It ought to be possible for you to do that some day.'

'I will,' said the young marine, 'I will.'

While living at the Clignancourt Barracks just outside Paris, Tunney met Eddie Eagan. Originally from Denver, Eagan was a couple of months younger than Tunney and they got along well together. Tunney saw Eagan win the middleweight championship at the Inter-Allied Games held at the Stade Pershing in Paris, the first of many amateur titles he would win. In 1920 Eagan won the Olympic light-heavy crown at Antwerp, became a Yale scholar and later went to Oxford on a Rhodes scholarship, winning the ABA heavyweight championship in 1923. In 1932 Eagan won another Olympic gold medal as a member of the four-man bobsled team, becoming the first athlete to win gold medals at both the Summer and Winter Olympics. A prominent lawyer after his sporting days, Eddie

Eagan never lost his love for boxing and would eventually serve as Chairman of the New York State Athletic Commission. Eagan and Tunney became great friends during the two months they spent at the Clignancourt Barracks outside the old Paris wall just after the Great War ended. On a July day in 1919, as Private Tunney prepared to leave on the long journey home, Eagan said to him, 'Gene, when you get back, why don't you come to Yale with me?'

'Eddie,' replied Tunney in all seriousness, 'I won't have any time for Yale. I am going to win the heavyweight championship of the world!' Some ten days before that final meeting in Paris, Jack Dempsey had destroyed the giant Willard to become heavyweight champion. On the face of it, the young marine had set himself a formidable task.

4

A Short Beginning

'I'll never forget my first peep at Dempsey's fists,' Gene Tunney told boxing writer Ed Van Every. 'It was my first meeting with Jack. It was shortly after my return from France and, of course, I was just a gangling kid that didn't mean anything to the champion. And yet, I'll never forget how genial he was to me. He said something about having to keep his eye on the young fighters who were coming along to threaten his title. It wasn't his words that interested me so much, though. It was his hands. They looked big to me, terrible weapons, to tell you the truth. He had been pickling his hands for a time and in places the skin had cracked into a hard scaley substance. And as he spoke to me Jack ripped off these loose pieces of flesh indifferently and my eyes must have almost popped out as I looked on. And it seemed to me the longer I looked at those fists, the larger they seemed to grow before my very eyes. "So you want to be heavyweight champion of the world," I said to myself. "You want to take the title away from Jack Dempsey, Gene," I thought, "you sure have your work cut out for you."'

The work started shortly after Tunney became a civilian again, on 13 August 1919, the day he was honourably discharged from the US Marine Corps at Quantico. He arrived home with $60 in his pocket, but after buying a suit, hat and a pair of shoes, he was broke again. If he was going to be a professional fighter, he needed to buy some training gear – he needed a gym. His mother gave him the price of a night out at the theatre now and then but he could hardly ask her for money to buy boxing gear. For one thing, she didn't know of his plans to be a fighter. She was hoping he would go into business of some sort.

Tunney wanted to get into the fight business, and help came from an old-time featherweight named Sammy Kelly who was associated with Charles A Stoneham, owner of the New York Giants. Kelly was also a prominent figure in horse-racing circles and was at Saratoga when he asked Tunney to visit him. Kelly met Tunney off the train from New York and took him to 'Uncle' Tom Luther's training camp at the White Sulphur Springs Hotel, where heavyweight Frank Moran trained for his fights. Sammy Kelly had heard of Tunney's boxing prowess from a guy who had been in France with the boy from Greenwich Village. He agreed to handle Tunney and after treating him to dinner, gave him $100 to buy some training gear. Tunney figured twenty bucks would cover it, but Kelly insisted that he took it, saying that no fighter of his would have a training outfit costing less than $100.

Back home, Tunney went out the next day and bought some equipment. He had not decided on a gymnasium, not knowing anyone at Grupp's or Stillman's, when Kelly came back from Saratoga. Kelly took his new fighter along to the City Athletic Club on West 54th Street, where Jack Denning was the boxing instructor. A former middleweight who had once defeated Mike Gibbons, Denning agreed to train Tunney at the club but after a while he found it too much, the club members being his priority, so he brought in a pro heavyweight named Bartley Madden.

Madden, who was 29 when he agreed to work with Tunney, had started fighting in his native Galway in 1910. Arriving in America two years later, he was soon mixing it with some of the best fighters in the business – guys like Battling Levinsky, Bill Brennan, Harry Greb, Billy Miske and Tom Gibbons. Standing just over five foot ten tall in his socks, Madden was a fair boxer but lacked power. There was nothing wrong with his chin as he had never been knocked out, and he gave Tunney some good workouts over the following few months. One of the club members who watched those workouts with keen interest was one day introduced to Tunney by Jack Denning. He was Bernard Gimbel, 34-year-old head of the New York store that bore his family's name, and he asked if he could spar with the young fighter.

'Although he weighed 190 pounds to my 172, the idea of fighting an older businessman amused me,' Tunney recalled in a magazine article. 'My condescension turned to surprise when he donned his boxing trunks, revealing a rock-hard physique. He was a good boxer, too. We fought three rounds, with each of us getting in some good punches. After that we boxed a couple of times a week and soon became close friends. Although I was virtually unknown, Gimbel predicted that I would become heavyweight champion. As I slowly climbed the boxing ladder, he was always at my side as friend, counsellor, and occasional sparring partner.'

As the year 1919 drew to a close, Gene Tunney was in fighting shape, but there was no boxing in the city at that time and Sammy Kelly was finding it difficult to get his new boy a fight. When horse-racing business took Kelly off to Cuba, he suggested Tunney go with manager Charley Harvey while he was away. Tunney didn't know Harvey but he did know Billy Roche, who had seen him box in France. Roche agreed to look after Tunney on the same terms as had Kelly – 25 per cent – but he had no more luck than Kelly did in landing a fight for the former marine.

'I continued broke and in debt,' Tunney wrote in *A Man Must Fight*. 'I wore a path to Billy's office in the celebrated Putnam Building and became a familiar figure to the numerous tenants of that rendezvous of sharp-wits and Broadway chisellers. One day I followed Billy to the office of Jack Curley, the wrestling promoter, which was just across Times Square. In Curley's office I was introduced to the great Joe Humphreys, the man who has made an institution of his powerful lungs and made prizefight announcing an art, of which he is the old master.'

Learning of Tunney's problems in finding some action, Humphreys said he was going over to New Jersey that night to announce a light-heavyweight fight and suggested Tunney go along and challenge the winner. 'Billy Roche and I went down on the Jersey Central with Joe,' recalled Tunney, 'hopeful that between my reputation as the AEF champion and Joe's good offices we could procure a match at the club for some later date. Joe, generous soul that he is, paid the railroad fares down and back. He duly introduced me, and in his challenge to the winner I am afraid he waxed too eloquent. The winner, Eddie Josephs of Staten Island, would have no part of me.'

Then Christmas arrived a couple of weeks early for Tunney. Billy Roche finally booked a fight for him, against Dan O'Dowd of Boston, on 17 December at the Bayonne Athletic Association, an unheated arena in a summer amusement park, where Charley Doesserick was running fights. O'Dowd was a tough heavyweight who had just fought eight rounds with Bill Brennan and he took everything Tunney threw at him, which was plenty. It was a No-Decision contest but Tunney was satisfied with his showing, and he was even happier when the promoter handed over his 25 per cent of the gate receipts, $201. Paying Roche his cut, Tunney was left with $150.75. He felt like a millionaire, and couldn't wait to get home. The money was in $1, $2 and $5 bills, and when he tipped it on to the dining room table, his mother's eyes almost popped from her head. Crossing herself, she said softly, 'God bless and spare the hands that can make so much money in one night.'

Tunney had shaped up well against O'Dowd and a few days later Roche received a call from the Jersey City Armoury matchmaker, Dave Driscoll, offering a fight with Bob Pierce for a guarantee of $200. Roche accepted immediately and Tunney was delighted at the news. The fight took place on 29 December and Tunney floored the Chicago fighter several times before knocking him out. Next day one boxing writer declared in his column, 'Here is a young heavyweight with some class. He will do.' Three days later, on the afternoon of New Year's Day 1920, Tunney was in action again for Charley

Doesserick at his Bayonne club, fighting Whitey Allen of the Bronx, a guy with a rock in his right hand.

Tunney recalled that fight years later, in an issue of *Guideposts Magazine*, writing, 'I was one scared young man on the morning of the New Year in 1920. The opponent, whom I was scheduled to box that afternoon was a tough veteran named Whitey Allen, as cagey and experienced a fighter as they come. I was still wet behind the ears in the professional fighting sense. I can remember praying that morning as fervently and humbly as any man ever has. I prayed that in the fight that afternoon I might not be permanently injured when I was knocked out. I didn't ask that I might win. I took it for granted that I'd be knocked out, and I was terribly afraid of being hurt for life. To every fighter comes occasionally the supreme horror of not being able to fend off the blows showered on him, of being helpless to raise his hands to ward them off. Thus when I prayed that I might not be permanently injured, I gained confidence that I wouldn't be. This took the edge off mad, irrational fear. If it hadn't been for this confidence I gained from prayer, I imagine that I'd have gone into the ring inwardly shaking and quaking, thoroughly beaten in advance. As it was, I climbed into the ring that day with enough courage to go through the orthodox procedures of fighting a normal fight. In the second round I suddenly realised how groundless my fears had been. My opponent was no superman. I went on to win the fight.'

At the opening bell, Whitey Allen rushed at Tunney and threw a vicious right to the head. Tunney ducked the blow and landed a solid left to the body. Breaking from a clinch, Allen again threw his haymaker, but Tunney stepped inside the blow and hammered the body. As the round ended, Tunney had not been hit and Whitey had a red welt around his solar plexus. Allen tried that right again, as round two opened, but this time Tunney stepped back and threw his own right. Whitey went down and the referee counted him out. Happy New Year!

'I decided for the future,' Tunney would say, 'that no matter how uncertain the outcome of a match might be, I would shut the doors of my mind to the possibility of defeat. This process of mental training I started the moment Whitey Allen was counted out.'

Fighting around the New Jersey clubs that year, Tunney reeled off nine straight knockouts after taking care of Mr Allen. Two of those fights were against Al Roberts and 'KO' Sullivan. In later years, Tunney always said that Roberts nearly made him seek employment in some other line of business. Roberts, who worked on the Staten Island Railroad, was a big, powerful fellow who packed a wallop and regularly drew sellout crowds of 3,000 to the Port Richmond Coliseum. They followed him over to New Jersey that February night in 1920 when he fought Gene Tunney at the Newark Armoury and, according to journalist Jersey Jones, their noisy encouragement conceivably robbed their favourite of a knockout over the future world heavyweight champion.

Writing in a 1959 issue of *The Ring*, Jones recalled, 'Roberts was slow and crude in boxing technique, but a strong, willing slugger and the most dangerous puncher Tunney had faced up to that time. In the second round of the Tunney affair, Roberts nailed Gene with a lusty right on the chin. Tunney was hurt. His eyes glazed, his knees buckled, and he reeled back on rubbery legs. One more solid clout and the Greenwich Villager would certainly have hit the canvas.

'Roberts never started that punch. As Tunney staggered, Al's enthusiastic cohorts promptly turned loose a deafening racket with horns, whistles, bells, and a varied assortment of noise-producing gadgets. Just as he was about to belt Tunney again, Roberts suddenly spun around and walked to his corner. In the excitement, Al thought he heard the bell ending the round. Actually what he heard above all that din was a cowbell. It must have been at least ten seconds beore his frantic handlers were able to convince Roberts that the round still had a half-minute or so to go. By the time the Staten Islander resumed hostilities, however, Tunney had recovered. From then on a cautious, systematic Tunney gradually wore Roberts down and finally stopped him.'

Tunney would later tell ring historian Nat Fleischer that Al Roberts gave him his toughest fight on the road to the title. 'As long as I live I shall never forget the fine tanning I received at the hands of the big, sturdy Staten Islander,' he recalled. 'I was not ready for the big time, but I was informed that I could enjoy a good workout at the expense of Roberts, in spite of the fact that the record books showed he had run up a string of knockouts about a mile long, nineteen straight, I think. "He's made to order for you," said my manager. Roberts had no pity for a young man just trying to get along. How that old boy pummelled me in the first three rounds!

'He closed one of my eyes and split my lip. He staggered me time and again with solid rights to the jaw. Around the fourth session he brought a left hook from the floor, curled it around his gloved fist once or twice and let it fly. I saw it coming but before I could move it landed flush on my jaw. I saw stars and felt I was a goner. That aroused my Irish. In desperation I took a healthy swing and luckily Roberts' jaw came in contact with it . . . it sat Roberts on his all fours and before he could scramble to his feet the referee tolled off three. He came back at me like a maddened bull, raining blows on me from every angle. If I tried to block his right, his left kept spitting fire on my nose and mouth . . . I was praying and sure enough my prayers were answered in the seventh round when I caught him off balance with a terrific left hook to the chin. He fell as if shot. It must have hurt him terribly for he couldn't get up until the nine count was reached . . . I hit him another corking left hook and flop he went for a two count. The beating he received in this session paved the way for his defeat in the eighth. When he came out of his corner he looked as if a trolley car had run over him. I hit him with everything but the water bucket. As often as I floored him he would get up to run into another fusillade of punches. A left hook to the body doubled him up, and as he tried to land a left, I let go a terrific right, which caught him on the right spot and nearly carried his head off. He was practically out on the ropes, yet just before the referee intervened he staggered me with a couple of wild left swings. That was a fight of all fights, believe me.'

The fight with 'KO' Sullivan was equally dramatic, even if it lasted only a minute and a half. Tunney had beaten Sullivan over ten rounds in the AEF tournament in France and the Newark Armoury promoters figured it would make a good attraction to match the boys up again. A rough and tough southpaw from Pennsylvania, Sullivan stormed out of his corner at the sound of the bell and before Tunney could get his hands up, a bomb of a left hand exploded against his jaw. Tunney's knees buckled and he reeled back across the ring and into the ropes near his own corner. With visions of a sensational victory, Sullivan rushed in to finish his dazed opponent. But as he did so, Tunney fired a desperation right that smashed into Sullivan's incoming jaw and he was knocked cold.

Looking back on the fight, Jersey Jones wrote in *The Ring* magazine, 'What would have happened to Tunney had he been flattened so quickly that night? Knowing Gene as we did, we don't believe he was psychologically equipped to absorb so humiliating a defeat at that stage of his career. In all probability he would have quit the ring then and there and switched to a more prosaic and less hazardous occupation.'

Shortly after the Sullivan fight, Sammy Kelly returned from Havana and informed his now-promising light-heavyweight that he was resuming control of his career. Tunney argued that Billy Roche had done a good job so far and he thought Roche should still be involved. But when Kelly agreed to share the management of the Greenwich Village boxer, Roche didn't like the idea. Either he was the boss or he wasn't interested. Roche already had a deal going with another guy to open a theatrical agency, so wishing the young boxer luck, he departed. Tunney wasn't too happy at this turn of events. Sammy Kelly had too many irons in the fire, and his gambling habits gave cause for concern. If Tunney was on the road to the world championship, he wanted someone at the wheel he could trust. He talked it over with Kelly, who finally agreed to release him to a manager of Tunney's choice. He chose Frank 'Doc' Bagley.

'I believed Bagley to be the outstanding manager of my acquaintance,' Tunney recalled. 'Moreover, I had a personal liking for him, so finally decided to go up to Harlem to see him. Upon my stating my case, Bagley expressed his willingness to handle my affairs for twenty-five per cent. A verbal contract was agreed upon.'

Bagley was a good manager who knew the fight business and he was invaluable in the corner whenever blood started leaking from his fighter. In Ronald Fried's excellent book, *Corner Men*, legendary trainer Ray Arcel recollects, 'Doc Bagley chewed tobacco, and he could stop the worst kind of cuts. If the fella got cut he'd take a piece of chewing tobacco out of his mouth and press it up against the cut. I don't know whether it was the pressure applied or whether it was tobacco juice or whatever it was, but he was successful in stopping cuts.'

Doc Bagley had attended Manhattan College, and according to Whitey Bimstein, a contemporary of Arcel, 'was the first trainer to actually study medicine. He originated the use of adrenaline chloride to stop bleeding.' When he agreed to handle Tunney's business, Bagley was managing lightweight star Willie Jackson, and he didn't think a lot of the former marine. But he lined up some decent matches for Tunney and the New York boy obliged by doing the business in the ring, taking care of guys like Jeff Madden, Ole Anderson, and Sergeant Ray Smith. Paul Samson-Koerner snapped Tunney's knockout streak at eleven when he lasted the ten rounds in their Paterson, New Jersey fight, in October 1920. A few years later, fighting as Paul Samson, he was back in Germany winning his native heavyweight title.

Like all good workmen, a fighter needs a good set of tools if he is to get the job done, and his hands are his tools. If anything was going to slow Tunney's climb to the championship, the answer was quite literally in his own hands. The injury to the knuckle of his right hand, suffered in France and never properly treated, was giving him trouble again and it flared up in his second bout with Leo Houck in December of 1920.

From Lancaster, Pennsylvania, Houck was one of those rare fighters who campaign through every division from flyweight to heavyweight, even if it took him twenty years to do it. Along the way he crossed gloves 27 times with ten fighters who were, had been, or would be, world champions, from welterweight Jack Britton, middleweights Joe Thomas, Billy Papke, Frank Klaus, George Chip, Johnny Wilson and Harry Greb, light-heavies Jack Dillon and Battling Levinsky, to heavyweight Gene Tunney. Sportswriter Dave Gregg described Leo as 'one of the most highly skilled middleweights who ever pulled on a glove. The dark-haired, fair-skinned Houck was a master boxer whose near-impregnable defence enabled him to spot some of the most dangerous punchers in the trade as much as thirty pounds. Lionhearted Leo wasn't a slugger. He never wasted a punch and never took a blow he could avoid. Though the Quaker-Stater excelled in every department of the game, he was proficient in one phase to an almost unbelievable degree. Leo developed perhaps the greatest left jab of all time. No left lead in the annals of boxing was faster, more accurate, or more destructive. With Leo, the jab was an offensive rather than a defensive weapon. He shot into his opponent's face with the sickening force of a pile driver, often scoring knockdowns. Nobody could be effective with that slashing, unavoidable jab smearing his features. Houck rearranged a lot of profiles.'

There is no evidence that Leo Houck rearranged the handsome features of Gene Tunney in their two bouts in 1920, but he did rearrange Tunney's left thumb in the second fight. After boxing a six-rounds No-Decision bout in Philadelphia, they clashed again a fortnight later, this time in Jersey City. Tunney's right hand was already troubling him when, in the fourth round, he slammed a left to the body. The clever veteran dropped his elbow to block the punch, breaking Tunney's left thumb in the process.

'Here I was in the fourth round of a ten rounds bout with both hands practically useless,' remembered Tunney in his autobiography. 'By luck I happened to hit Houck on the temple with my right, putting him down for a nine count in the ninth round. I could not use either hand after this. In the tenth round of that match I realised that I'd gone away back in fighting form. I knew the cause. I decided to get out of boxing altogether until my hands got well. I had been considering going to a lumber camp. Now I was determined to do so.'

5

American Champion

Tunney celebrated Christmas with the family, greeted the New Year 1921, and set off for Canada to join a lumber company in Algonquin Park, Ontario. Along with the other men in camp he got out of bed at five in the morning, ate breakfast, and trudged along the snowy trails to the timberline in time to start cutting trees as soon as there was sufficient daylight. The heavy work, using axes and saws, and the fresh air soon put a healthy tan on the city boy's white face, and he could feel his hands getting stronger. Every night he fell asleep as soon as his head hit the pillow, too tired to even read a book. There would be plenty of time for that.

When the camp broke up in the spring, Tunney returned to New York, but he still was not happy that his hands were strong enough for what he had in mind – hitting some guy with a head like a rock, and not feeling it! He arranged through a friend to take a job at Poland Springs in Maine, where he spent another three months working as a labourer, strengthening his body and, most importantly, those wrists and hands.

Tunney also devised a means of training whereby he would stand for long periods pressing the full weight of his body on his knuckles and hands against a wall or partition. In floor exercises he would raise his body again and again on the tips of his toes and the flat of his knuckles, and finally on his fingertips. He also took to carrying around two small rubber balls, which he would continually squeeze in his hands.

'The purpose of these exercises was to strengthen the tendons, ligaments, and small muscles of the hands and knuckles,' he would say. 'It was something that could not be shirked. I had been given a glimpse of Dempsey's powerful mitts and I knew I was going to need good tools for that party.'

June 1921 found Tunney back in New York, back in the gym, and back in the fight business. He contacted Doc Bagley and told him to book a fight. Bagley fixed him up with Young Ambrose at the Pioneer Athletic Club in New York, on 29 June, but it was not the test Tunney was looking for. The sound of the opening bell had hardly died away when Tunney set his man up with a left jab, crossed a heavy right to the jaw, and Young Ambrose went into orbit, turned a somersault, and was counted out. Bagley had good news for Tunney however, when he came out of the ring. He was to fight the ten-rounds semi-final bout in Tex Rickard's 'Battle of the Century' promotion at Boyle's Thirty Acres in Jersey City, just three days later!

Rickard had Jack Dempsey defending his world heavyweight championship against the Frenchman Georges Carpentier and had built a huge wooden arena to hold the crowd of 80,183 who would pay boxing's first million-dollar gate. With a ringside priced at fifty bucks, the fight drew $1,789,238. While they waited to see Dempsey knock out Carpentier in the fourth round, those eighty thousand people had to watch Gene Tunney, the former marine who had won the AEF champion-ship in France, box another war veteran, Soldier Jones of Canada, in ten rounds or less.

At 25, the Canadian was a year older than Tunney and had mixed in better company – Harry Greb, for instance. The Pittsburgh Windmill blew Jones away in four rounds a couple of months before the Tunney fight and had slapped him around for ten rounds a couple of years previously, but Jones decked Greb in both fights and Greb would say, 'The Soldier hits hard. He looks like a bum against somebody you never heard of, and then turns around and looks like a champ for a few minutes against me!'

Jones had won the Canadian light-heavyweight crown with a five-rounds knockout of Tex McEwan and followed up by stopping the respectable Jack Renault in four rounds for the heavyweight title.

Tunney's big fight on that hot July afternoon in Jersey City was a big disappointment. Still a natural light-heavyweight, he had put on weight while working in Canada and Maine, and had scaled 189 pounds against Ambrose in his comeback fight. It didn't bother him in the less than one round it had taken to see off Ambrose, but it bothered him against Soldier Jones. The knuckles of both hands were still giving him trouble, although the fracture of the left hand sustained in the fight with Leo Houck stood up well against the dour Canadian. Tunney won the fight, the referee stopping it in round seven, but as he later recalled, 'It was a sorry exhibition that I gave that afternoon. It was particularly disappointing to me because of the number of people who saw it. I was so slow that I could not get out of my own way, much less out of the way of the wild swings that Jones was pitching at me, several of which landed on either side of my jaw in the first round. Had I not possessed a rather tough chin, I am convinced that my career would have ignominiously ended that day before the ninety thousand [sic] spectators who were forced to sit through our spectacle while waiting for Georges and Jack to start their Battle of the Century.'

George A Barton, respected Mid-Western boxing authority and sports editor, was ringside that day to cover the Dempsey fight. He reported, 'I was not particularly impressed with Tunney's performance against Jones, although I liked the fine competitive spirit he displayed. The Canadian was nothing more than a tough trial horse; he lacked boxing finesse and was a powder-puff puncher. Gene made hard work of it in besting Jones. Tunney hit Jones with almost every type of punch, he cut and bruised the Canadian and his punches knocked Jones off balance occasionally but Gene was unable to score even a knockdown. The referee, finally taking pity on Jones, halted the one-sided bout in the seventh round, making Tunney the winner by a technical knockout.'

Grantland Rice was the most beloved and best-respected sportswriter of his generation. He died on 13 July 1954, aged 73, having completed his autobiography just twelve days before. In that wonderful book, *The Tumult and the Shouting: My Life In Sport*, he remembered Gene Tunney. 'The Giants were playing at home and Heywood Broun, covering for the *World*, and I were in the press box at the Polo Grounds when Walter Trumbull, sports editor of the old *New York Post* appeared in our midst with a young fellow in tow. Trumbull introduced his guest, Gene Tunney, all round, and I recall that Broun made quite a fuss over the handsome youngster.

'I had glimpsed Tunney several days earlier when he fought Soldier Jones, a tough trial horse in a supporting bout to the Dempsey–Carpentier fight at Jersey City. Tunney scored a knockout in seven rounds. He was known only as a soldier-boxer who had won the light-heavyweight title of the AEF in France. However, he had not fought as a bona fide heavyweight and certainly looked no part of one.

'"What are your plans," I asked.

'"My plans are all Dempsey," he replied.

'"Very interesting," I said. "But why not sharpen your artillery on Harry Greb, Carpentier, or Tom Gibbons before you start hollering for Dempsey?"

'"I suppose I'll have to beat them on the way up," Tunney said. "But Dempsey is the one I want."

'I said no more and turned my attention back to McGraw's Giants, who with George (High Pockets) Kelly at first base, were headed for their first pennant since 1917. I recall that Tunney later volunteered that he was twenty-three years old. I couldn't help thinking that this forthright young fellow would make a fine insurance salesman but certainly had no business having his features and brains scrambled by Dempsey's steel fists.' Mr Rice and Mr Tunney would meet again.

The New Yorker had enjoyed the outdoor life in Canada and readily accepted the offer of retired contractor Harry F McCormack to train at his farm at Red Bank, New Jersey. Tunney loved the place so much that he used it as his training base for the next three years. There he set about shedding the surplus weight he was carrying around and started doing more physical work such as roadwork and chopping trees. 'I knew it would take months to strengthen my hands sufficiently to withstand the force of blows,' he said. 'Unfortunately for me, as a boxer, my hands are unusually small for a man of my size.'

If you had asked any pug in 1921 what he knew about William Pardon Bower, the response would have been a blank stare followed by the question, 'How much does the bum weigh?' Bower wrote a book entitled *Applied Anatomy and Kinesiology, the Mechanism of Muscular Movement*, and according to Nat Fleischer in his 1931 biography of Tunney, Gene would sit 'for hours in Madison Square Park, opposite the old Garden, with a copy . . . He studied about the solar plexus, the kidneys, the effects on the stomach of a heavy blow. And to that study, more than to his ring science and hard hitting, Tunney attributed the decisive defeats he administered to many of his opponents. He knew the vital spots, was aware of the reactions of the nerves to punishment, and this knowledge, combined with his natural ability as a fighter made him the most perfect stylist of modern times.'

A month after the Jones fight, Tunney tested his hands and his new-found knowledge of anatomy against Martin Burke at the Bronx Oval. Burke came out of the old French quarter of New Orleans, where his father was a cop. At a local church, where the French padre was running a boxing gym for kids, young Burke turned out to be a natural, going on to win the national amateur middleweight and heavyweight titles. When Jack Dempsey came to town to fight Carl Morris, he hired Burke as a sparring partner. Dempsey and manager 'Doc' Kearns were so impressed with the kid, they took him along with them, and by the time Dempsey took the championship off Jess Willard young Burke had sparred over a thousand rounds with the Manassa Mauler, and lived! Burke used the Dempsey experience to good effect when he turned professional in 1919 and by the time he hooked up with Tunney in New York, manager Jimmy Dunn had made him a box-office favourite in

New Orleans by having him fight guys like Bartley Madden, Carl Morris, Chuck Wiggins and George Chip.

Burke was a fast, clever boxer rather than a puncher, and he had height and reach advantages over Tunney in their ten-rounder. But Tunney was able to slow Burke down with his harder punches, and outbox and outpunch him in an entertaining bout, even if by the final bell he had suffered a badly bruised ear that would become slightly cauliflowered. Tunney came out with the decision, and sore hands.

Against Eddie Josephs in his next fight at Staten Island, Tunney decided to concentrate on a body attack for almost the entire twelve rounds. The local favourite had the crowd yelling from the start but they calmed down in the third round when Tunney sent Josephs tumbling to the canvas from a short right under the heart. He took the nine count before getting back into the fight but was on the receiving end of a systematic beating, and when the doctor checked him over in the dressing room afterwards, Josephs had lost two teeth and had three broken ribs over the heart. Josephs was the same guy Tunney had challenged in Perth Amboy when he was trying to get a fight after coming home from France and Josephs' brother-manager had turned him down.

Tunney fought an English light-heavyweight, Herbert Crossley from Mexborough, in New York, in September 1921. One of three boxing brothers, Crossley was regarded as a fine prospect, but Tunney hammered him until his seconds pulled him out in the seventh round. Crossley died suddenly a few weeks later, though his death had nothing to do with his fight with Gene Tunney. Oddly enough, Herbert's younger brother, Harry, who became British light-heavyweight champion in 1929, was only 47 when he died.

Tunney's manager, Doc Bagley, figured it was time his fighter had a press agent. 'How do you think Willie Jackson, Johnny Dundee, Benny Leonard, and Jack Dempsey keep their names before the public?' Bagley said to Tunney one day at the gym. 'Don't you realise that they must have press agents daily sending out copy, otherwise you would hardly hear of them?'

Tunney could see the wisdom of Bagley's advice and engaged the services of two newspapermen who had daily columns. They would get five per cent of Tunney's purses in exchange for getting his name onto the sports pages. This paid dividends sooner than Tunney could have hoped for when Tex Rickard offered him a fight in Madison Square Garden with Jack Burke of Pittsburgh. With Rickard and his heavyweight champion Jack Dempsey watching from ringside, Tunney punched Burke full of holes for a second-round stoppage. Rickard liked the look of the clean-cut former marine and booked him for a December fight with Eddie O'Hare. In the meantime Tunney stopped Wolf Larsen in seven rounds and went into camp for two months to get ready for O'Hare. Now that Tex Rickard knew he was alive, things could begin to happen.

Like Tunney, Eddie O'Hare was from Greenwich Village. A tall, lanky kid who had been a standout in the amateurs, he was being touted as an upcoming professional champion by his manager, a wise old bird named Leo P Flynn. O'Hare had been going great guns until running into veteran Cap'n Bob Roper at the old Commonwealth Club in Harlem. He handed Roper a sound beating until the dying seconds of the bout when Cap'n Bob finally got the range and knocked the kid spark out. O'Hare got the decision but he didn't know, not until he woke up! He wasn't quite the same after that experience but Flynn still had faith in the kid and took the match with Tunney at the Garden, a few days before Christmas 1921. Tunney was keen for the fight with his Greenwich Village neighbour, for O'Hare had been one of Dempsey's sparring partners for his fight with Carpentier. Maybe Tunney could learn something of the champion from O'Hare.

'Eddie was a remarkably fast, shifty and alert boxer, a fine, hard hitter, and dead game,' wrote Nat Fleischer. 'His left hand was poison when the punch landed, for it carried dynamite and he could snap it out with the precision of a snake's darting fang. His right, too, sank in deep every time it hit the stomach and against these Tunney had to be mighty wary. Yet the Fighting Marine proved Eddie's master. Eddie befuddled Tunney at the start with his cleverness, but Gene soon solved the riddle and then took the play away from his opponent. In the sixth round he jockeyed Eddie into a position against the ropes, feinted him, and then crashed his right to the jaw. Down went O'Hare. He arose at the count of nine, but his underpinning was weak and he seemed ready to fall.

'Gene stepped back and with a look of anxiety, appealed to the referee to halt proceedings, but to his astonishment, the official motioned for him to go on. Although eager to refrain from hitting Eddie again, the AEF champion took one more punch at him. He crashed a terrific right to the jaw and the bout was over. They carried Eddie from the ring. A few weeks later, O'Hare, to recuperate, took a trip to Maine, where he went tobogganing. He struck a tree and broke his neck. He was the second opponent who had died shortly after engaging in combat with Tunney, and naturally the coincidence had its effect on Gene.'

However, there was good news for Tunney as Christmas approached. Rickard had matched him with Battling Levinsky for the American light-heavyweight championship at Madison Square Garden, scheduled for 13 January 1922. Levinsky was a ring-wise veteran of some twelve years with 240-odd fights against the biggest and the best. His real name was Barney Lebrowitz and he was born to Jewish parents in Philadelphia. His father apprenticed him to a jeweller when he finished school and it was his employer who insisted he join a boxing gym so that he could protect the stock should there be a hold-up. One night he was invited to a social club and wandered into the wrong building, where a secret union meeting was taking place. Suspected of being a spy for their employers, Barney was set upon and had to defend himself, which he did rather well before making his escape. On the way home he passed a fight club, where he paid his dollar, took his seat and was promptly bitten by the boxing bug. By the end of that night, he had made up his mind to become a fighter.

Lebrowitz knew the family wouldn't take kindly to the news of his decision, so he started boxing as Barney Williams, and by the time his father found out, he was doing rather well with his mitts. Lacking a punch, he developed his boxing skills based on a sound defence and by the time he faced Gene Tunney in 1922, only two men had managed to beat him inside the distance, Jack Dempsey and Georges Carpentier. It was when he hooked up with Dumb Dan Morgan in 1913 that Barney Williams became Battling Levinsky.

'For one thing the fans don't know you're Jewish,' said Morgan, 'and that's bad for publicity because they all know Hebrew fighters are some of the best you can get. And we'll call you Battling to cover up the fact that you're a counter-puncher.'

Levinsky lived and fought out of a suitcase. He wrapped up 35 fights in 1914, the last one on Christmas Day, then incredibly he boxed three times on New Year's Day 1915. In the morning he boxed ten rounds with Bartley Madden in Brooklyn, crossed into Manhattan for a ten-rounder with Soldier Kearns in the afternoon, then hopped on a train to Waterbury, Connecticut, where he went twelve rounds with Gunboat Smith!

'How Levinsky loved to fight,' exclaimed Morgan. 'He once fought five times in one week. I normally gave him Wednesday nights off! Bat was taking his wife to the theatre this Wednesday when I got a call for a fight, $500, so I jumped in a cab and got to the theatre as they were going in. Mrs Levinsky took her seat and Bat took his seat beside me in the cab. We went to the arena, he knocked the guy out, and was back at the theatre in time for the third act!'

Fighting all over the country never bothered Levinsky, who looked after himself, but it took its toll on Morgan who enjoyed a more colourful lifestyle. 'Bat,' he would say, 'for the love of Mike get sick, or something. This change of food and water on these one-night stands is killing me!'

Levinsky fought many of boxing's top men more than once: Jack Dillon ten times, nine with Porky Flynn, eight against Clay Turner, Gunboat Smith and Harry Greb six times each, five with Billy Miske, and four times against Leo Houck, Fireman

Jim Flynn, Charley Weinert and Bartley Madden. He and Dillon kicked the light-heavyweight title around between them until the Battler finally won a decision in Boston in 1916 to become world champ. By the time he climbed into the Garden ring with Tunney, Bat had lost his title to Carpentier but Morgan was still claiming the American title for him and it was on the line that night, along with a diamond-studded belt Tex Rickard had promised the winner. At the official weigh-in, Levinsky was actually one-and-a-half pounds over the class limit, scaling 176½ pounds to 172 for Tunney, but the New York Commission recognised it as a title match, and Tunney refused to accept the Battler's weight forfeit.

A record number of people crowded into the old Garden that Friday night, with 14,428 paid admissions, and most of them were cheering for the New York boy. Tunney didn't let them down. From the first bell he carried the fight to the veteran and Levinsky was forced to call on his survival skills to stay with his younger rival. After a few seconds of sparring in that first round, Tunney forced his way inside to hammer the body. Tunney kept his man on the defensive, scoring repeatedly with lefts and rights, although Levinsky weathered the storm.

Nat Fleischer reported, 'Though concentrating most of his attack to the body, Tunney jarred Levinsky with a hard right to the head, midway of the second, and just at the end of the round crowded him into a neutral corner and rocked him with a clean right hand smash to the jaw. Tunney was pounding Levinsky hard at the bell.'

Tunney continued to outbox the champion through rounds three and four and in the fifth staggered Levinsky with a terrific left hook, then a hard left before the Battler could fall into a clinch. The veteran was glad to hear the bell.

At ringside for the *New York Times*, James Dawson wrote, 'Levinsky weathered a trying storm in the sixth session. For a time it appeared that the bout would end there in a knockout for Tunney. Tunney, forcing Levinsky before him continuously, crashed over a left to the jaw, which sent Levinsky up against the ropes. When the Battler rebounded Tunney sent home a left and right to the jaw and quickly crashed past Levinsky's defence with a left hook to the jaw, which staggered the champion. Tunney continued his assault until the bell ended the round. As he went to his corner, Levinsky was bleeding from a cut over the left eye, a bruised mouth and a banged-up nose.'

By the seventh round, the fast pace maintained by Tunney along with his relentless body attack had slowed Levinsky and the veteran held repeatedly. His face was a bloody smear and his legs were shaky again as Tunney found his jaw with hard right smashes. A heavy right to the jaw followed by another under the heart made the Battler grab his tormentor and hang on till the bell. There was a brief moment of glory for the Philadelphian in round nine when he caught Tunney napping and landed two right-hand swings to the head, but Tunney was soon back on the attack and had his man hanging on at the bell.

Dawson reported, 'In the tenth and eleventh rounds Tunney forced the fighting steadily and had Levinsky in full retreat. Repeatedly at long range Tunney sank his left to the stomach and crashed over the right to the face in an assault which had the crowd yelling wildly. Tunney gave his rival no time to set in the twelfth round, the West-Sider forced Levinsky before him and the weary battler clinched with each exchange at long range. Tunney had all the better of the milling and had a clear lead in points at the final bell. It was a manifestly just verdict, as was indicated in the approving shout that was sent up by the capacity crowd. The result was not unexpected. Levinsky, aged in ring activity and in years, assumed too great a task in the effort to overcome the youth and vigorous strength of the aspiring Tunney. It was another of those examples of the ring, a victory for youth and strength over age and experience.'

Yet Fleischer would proclaim, 'Tunney that night whipped a Levinsky who was far better physically than the Battler who had lost the world title to Carpentier. Against Tunney there was the real Levinsky, the cool ring general who was a marvel in his prime. It was his defensive skill, his canny ring generalship that enabled him to go the route against the younger, faster, aggressive, hard-hitting opponent.'

In his autobiography, Tunney recalled, 'At the beginning of the twelfth and last round, as we came to the centre of the ring, Levinsky whispered to me, "Please, let me stay, Gene." Having only the kindest feelings towards the old warrior, I relaxed. Whereupon, at the very next exchange, with my guard lowered, the old battler planted a right with all his might on the side of my jaw. It was fortunate for me that Levinsky could not hit. Instead of getting furious, I laughed at myself for being taken in by such an ancient and obvious trick. I was given the decision and the title of light-heavyweight champion of America. I never got the promised diamond-studded belt from Tex Rickard.'

6

Harry Greb

In the aftermath of Tunney's fine victory over Levinsky, Nat Fleischer wrote, 'His fame as a two-fisted fighter had spread and promoters were on his trail. Tunney was in demand, but not in his hometown, where the scribes and promoters still figured that he was just an ordinary attraction. Such is Fate! A hero everywhere except in his own city!'

Just a few weeks after winning his title, Tunney stopped Jack Clifford in six rounds at the Rink Sporting Club, in Brooklyn. Three days later he was in Philadelphia to box Whitey Wenzel at the Ice Palace. Whitey had shared a ring no less than ten times with Harry Greb between 1914 and 1917, all No-Decision bouts with his people claiming he beat Greb at least twice. He couldn't beat Gene Tunney, who knocked him out inside four rounds. Grand Rapids, Michigan, was the scene of Tunney's next assignment: ten rounds with Fay Kaiser, another guy who claimed four newspaper decisions over Greb in their eight fights. Kaiser had just boxed Tommy Loughran in Philadelphia and he made Tunney step along for ten rounds, with the reporters at ringside marking Gene a winner. Then Tunney headed back to New York to see the fight between Tom Gibbons and Harry Greb at the Garden. Joe Humphreys introduced Gene from the ring before the first bell and informed the crowd that the winner would get a crack at Tunney's American title.

In a February 1926 issue of *Collier's Magazine*, Grantland Rice wrote, 'The first time I ever saw Harry Greb was when he

met Tom Gibbons at the old Madison Square Garden.
Gibbons at that time was in his prime, a great boxer, a hard
hitter, a cool, courageous campaigner who outweighed Greb by
ten or twelve pounds. He was a younger Gibbons than the man
who stayed fifteen rounds with Dempsey at Shelby. Yet Greb
fell upon the St Paul star with such speed and fury that Gibbons
was literally buffeted all over the ring. The brilliant defensive
boxer from St Paul had no defence that could face the speed,
skill and savage fury of Greb's onslaught. In one exchange Greb
hit Gibbons seven times before the latter could counter once.
After noting Greb's speed through the first two rounds the
general opinion was that he would soon blow up, that no
human frame could stand that dizzy pace. But in place of
blowing or slowing down the Pittsburgher put on additional
speed, and his final charge in the fifteenth round was the fastest
of the lot.'

Greb versus Gibbons was the first of the Milk Fund fights
sponsored by Mrs William Randolph Hearst and the Garden
ringside was more like opening night at the opera. There was
Mr and Mrs Vincent Astor, with Mr and Mrs Kermit Roose-
velt. The William K Vanderbilts had a box, and W Rhinelander
Stewart was also present, along with some of the Dukes.

James R Fair, in his brilliant biography of Greb, *Give Him to
the Angels*, wrote, 'The bell rang and out of their corners wheeled
Greb and Gibbons, disrespect in their eyes, fury in their hearts,
murder in their fists. It was New York's first view of them and it
watched amazed while at intervals, first one and then the other
stepped back and spat out blood and/or teeth. The fight was
featured by rough tactics, at which Greb was the aggressor and
the more adept. Tunney had said he wanted to box Greb
because Gibbons, an almost technically perfect boxer as well as
a knockout artist, was too experienced for him. He sat in a
ringside seat, not missing a thing up there under those strong
lights, and his face was sombre as Greb larruped Gibbons with
jarring blows from every angle and bullied him around the ring.
It was a hard, mean fight. It was one-sided, with Greb winning
twelve of the fifteen rounds, but it was vicious and frightening.

Gibbons had entered the ring such a heavy favourite that not even the Pittsburgh millions could knock down the odds which in some quarters were as high as four to one. He fought hard to justify those odds. But Greb fought harder to ridicule them. He had bet his share of the purse, $17,500, on himself to win. That was the way he had always bet and that was why those Pittsburgh millions rode on his nose.'

That sensational victory earned Harry Greb a crack at Tunney's American title and Rickard set the match for 23 May 1922, two months later. Tunney had one more engagement before going into training: a return bout with Jack Burke. The Pittsburgh fighter had lost to Tunney inside two rounds of their fight in the Garden, but his fans and backers refused to believe the New Yorker was the better man. So Tunney went into Burke's own backyard and stopped him again, this time in nine rounds, at the Motor Square Garden. Then it was time to get ready for Greb.

Tunney prepared at Red Bank in New Jersey. Mickey Walker, who would go on to win the welterweight title a few months later, also trained there, and recalled his first impressions on meeting Tunney in a 1955 issue of the *National Police Gazette*. 'We were introduced by a mutual friend, Harry McCormack. Gene's name slipped by me, because I had never heard it before. I had the feeling I might be shaking hands with a young artist, a young philosopher or a wealthy young man who had an interest in boxing. Tunney didn't look like a fighter, nor did he have the mannerisms of one.'

At that time Tunney owned a second-hand Cadillac. Returning to camp after his fight with Kaiser in Grand Rapids, he walked into the garage to check on his car, emerging a few minutes later to ask, 'Who has been driving my car?' When no one answered, Gene said angrily, 'I took the speedometer reading before I left, now it's way over the previous mark.' One of the sparring partners finally spoke up. 'I only took a girl friend for a ride around town,' he said.

As Walker recalled, 'Gene said, "Didn't I tell all you boys to keep away from girls while you're training here? You're fired!"

Another time when he was training for his first fight with Harry
Greb, one of the spectators who came to the gym to watch
Gene work passed an obscene remark while Gene was in the
ring sparring. He stopped, and turning in the direction of the
voice said, "If anyone uses that kind of language again, they'll
have to leave." These incidents formed an impression in my
mind that Tunney might be kind of softhearted in a tough fight.
But the impression didn't last.'

On fight night, Gene had more serious problems than foul-
mouthed spectators. 'My left eyebrow had opened, and both
hands were sorely injured,' he recalled. 'I had a partial
reappearance of the old left elbow trouble which prevented my
using a left jab. Dr Robert J Shea, a close friend, who took care
of me during my training, thought that a hypodermic injection
of adrenalin chloride over the left eyebrow would prevent
bleeding when the cut was re-opened by Greb. At my request
he injected a hypodermic solution of novocaine into the
knuckles of both hands as well. We locked the dressing room
door during this performance.'

Greb's manager, George Engel, was not a happy man when
he found the door locked, preventing him examining Tunney's
hand bandages before the fight. Banging noisily on the door, he
demanded admittance. He was finally allowed in when the
doctor had completed his task, and he insisted Tunney remove
the bandages from his hands. The New Yorker refused at first,
but when Engel read the Riot Act he submitted to the
manager's wishes. The tapes were removed; Engel was satisfied, and returned to see to his fighter. This was a big one for
the Pittsburgh Windmill. He wanted Tunney's title.

Growing up in Pittsburgh, young Edward Henry Greb
always wanted to be a fighter. His sister, Ida, recalled that at the
age of ten he would go down into the basement, stand on a box,
strike a fighting pose, and proclaim himself champion of the
world. His father, Pious Greb, hoped he would be a baseball
player, but lifetime pal Happy Albacker always said, 'Harry
could never even catch a ball, never once! He was the worst
baseball player you ever saw.'

But Harry Greb was a helluva fighter! Starting in May 1913, Greb fought anybody, anywhere, at any time. A natural middleweight, he regularly stepped out with men who outweighed him by twenty or thirty pounds, and whipped them to a standstill. In the nine years up to his first fight with Gene Tunney, Greb packed in an incredible 225 fights and his record resembled a veritable boxing Who's Who: George Chip, Tommy Gibbons, Mike Gibbons, Al McCoy, Jack Dillon, Battling Levinsky, Mike O'Dowd, Mike McTigue, Gunboat Smith and Bill Brennan, most of them champions at one time or another. Harry Greb licked them all and when they came back for more he whipped them again.

'I am a great believer in putting about all I have in the attack,' he would say. 'I never think along defensive lines. My plan is to start an offensive rush from the first second and keep both gloves as busy as my two arms can drive them. And I like to fight as often as I can, for that keeps me in shape.'

'When Greb is fighting,' wrote Grantland Rice, 'you have the impression that the arc-lighted air of the ring is full of boxing gloves, boxing gloves thrown from thirty or forty directions in fusillades, salvos, volleys. He comes upon an opponent like a swarm of bees. No matter how fast his opponents have been, Greb has always been a little faster. And no matter how hard they had trained, Greb, without any training, was usually in better condition with more stamina to call upon.'

Harry Keck was a nationally recognised boxing authority, sports editor of the old Pittsburgh *Sun-Telegraph*, and a close friend and confidant of Greb. 'Each rehash of the Greb legend is more sickening than the one before it,' he would say. 'A foul fighter? Take a look at the record, there's your answer. Harry was disqualified only once in a career that spanned almost fourteen years and more than 300 fights! True, there were some months when he did very little training. But look again at the record. He fought so often that he used one fight as preparation for the next. As for his alleged drinking, do you think a drunkard could have compiled a remarkable record like that of Greb?'

Greb was a rough fighter who came at you with everything – fists, thumbs, elbows, head – but he never complained if you did it back to him. It was that way when he clashed with Kid Norfolk in August 1921 at Forbes Field, Pittsburgh. By about the fifth round, the Kid got fed up with Greb's thumb in his eye and retaliated. From that moment on, Harry Greb was virtually blind in his right eye, yet it was a secret known only to a few intimate friends. He sought no treatment, just went on fighting for the next five years, putting some of his greatest fights in the book. One of them was against Gene Tunney in Madison Square Garden that May night in 1922.

Defending his new title, Tunney weighed 172½ pounds against Greb's 162¼ pounds, and he was almost five inches taller, but Greb was nine years and 225 fights better that night and he took the young man from Greenwich Village to school. At the opening bell, Greb roared across the ring and in the first exchange Tunney suffered a double fracture of his nose. In the fury of Greb's attack it was not clear whether a butt or a glove had caused the damage. What was clear was that Tunney's nose poured blood for the entire fifteen rounds. The blood ran down his body, ran down his throat, smeared both Greb and referee Kid McPartland. And before that nightmare three minutes had ended, a deep gash was ripped over Tunney's left eyebrow.

'It was one of the bloodiest and one-sided championship fights ever seen in the professional ring,' wrote Greb's biographer, James R Fair. 'Save for the third, fourth, and seventh rounds, in which Tunney held his own, Greb couldn't have won more decisively if he had knocked him out a dozen times. With the first flurry of punches, delivered before the bout was twenty seconds old, he broke Tunney's nose in two places. A moment later, Tunney's face was drenched in blood and, fed by a long, ugly gash which Greb opened above his left eye, it remained that way throughout the fight.

'Greb's gloves were soggy from slushing in the blood. The blood, and sweat, like grease, was deflecting his punches. He would step back and hold out his gloves and blood-bespattered Kid McPartland, the referee, would wipe them off with a towel.

Tunney fought back gamely, doggedly moving forward. He wouldn't quit. He was a champion and the kind of champion he was doesn't know how to quit. Greb would rain a fusillade of blows against his face, down which blood cascaded, then push him away and ask McPartland, "Wanna stop it?" McPartland would ask Tunney how about it and Tunney would say, "Don't you stop it." Sometimes, when his throat was clogged with blood and he couldn't talk, he would shake his head no. Greb would leap in and resume the carnage.'

In his autobiography, Tunney recounted, 'I am convinced that the adrenalin solution that had been injected so softened the tissue that the first blow or butt I received cut the flesh right to the bone. In the third round another cut over the left eye left me looking through a red film. For the better part of twelve rounds, I saw this red phantom-like form dancing before me. I had provided myself with a fifty-per cent mixture of brandy and orange juice to take between rounds in the event I became weak from loss of blood. I had never taken anything during a fight up to that time. Nor did I ever again. It is impossible to describe the bloodiness of this fight. My seconds were unable to stop either the bleeding from the cut over my left eye, which involved a severed artery, or the bleeding consequent to the nose fractures. Doc Bagley, who was my chief second, made futile attempts to congeal the nose-bleeding by pouring adrenalin into his hand and having me snuff it up my nose. This I did round after round. The adrenalin, instead of coming out through my nose again, ran down my throat with the blood and into my stomach.'

Greb made the first and second rounds his own. Tunney fought back with a body attack in round three, while Greb targeted the nose. The fourth was a furious session and they fought on some fifteen seconds after the bell before McPartland could tear them apart. Greb had shaded that round and Tunney fought desperately enough to make the fifth even, his hammer blows to the mid-section giving Greb something to think about. But the Pittsburgh Windmill almost blew Tunney out of the ring in round six and the New Yorker was glad to hear the bell. Yet Tunney summoned the strength from somewhere deep in his fighter's soul to launch a savage attack to Greb's body in the seventh round, left and right hooks thudding home to let his opponent know he was still there. Greb didn't need reminding and he tore from his corner for the eighth round to punch Tunney all over the ring. At the bell Tunney was bleeding from a cut over his right eye.

'The Greenwich Village boy had the grotesque appearance of having eyebrows of brilliant red,' reported Nat Fleischer. 'As the fight progressed, Greb's speed seemed to increase, and in the twelfth round he was delivering more spectacular fireworks than in the first. He took the ninth easily, but was held to an even break in the tenth. The eleventh was Greb's, his blows numbering six to Tunney's one.'

At the end of the twelfth round, Tunney took a swallow of the brandy and orange juice, something he regretted almost immediately. Everything he looked at through that blood-red film started spinning around and they had to push him off his stool for the thirteenth round. Somehow he survived those last three rounds, knowing that if he stopped for even one second he would collapse, or McPartland would stop the fight, a sporting contest that had become a brutal slaughter.

'At the end of fifteen brutal, terrifying rounds,' recorded James R Fair, 'Greb gave Tunney over to his handlers, a bleeding, helpless hulk, and loped off with his title. Staggering uncertainly, Tunney mumbled through swollen lips, "Well, Harry, you were the better man, tonight." Half blind, sick, his body bruised from ceaseless battering, his face a pulpy mask, Tunney stumbled toward his dressing room, blood dripping off his face on to his chest. He collapsed before he got there and his handlers carried him the rest of the way. The moment supporting hands left him, he fell back with a thud, the back of his head striking the rubbing table.'

Dr William Walker of the Boxing Commission attended to Tunney in the dressing room and it was a good two hours before he was ready to leave the Garden. As the fighter had lain there, utterly exhausted but his mind clear, old-time featherweight champion Abe Attell came into the room and planted a kiss on Tunney's battered face. 'Kid,' he said, 'you're the gamest fighter I ever saw. I lost twenty-five hundred dollars on you, but to hell with it. In the second round I sent out for four bottles of adrenalin chloride and gave them to Bagley. I never saw any cuts like them. You were the better man tonight, and the gamest in the world.'

There was a grim humour in the immediate aftermath of that terrible beating that was not lost on the intelligent Tunney. In the taxi taking them away from the Garden, Doc Bagley lay back in his seat and, wiping a sweaty hand across his forehead, said, 'What a job you gave me tonight! I am all in! Do you know that we used six bottles of adrenalin chloride trying to stop those cuts?' 'I was too weary to get angry,' recalled the brave contender. 'Poor Doc. All I did was bleed.'

Gene Tunney had suffered his first professional defeat in losing his coveted championship to Greb. He would never be beaten again. In fact as he left the Garden that night, he had already arrived at a startling conclusion. He knew he could beat Greb, he had realised that much even as his tormentor was driving him around the ring with his hammering fists. He realised the terrible handicap he had been in from the very first round, his nose smashed and gashed over the eye. He wanted Greb again, and soon!

'In relating the story to me,' wrote Nat Fleischer, 'Doc Bagley said that Gene asked him for an appointment two days after the fight and when they met, Gene, still showing the marks of battle, said, "Doc, Greb couldn't knock me out, although he had me at one time helpless. The next time I meet him, I'll turn the tables with a vengeance. I was puzzled by his erratic rushes and his mauling style and made the mistake of standing off and trying to box him. You can't box with a buzz saw. The only way to stop a buzz saw is to throw a hunk of iron into it. That's what I'll do when I meet him again. Get me another match. I want it within a few weeks."'

Tunney did not recover from the Greb beating as quickly as he thought he would, and he was forced to stay in bed for a week when he returned to Red Bank. The great loss of blood had left him weak and exhausted, but rest and a blood tonic prescribed by Dr Shea soon had him back on his feet.

It was a few days after the Greb fight that Gene saw his father at home in Perry Street. Most of the bruises and discolouration had left his face by that time, but John Tunney had read the papers, the lurid descriptions by the tabloid reporters, and had heard the talk among his friends and workmates at the docks. 'Gene, why did you let Greb beat you?' he wanted to know.

'What does a beating mean when you receive twenty-two thousand dollars for it?' said his son.

'It doesn't make any difference whether you receive twenty-two million dollars,' his father exclaimed. 'You were beaten. You shouldn't have let Greb do that.'

Grantland Rice would recall Tunney's sole defeat 'in perhaps the bloodiest fight I ever covered. A great fighter, or brawler, Greb handled Tunney like a butcher hammering a Swiss steak. How the Greenwich Village Irishman with the crew haircut survived fifteen rounds I'll never know, except that Tunney always enjoyed more and better physical conditioning than anybody he ever fought. By the third round, Gene was literally wading in his own blood. I saw Gene a few days later. His face looked as though he'd taken the wrong end of a razor fight. To me, that fight was proof that Tunney meant to stick with prize fighting.'

Sports columnist Damon Runyon covered the Garden fight, writing, 'Fighters who lose fights have cut eyes, broken noses, torn lips and broken bones. Tonight, Gene Tunney simply had a broken face. He had no business being around for the full fifteen rounds, but he was and you have to take your hat off to this boy. He has the kind of courage of which great champions are made.'

7

Coming Back

Doc Bagley turned a deaf ear to Tunney's request for an immediate rematch with Greb, advising him to take a long rest, but Tunney wouldn't hear of it. A couple of days after the fight in the Garden, he was at the offices of the New York State Athletic Commission to collect his purse of $22,500 and lodge his $2,500 bond for a challenge against Harry Greb. Before the commission would accept it, however, Tunney was informed that a copy of a written contract between himself and Bagley must be filed with the commission. Although he and Bagley had a verbal agreement, when the necessary form was produced, Gene signed it rather than postpone his challenge any longer. That signature would cost him $5,000 a few months later, when he sought to end his relationship with Bagley.

In two weeks Tunney was back in the gym and in six weeks he was back in the ring, fighting Fay Kaiser in a rematch over twelve rounds at Rockaway, Long Island. After four rounds of having Kaiser's hard head being shoved into his face, opening cuts both sides of his chin, Tunney asked the referee to request that Mr Kaiser stop using his head or put a glove on it! 'I have cautioned him several times, Gene,' said the third man, 'but I can't do nothing with him.'

'Then I will,' replied Tunney. In round five, as Kaiser came in with his head again, the New Yorker felt for his left eye, threatening to stick his thumb into it. Kaiser let out a yell to the referee, claiming Tunney was gouging him. When he was told to get on with the fight, they clinched, and with the head going in again, Tunney once more made as if to poke a thumb into Kaiser's right eye. Another protest to the referee fell on deaf ears and from then on Kaiser stuck to the rules as laid down by the commission.

At the end of twelve rounds, Gene Tunney was back on the winning trail. An easy third-round knockout over Ray Thompson followed at Long Branch, and then Bagley matched him with Charley Weinert, in what was to be a twelve-rounds No-Decision bout in Newark.

Coming from West Orange, New Jersey, Weinert started fighting at thirteen and a few years later shocked New Yorkers when he gave veteran Battling Levinsky a boxing lesson at Bill Brown's Gym. Moving to Newark he became known as the Newark Adonis and he liked his growing celebrity so much that he was soon known as Good-Time Charley. He figured he didn't need to train – he was beating guys like Gunboat Smith, Jim Coffey, Boer Rodel and Porky Flynn. A big, strong fellow, he was dynamite when in the mood, but he abused his natural talents and never did fulfil his potential. Nevertheless he gave Gene Tunney a helluva fight that August night in 1922 and, according to Tunney, Good-Time Charley had a little help from a friend.

'Against my specific instructions,' he recalled in *A Man Must Fight*, 'my manager agreed to let Henry Lewis, Weinert's pal, into the ring as referee. I had to battle two men that night, Lewis when he held my hands so Weinert could hit me, and Weinert as he was hitting me. However, I had the satisfaction of throwing Weinert out of the ring twice, the second time he landed head first on the platform outside the ring.'

It was a vicious affair and Tunney was fouled repeatedly, roughed up in the clinches, but he fought back well to give Good-Time Charley some of his own medicine, and at the final bell most of the ringside press gave their vote for Tunney. A week later Tunney was off to Philadelphia to box local favourite Tommy Loughran. Just nineteen, the Irish-American was already being hailed as a fine boxer with a brilliant left hand.

Loughran had just furthered his education in a fight with Harry Greb when he faced Tunney in the National League Ball Park, set for an eight-rounds No-Decision contest.

Tunney put his stamp on the fight in the opening round when a heavy left and right to the jaw dropped Loughran in a cloud of resin dust for a nine count. Loughran seemed none the worse for his tumble, however, and fought back against the heavier man, more than holding his own in some stirring exchanges. He hurt Tunney several times with blows over the heart and at the final bell there was little between them. Nat Fleischer gave Tunney five of the eight rounds, some reporters called it a draw, while the two local papers, the *Evening Bulletin* and the *Enquirer,* both saw Loughran as the winner. Tunney would recall, 'Lacking a punch, the strongest and best natural defence in boxing, Loughran did more with what he had than any fighter in my experience.' The Philadelphia boxing master, who would go on to win the world championship at light-heavyweight, became one of Tunney's biggest supporters. 'Tunney was as strong as a bull,' he recalled. 'Gene couldn't punch as murderously as Dempsey did, but don't think he couldn't hit. I fought him once and he nearly knocked my head off with a straight right that he got home early in the game. However, Gene was of the intellectual type and depended on his boxing ability and boxing brains to win.'

Chuck Wiggins was a rough, tough guy who fought the best from middleweight up to heavyweight, tangling with such head-liners as Tommy Gibbons, Harry Greb, Tommy Loughran, Les Darcy, Mike Gibbons and Tiger Flowers, and in 1920 he took world light-heavyweight champion Battling Levinsky to a draw over twelve rounds. He enjoyed a foul-filled, nine-bout series with Greb, all No-Decision affairs, and claimed victory in at least two of them. Greb would say of Wiggins, 'He was the best butter I ever butted against!'

Lester Bromberg in his book, *Boxing's Unforgettable Fights,* remembers, 'The Greb–Wiggins contention for the honours as "dirtiest fighter in the world" had been a long-standing feud. Gene first met Wiggins at Boston in the fall of 1922. Chuck thumbed him, butted him, and elbowed him. Tunney kept his straight left flying in Chuck's face for a ten-rounds decision. "Thanks, Chuck," he said afterwards, "you remind me of somebody we both know." Wiggins scowled. "That Greb, huh?" he replied, "Well, I can do anything he can do." Gene said, "You'll get a chance to show me some more."

Recalling that Boston fight in October 1922, Tunney would say, 'A very amusing thing happened in this fight. At this period I was developing a new punch. After feinting, I would bend down, slip in, and bring a left uppercut to the solar plexus or liver. My judgement of distance was not yet good. On two occasions I tried this on Wiggins, and was cautioned by the referee both times for hitting low. In the seventh round I slipped in and again accidentally hit Chuck low. The referee immediately jumped between us, he was ready to give the fight to Wiggins on a foul, but Chuck pushed him aside and said, "Christ, Gene, no kidding, that was low! Keep 'em up!" He then resumed fighting, though he had been getting a fairly good whaling. Chuck was not of the school that would take a fight on a foul unless he was really incapacitated.'

Next up on Tunney's hit parade was the unfortunate Jack Hanlon. They tangled at the Clermont Avenue Rink in Brooklyn just a week after the Wiggins fight and Tunney was in devastating form. They had been matched just over a year previously in Jersey City but the show was cancelled when the main event fell apart. Hanlon had been bad-mouthing the New Yorker ever since, telling all and sundry what he was going to do to 'that bum, Tunney!' But the ex-marine didn't give him a chance to do anything, coming from his corner like a bat out of hell. A thudding left and right crashed to the jaw and Hanlon crashed to the floor, blood oozing from his mouth. The fight had lasted all of thirty seconds! Jack Hanlon didn't say much about 'that bum, Tunney' afterwards. In fact, he didn't say much about anything, on account of his lower jaw being broken!

'Later, I learned the facts of the case,' revealed Tunney in his 1941 autobiography, *Arms For Living*. 'Hanlon, once a pretty good heavyweight but now washed up, had not been in a ring for a year. He was in no condition to box, should not have been permitted to try. His recent boasting about bums and Tunney had been the vainest of talk, as he himself had known. He undoubtedly honestly felt Tunney was a bum. He had taken the bout with me only to pick up some extra money, and probably thought he had a good chance to win. Actually it was a shame to hit him at all, but I didn't know. For weeks I was haunted by the mental picture of the unconscious Hanlon lying on the canvas, blood oozing from his mouth, his jaw broken. I had never before boxed with anger, and I never did again.'

Tunney hadn't been satisfied with his performance against Charley Weinert in their Newark fight, and readily agreed to meet Weinert again, this time in Madison Square Garden, on 19 November 1922, Thanksgiving eve. The boys weren't feeling very charitable towards each other when the bell rang for round one. Weinert started the rough stuff straight away. He wanted to make Tunney angry, upset his game plan. But Gene was cool, calm and collected, and he jabbed methodically, knocking Weinert off balance and shaking him up with solid left and right hooks. In the third round, the Newark Adonis smashed home a terrific left, breaking Tunney's nose. As the blood spurted, Gene knew he would have to stop Weinert before the referee stopped him. Answering the bell for the fourth round, the New Yorker feinted Weinert, drew him into an opening, and ripped a left hook to the jaw. Weinert dropped in a heap and was counted out. It was the first knockout Tunney had scored with his left, and he and Bagley were delighted with themselves. He would say afterwards of his victim, 'Weinert, in my opinion, was the cleverest heavyweight developed in the last twenty-five years. He had amazing speed and skill, courage, too. His left jab was vicious. It broke my nose.'

Tunney had won seven fights, three by knockouts, since losing to Greb, and he was becoming impatient with the failure of Doc Bagley to land the return bout he so badly wanted. Probably Bagley wasn't trying too hard because he didn't think his fighter could do any better against Greb, no matter when they fought. Mid-Western boxing authority George A Barton remembered, 'Bagley, who had a reputation as a shrewd manager of boxers, confided to me that he was convinced Tunney didn't possess much pugilistic ability.'

Shortly after the Weinert match at the Garden, Tunney and Bagley came to a parting of the ways and, because that new three-year contract was now on file with the Boxing Commission in New York, it cost Tunney $5,000 to obtain his freedom. He considered it money well spent. On the advice of a friend, he arranged a meeting with Billy Gibson, who was well known in political circles as well as in the fight business. Gibson had served as matchmaker, manager and promoter, and for many years ran the Fairmont Athletic Club in the South Bronx, one of the city's leading fight clubs. When Tunney fought Billy Rowe at Gibson's club back in 1915, Gibson wouldn't even leave his office to watch him. Seven years later he was ready to listen to the former marine as he mapped out his campaign for an attack against the impregnable Jack Dempsey, heavyweight champion of the world. Gibson already had one world champion in lightweight Benny Leonard, but all managers yearned for a heavyweight who could conquer the world. A three-year contract was drawn up that day in Gibson's office.

'Billy was very smart and resourceful about the business of managing boxers,' Tunney would recall. 'He stood out as the most prominent man in professional sports in America at that time. He was a most lovable character and from the moment I first met Billy until I retired from the ring, except for a short period, we remained friends and had a mutual regard for each other.'

Gibson took his new boy out of town for their first match. They went to Philadelphia, where Tunney boxed Jack Renault, a former Mountie from Quebec who had been fighting since 1919. Renault, standing an inch over six feet and tipping the scales at around 190 pounds, had more than held his own in sparring sessions with Dempsey when the champion was preparing for his title defence against Carpentier. The Canadian had boxed Billy Miske ten rounds on that Battle of the Century show and maybe he remembered Tunney stopping Soldier Jones in another prelim that day.

If Renault didn't recall that fight, one of his seconds did. He walked into Tunney's dressing room as the New Yorker was taping his hands and suggested he pull his punches. Tunney sent him away with a flea in his ear and in the ring against Renault put every ounce of his 177 pounds into his punches, hammering his body so heavily that the referee, Pop O'Brien, stopped the contest in the fourth round. There was some confusion, however, when O'Brien announced a No-Contest decision. The reports in next day's newspapers generally considered that the referee had acted hastily and that Tunney's showing had been excellent, and much better than when he had boxed Tommy Loughran some five months previously in the same ring.

As Tunney explained in his autobiography, 'The referee stopped the fight in the fourth round. I thought he had given it to me on a technical knockout, because of Renault's disinclination to fight. The record book records this as No Contest. A clipping I have in my scrapbook from a Philadelphia newspaper of the next morning states that the referee stopped the match to save Renault from further punishment. According to the law under which boxing operated in Philadelphia at that time, an official decision could not be made. Renault's chief handler, Pete the Goat, returning aboard the train with Billy Gibson and several New York newspapermen, stated that in his opinion, "Tunney could lick any heavyweight in America barring Dempsey and Gibbons." He evidently was convinced that his fighter had lost.'

Tunney had promised Chuck Wiggins they would fight again as preparation for Tunney's return fight with Harry Greb and they did, on 3 February 1923, just four days after the Renault match. The scene was Madison Square Garden and it was a replica of their Boston fight, with Wiggins taking Tunney through his extended course of anything but the noble art. The contest was bitterly fought through twelve action-packed rounds, with Tunney's relentless body attack resulting in

Wiggins suffering several broken ribs, yet he was still fighting furiously at the final bell when Tunney received the decision.

The return engagement between Gene Tunney and Harry Greb for the American light-heavyweight championship would take place in the Garden on 23 February 1923. The signing of the contracts for that fight was carried out in somewhat peculiar circumstances, as Tunney would later discover. George Engel, Greb's manager of the last two years, learned from a friend in Pittsburgh that the fighter was about to sever their relationship, which was based on a verbal agreement. Engel promptly contacted Doc Bagley, who was still managing the New Yorker, and arranged a meeting on a Sunday afternoon at the Garden. Tex Rickard's matchmaker was present and the contracts were drawn up, signed and filed at the offices of the Boxing Commission next day. By the time the actual fight took place, Greb was back with former manager James Red Mason and Tunney was newly signed to Billy Gibson, but Engel and Bagley duly collected their managerial shares of the purse money, as mandated in that contract signed a few months previously.

Gibson lost no time getting to work for Tunney, writing to the *New York Journal*, 'It is a matter of public knowledge that Greb is a flagrantly foul boxer. I am requesting the State Athletic Commission to take special note.' Red Mason countered by accusing Gibson of trying to intimidate the New York officials by creating anti-Greb feelings. Greb's wife, Mildred, also complained to the commission that she had received threatening letters from alleged Tunney supporters, all of which moved the commission chairman William Muldoon to publicly address Greb as follows: 'You have won all your fights and I have never heard of you being disqualified for foul tactics. The referee will judge the bout on what is done in the ring and not by threats or accusations made by Tunney or his partisans.'

One of boxing's greatest ever trainers and seconds was Ray Arcel and he recalled the Tunney–Greb series for author Ronald Fried in his fine book, *Corner Men*. 'Greb was great, but as great as he was, that's how dirty he was, all of the dirty tricks of the game. This was the only fight Tunney ever lost, and he took a bad lickin'. Tunney made up his mind. He was a very determined guy, clever, determined, and very difficult to talk to.'

Fighting his way back from that horrendous defeat by Greb, Tunney lived for the day he would fight Greb again, convinced he had the key to success over the man from Pittsburgh. He had badgered Bagley to get the rematch, and now the obsession continued with Gibson. 'Gibson finally called Benny Leonard up,' remembered Arcel, 'that was his fighter. He says, "Ben, do me a favour. Go up in the gym. Gene is working out. He's tearing the bags down. And he's fighting for a return match with Greb. Go up there, look at him, influence him to take his time."

'So Benny went over there, and of course when Leonard walked into a gymnasium everybody stopped working. This was the great, the great . . . you know. And he walked over to Gene, and Gene is punching the bag and Leonard stood there looking at him and he says, "How are you, Gene?" Tunney kept punching and he said, "I'm all right, Ben, I'm trying to get into shape. I'm gonna knock that Greb out." Leonard says, "You're throwing a right hand. Where you gonna hit him with a right hand? On the chin? You ain't never gonna hit Greb on the chin with a right hand. If you're gonna hit Greb with a right hand, the place to try to hit him is in the body. Try to do *that*." And he says, "Take your time. The longer you wait to fight Greb, the better it is for you."

'Greb had a great reputation for being a dissipater, drinking and all that. Greb was that way. He fought every night in the week. If you look at his record you see that he fought twenty, twenty-five fights a year. So Leonard says, "The longer you wait, the better off you are because this guy dissipates. He drinks. He runs around with women."'

It was common knowledge that Greb liked doing his roadwork along the primrose path, but Bernard 'Happy' Albacker, who grew up with Greb in Pittsburgh, would say, 'I was probably as close to Greb as any person. Greb never drank a drop of liquor. He would drink an occasional bottle of ale to build up his strength after trying to make weight or sometimes a glass of champagne, but never the hard stuff. You might have heard stories of Greb sitting in a nightclub roaring drunk. But not Harry. He would either dump his drinks under the table, spill them or pass them to others at the table. Harry always was in shape for a fight, and he never failed to train religiously for a fight, either. He was in the gym every day.'

The *New York Sun*, however, was no great supporter of the American champion, an editorial on the sports page commenting, 'He cares nothing at all for the rules and regulations. He has two active hands that fly around in all sorts of weird motions, but the top of his head is his most dangerous weapon. If the rules of boxing were strictly enforced, Greb wouldn't last a round without being disqualified.'

8

Revenge

It was in 1874 that showman P T Barnum acquired an old railroad shed at 26th Street and Madison Avenue in New York City, and in April that year it was officially opened as Barnum's Monster Classical and Geological Hippodrome. It would become known as Gilmore's Garden the following year and in 1879 they called it Madison Square Garden, a name that has been synonymous with boxing ever since. Ten years later they tore the roofless arena down and spent $2 million on a new building, which opened in June 1890, rapidly becoming the national showplace for sports and entertainment – especially boxing!

Boxing was the main event the night of 23 February 1923 and the lines stretched around the block as the fans rolled up to see Gene Tunney go against Harry Greb in the return fight for Greb's American light-heavyweight championship. It was the fight Tunney wanted more than any other and the capacity crowd of some fifteen thousand gave him a standing ovation when he followed the Pittsburgh man into the ring. 'It was one of the greatest receptions ever accorded a boxer in the Garden,' wrote Nat Fleischer. 'It showed the crowd were solidly behind the Greenwich Village battler.'

Grim determination was etched on Tunney's handsome face as he sat in his corner while Joe Humphreys made the announcements. 'To advance a step in my plan,' he would recall, 'I realised I had to win the return match with Greb. I entered the ring determined either to win or die in the attempt. I reasoned with myself that it would be much better to die than to lose. While training for this match I contracted influenza. It increased as my training progressed. I could not call off the contest or ask for a postponement. The Garden dates were filled.'

In the nine months since he had mugged Tunney in the Garden ring, Harry Greb had kept in shape as he normally did, by fighting and getting paid for it. Eleven fights, two knockouts, three decision victories, six newspaper verdicts; 109 rounds, from Philadelphia to Providence, Toronto to Grand Rapids, Buffalo to Jersey City, a couple of stops in Pittsburgh for the hometown fans, and a unanimous fifteen-rounds decision over the clever Tommy Loughran in the Garden with his title on the line. On 16 February 1923 he whipped Young Fisher over twelve rounds at the Olympian Arena in Syracuse and seven days later he was in the Garden ring ready to give this guy Tunney another dose of the Greb medicine.

At the afternoon weigh-in, Tunney had scaled 174 pounds and the champion 165½ pounds. Former fighter Patsy Haley had been assigned to referee the bout, while the judges at ringside were Charles E Miles and former sports editor of the *New York Morning Telegraph* Charles Meighan. The Greb Specials had been rolling in from Pittsburgh and they carried enough money to send Harry Greb into the ring an 8–5 favourite.

Referee Patsy Haley didn't mince his words when he called them together for their pre-fight instructions. 'Greb, watch yourself,' he warned the champion, 'there are rules that you got to listen to. And it goes for you too, Tunney,' he added. Greb protested, grabbing Tunney and using him as a dummy to illustrate how he couldn't avoid doing some of the things Haley was telling him not to. When Greb almost threw the New Yorker to the canvas, Haley sent them to their corners and the bell rang for round one.

Tunney was first to score, landing a solid left hook to the head and following quickly with the same hand to the body. Greb came in close and they exchanged lefts and rights to the body, but when Greb jumped in with a left and right to the face he was wild and missed the target. Then Greb banged a right into Tunney 's face, but took a heavy right and left to the body in return. In a clinch, Tunney drove his right to the ribs, Greb coming back with a long right and left to the jaw. Tunney was concentrating on the body as Greb came in and he ripped in two more vicious hooks before the bell.

As Greb flew at Tunney at the opening of round two, he was wrestled to the canvas, and as he got back into the fight Tunney crashed a right over the heart. Undismayed, Greb hurled a right to the face and as Tunney missed a right meant for the jaw, the champion swarmed in, forcing his man back around the ring with a barrage of lefts and rights. Tunney steadied himself and smashed a right to the jaw, but Greb was moving through the gears and hurled himself forward, lefts and rights thudding home, and Tunney was forced to think survival. He sent left and right to the body but took a left hook from Greb at the bell.

Round three and Greb rushed in, only to be met by a solid body attack that made him seek a clinch. The champion fired right and left to the face, then a long left to the jaw before Tunney rammed in a left jab, followed by a right smash to the body. They exchanged lefts and, as Greb missed a right to the jaw, Tunney put everything into a right to the heart that lifted Greb off his feet and made him fall into a clinch. Tunney was on top in this round and bounced right hands off Greb's jaw before another terrific right under the heart made Greb glad to hang on. The New Yorker finished the round with two searing punches into the body and Greb was happy to hear the bell.

Tunney was remembering Benny Leonard's advice in the gym and was concentrating his attacks on the body as the Pittsburgh Windmill sailed in with gloves flying. In the fourth round, Tunney varied his attack and a right to Greb's flat nose brought blood. The champ fired back with a wicked left to the body but had to take a solid left and right to the jaw, then lefts and rights to the body forced a clinch. Tunney tore himself free and drove Greb before him to the ropes with a two-fisted barrage of leather that ended only with the bell. In the fifth round a smashing right to the face brought blood gushing from

Greb's mouth, but he stormed back with his own right to the jaw. Tunney hammered away at the body again and Harry was wild with his own shots as the bell sent them back to their corners.

Sixth round and Tunney sent a left hook to the body, then left and right to the same spot before Greb smashed over a hard left to the head, then right and left to the face. Tunney fought back and his weight advantage forced Greb to the ropes, and he bent under two terrific rights to the stomach. Greb hit home a solid right to the jaw and finished the round with a hard left into the body. It had been a better round for the champion and he roared out for the seventh round, the Pittsburgh faction in that big crowd making itself heard. A sizzling left hook opened a cut over Tunney's right eye, then Greb leaped in with a left and right to the body before crashing his right to the jaw. Tunney fought back and they exchanged punches to the body, finishing the round in a clinch.

Both men were cautious answering the bell for the eighth round before Tunney sent a left hook to the body. Greb just missed with a vicious right swing to the jaw but landed a right that knocked Tunney's head back. At close quarters Tunney hammered away at the body but Greb was leaping in on him, giving him the head and the elbows as Haley wagged a finger at him, then Greb struck two left hooks to the body as the round ended. The fight was swinging Greb's way and he landed a right to the jaw as round nine opened. Inside, the champ's gloves pounded his opponent's face and body, but Tunney did catch him coming in with a right to the head. Then Greb was back at his man hammering both fists to the head, a hook to the body, then the New Yorker brought a roar from his fans as he forced Greb back to the ropes.

Tenth round and Nat Fleischer reported, 'They clinched, then missed with rights. Greb kept on top of Tunney and hooked a left to Gene's body. He followed with several rights and lefts to the body. Greb sent a right to the jaw. They exchanged rights and lefts to the body. Tunney then hooked a left to the body and Greb grazed Tunney's jaw with a right.

Greb jabbed a left to the face in a clinch. Greb pounded Gene's face. Tunney sunk his right in Greb's body. Tunney drove a right and left to the body. Greb hooked a left to the jaw and a right to the body at the bell.'

The champion carried his drive through into the eleventh round but even he was tiring from the tremendous pace, and the bigger, heavier Tunney was coming back into it and beginning to put points on his side of the scorecards. Tunney's hammering body attacks were paying dividends and Greb's left side was covered in red welts. More and more, the Pittsburgh Windmill was forced to hold and referee Haley was kept busy tugging them apart.

'After doing well for the first six rounds,' Tunney would recall, 'I suddenly became physically exhausted. Greb relentlessly battered me about the ring from the sixth to the eleventh round. They told me in my corner I was losing, that if I wanted to win I would have to capture the remaining rounds or knock him out. In sheer desperation I came out at the start of the twelfth and luckily hit Greb with a long right on the cheekbone that had everything I had in it. It knocked him to the ropes. He slowed up considerably. Fight, fight, hit, hit, I kept repeating to myself, and did.'

At the end of the twelfth round, Haley followed Greb back to his corner and threatened him with disqualification if he didn't stop the rough stuff. Author James R Fair described Harry's reaction to that in *Give Him to the Angels*. 'Turning his back to Haley, Greb said to Red Mason, "Did'ja hear what this two-bit pimp said about heavin' me out'n the ring? I'll turn him inside out if he tries it." Meantime, the boos by the New Yorkers and the answering boos by the Pittsburghers were deafening. One reporter declared, "If I get out of here without falling apart I'll never cover another Greb fight. I can't stand the excitement." A colleague had his head under the ring and was peering at the glut of wires. When I asked him what he was looking for, he said, "A safer place to squat in case the booers get out of hand."

'Mason's performance as a second was almost as revealing as was Greb's while fighting. As a round was about to end he took

an enormous swig from the water bottle and held it in
ballooned cheeks that made him look like an ogre. When the
round ended he jumped into the ring and went pfuff, squirting
Greb in the face and half strangling him. Sometimes Greb tried
to duck, but it was no use. Mason was a Dead-Eye Dick, a
human water hose with a Norden bomb sight.'

Tunney knew the fight had to be close and over the last four
rounds he let his punches go in an attempt to knock Greb out.
It was mission impossible. The champ would only be stopped
twice in his entire career, once in his first year as a nineteen-
year-old pro and once when he broke his arm. Tunney tried
anyway. In round thirteen Greb banged over a right to the jaw
then a left to the body, but Tunney smashed lefts and rights
to the body, and Greb was glad to hold. He just got his head
out of the way of a right-left combination, fired a right of his
own to the jaw but took more punishment to the midsection.
Tunney wrestled Greb out of a clinch and this time Haley
warned him for roughness as the bell sent them back to
their corners.

In the fourteenth round Tunney leaped in with a thunderous
right to the jaw that almost decked Greb, bringing a roar from
the crowd. But the Pittsburgher was still standing when the
smoke cleared, though a tremendous right over the heart nearly
broke him in half and Tunney was hammering the body at the
bell. In the corner Billy Gibson rubbed Tunney's back. Only
one more round, son, he urged. Three minutes and you've got
the title back!

At ringside, Nat Fleischer reported, 'The men shook hands
as the last round started. Tunney hooked a left to the body, and
they clinched. Each clubbed his right to the face in a clinch.
Tunney leaped in with a left to the body, and they clinched.
Greb hooked a left to the jaw at close quarters. Tunney battered
Greb's body with rights and lefts. They both missed lefts for the
face, and clinched. Tunney hooked a left to the body, and
followed with a left and right to the wind, which made Greb
hold. Greb drove a right to the jaw, but took a wicked right to
the body in return. Tunney hooked a left to the wind and

pounded his right to the heart at close quarters. Greb hooked a left to the jaw as the bout ended.

'Pandemonium reigned when the decision was annnounced by Joe Humphreys and for a time, the police were kept busy quelling riots in various parts of the arena. The Pittsburgher's friends felt that he had been jobbed, but those who watched the bout closely, saw no basis for complaint. Sharp as was the division of opinion among the boxing fans as to who won, there was just as sharp a difference of opinion among the newspapermen. Some agreed with the official verdict; others felt that the least Greb should have gotten was a draw, and still others believed that Greb had won. Yet the officials voted unanimously in Gene's favour and that was sufficient to gain for him the title he had lost almost a year previously to the same Pittsburgh Windmill.'

Fleischer reported a unanimous decision for Tunney, yet James R Fair, in his biography of Greb, wrote, 'Tunney got the decision of the referee and one of the two judges at the end of fifteen vicious, bruising rounds, regaining the American light-heavyweight title. Hell broke loose between New York's anti-Greb and Pittsburgh's pro-Greb element. There were no deaths but the way noggins were being cracked there should have been. Leaving the ring, unmarked but tired, Greb wasn't even accorded by the New Yorkers the reception with which they normally greet fallen champions. I thought he had won, and Tunney said, "No one was as surprised as I was when Joe Humphreys lifted my hand in token of victory."

'William Muldoon, then chairman of the New York State Athletic Commission, was even more surprised. "The decision in Tunney's favour," he said, "was unjustifiable." There was talk of a reversal but Muldoon stood by the decision of his subordinates. Greb was mad as a hornet but, after castigating Haley and the judges, he took it philosophically, lauded Tunney on his courage and improvement, and went out and had a good time.'

Greb's manager, Red Mason, was in no doubt as to who had won the fight, telling reporters, 'Well, it can happen, even in

New York. They say that crime is abating in the big cities and that Broadway is exempt from robbers. Perhaps Broadway is, but Madison Avenue and Madison Square Garden evidently are not!'

The complete boxing record of Greb, as meticulously compiled by researcher James E Cashman, gives the result of the Tunney fight as a split decision for the New Yorker, and Tunney himself was quoted as saying, 'I was given the decision at the end of fifteen rounds. The judges, newspapermen, and spectators were divided. Realising there was some justice in Greb's claim of a bad decision, I offered him a return engagement.'

Wilbur Wood, sports editor of the *New York Sun*, wrote, 'This was one of the most savage fights in the history of old Madison Square Garden with no quarter asked or given by either gladiator. It was a close fight as well as a savage one, with some in the crowd holding that the unanimous decision by which Gene regained the American light-heavyweight championship was unjust to the Pittsburgher. But to most it seemed fair enough. That victory was the great turning point in Tunney's career. It proved to himself and everyone else that he had courage of the highest order as well as a keen analytical brain. Even the members of his family who had urged him, after the first Greb fight, to give up boxing before it was too late, now encouraged him to go on.'

Three weeks after Tunney beat Greb to reclaim the American light-heavyweight title, Mike McTigue beat Battling Siki over twenty rounds, on St Patrick's Day in Dublin, to become world champion at the weight. Through manager Billy Gibson, Tunney immediately issued a challenge to the Irish-man, but it fell on deaf ears. Tunney even offered to let McTigue take the entire purse, to no avail. McTigue went so far as to disparage the American title held by the New Yorker, which prompted a most uncharacteristic outburst from Tunney to 'step outside and settle things right here!'

Tunney was absent three months before getting back into ring action, hammering Jack Clifford to defeat inside eight rounds of their Detroit fight, then taking on the clever Jimmy Delany in a ten-rounds No-Decision bout in Chicago. Back in New York he tangled with Dan O'Dowd at the Queensboro Club, winning a good bout over twelve rounds. After that fight, on 31 July 1923, Tunney took himself off to his favourite spot, the Maine woods, to do some hunting and fishing, but mostly just running and walking.

'My legs were the mainspring of my operation,' he would say. 'I never lost sight of it. What good was the slickest left jab or stiffest right cross if you couldn't move up to the line of fire quickly and confidently with it? And how useful are any punches if, when somebody else is attacking, you can't get out of the way? I moved around only to get in the correct position, but I didn't fail to keep up a fair attack while on the move. My dancing was more a deceptive measure than anything else. And I did not go running about.'

That great Jewish fighter Barney Ross, who would win the lightweight, junior welterweight, and welterweight championships, observed, 'The so-called dancing fighter, such as Gene Tunney, was not a fighter who carelessly ran pellmell around the ring, for no man could keep endlessly on the move and work as well as Tunney did, especially if he were a heavyweight. I watched Tunney only once or twice, but I quickly noticed that he knew how to step away correctly from oncoming blows, and at the same time kept his head enough to judge when to attack. After all, the purpose of legwork is not solely one of escape, but also of offence.'

In his striving for physical perfection, normal roadwork was never enough for Gene Tunney. He would run backwards for miles at a time, as much as some fighters would run forwards, having learned from medical studies that backwards running really gave the cardiovascular system a tough workout. It was something Tunney learned while watching a service bout in the Marines, and it stayed with him. He saw a clever little boxer, Jackie Clark, take a stunning punch and suddenly start circling backwards in order to keep out of range until his head cleared. Clark's coolness under fire and the success of his evasive tactics impressed Tunney. 'What an asset!' he pondered. 'If you can just control the muscular action of your legs when you get in trouble.' Years later he would explain to boxing writers, 'Locomotion is the first thing to leave a fighter who has been badly shaken up. He may be all right up here,' said Tunney, drawing an imaginary line across his waist, 'but the legs just won't respond. I built those muscles up for years, just on the chance that I might desperately need to get on that bicycle some day.' That day would surely come.

During the summer of 1923 Tunney spent a couple of months at Charley Miller's place in the Maine woods. Miller had been a decent lightweight in a 28-bout pro career before giving up the ring for the great outdoors, and he would say, 'There's nothing that will beat the woods, anybody's woods, not just those in Maine, to get a man in shape for a fight. His legs will be strong, his wind good, his reactions sharp, and his mind restful after a good spell of living in the woods. Conditioning, for conditioning, that's what I'm here for,' Miller would insist. 'After a boxer gets through with me, he's got to be trained. But then he'll be ready for it. Gene Tunney loved the woods, loved to be alone, and so he relaxed, and that's ninety-nine per cent of my conditioning for conditioning.'

Tunney was in great shape when he returned from the Maine woods, which is just as well. As he moved into his training camp at Red Bank in New Jersey, word came from manager Billy Gibson that he would be defending his American championship at Madison Square Garden on 10 December. The opponent? Harry Greb!

9

Harry Greb Again

In a magazine article on Harry Greb, newspaperman Harry Cleavelin wrote, 'He was the wildest tiger, acknowledged king of the alley fighters, the dirtiest boxer in all ring history. Not a boxer, not a puncher, he beat 'em with blazing speed, a pair of rubbery legs that never seemed to tire, and what had to be one of the most magnificent fighting hearts God ever put into a man. He was the nearest thing to perpetual motion that ever stepped into a ring, throwing punches from all angles in a wicked tornado of ripping, tearing, jolting leather. There you have it, the imperishable legend of Harry Greb.'

New York sportswriter Frank Graham commented, 'Let's take Greb off by himself and try to see what kind of a guy he was. Well, he was this kind of guy. He would fight anybody, anywhere, in the ring, in a dancehall, or up an alley. Weight made no difference to him. He fought middleweights, light-heavyweights, heavyweights. He fought everyone who stood in his way and, when there wasn't anybody in his way, he went searching. There was an afternoon in a burlesque theatre in Brooklyn where Harry and another were sitting on a trunk backstage. The time was roughly 1925 and Dempsey was the champion of the world. "Grantland Rice," the other said, "thinks you are the greatest fighter, pound for pound, he ever saw. He would like to see you fight Dempsey." "Tell Mr Rice," Harry said, "I'd like to fight Dempsey, too. For six rounds. If I didn't blind him by then, he would kill me in the seventh."'

Greb didn't fight Dempsey. He fought Bill Brennan, who gave Dempsey a helluva fight in the old Garden one night before Dempsey, with one ear almost torn from his head, knocked Brennan out to save his title. Greb fought Brennan, a genuine heavyweight, four times, and big Bill got the worst of it every time. Before one of their fights, in Pittsburgh, Brennan told reporters at the weigh-in, 'I'm gonna knock your boy loose from his head this time. I'm not gonna scatter my punches like I been doin' and trying to punch it out with him. I'm gonna wait for an openin' and when it comes, whoppo! And there'll be Greb deader'n a mackerel on the floor.'

That night in the ring at the Duquesne Garden, Brennan waited for his chance, and when it came in round five, blasted a terrific right to Greb's jaw. The punch lifted little Harry off his feet and hurled him into the ropes so hard that a ring post jumped out of its socket! But Greb didn't fall. He bounced off the ropes and flew at Brennan with such a fury that the big guy could only hide behind his gloves until the bell ended his misery. 'How does anybody figure to fight that little mule?' shrugged Brennan at the final bell. 'You just go in there and catch 'em, and that's all there is to it. Just go in there and catch 'em.'

Greb regularly mixed it with bigger, heavier men. They were generally slower and he could slap them around for ten, fifteen rounds without coming to any harm. But he was a natural middleweight and, like all fighters, he wanted to be a champion. In 1923 Johnny Wilson was middleweight champion of the world, and he wanted to stay champion, which is why he didn't like being in the same town as Harry Greb, let alone the same ring. Wilson's real name was Panica and he grew up in the Italian section of New York's Harlem. The kid next door, a few years older than Wilson, was Frank Costello. 'A nice boy, never looking for trouble. Frank wasn't a troublesome fellow,' Wilson would recall.

Costello rose to the top of the underworld, and in May 1920 Johnny Wilson rose to the top of the boxing world, upsetting Mike O'Dowd for the middleweight title. During his three years as champion, Wilson defended his title four times. Then

Tex Rickard matched Wilson with Harry Greb for the championship, on 31 August 1923, at the Polo Grounds in New York. According to legend, Greb had been seen whooping it up in nightclubs and Wilson and his manager, Marty Killelea, figured it would be a good time to fight him. But Greb had been playing it smart, paying waiters to bring him glasses of coloured water as he made the rounds of the saloons and clubs, acting the drunk as he rolled home in the early hours.

The *New York Times* did not expect Wilson versus Greb to be a boxing classic, commenting, 'Neither man is of the type that places its main reliance on science and boxing skill. Once Wilson gets started he is likely to hit anything that is inside the ropes, including the referee, and Greb has long been known as the human windmill.'

That summer night at the Polo Grounds, Johnny Wilson realised that Harry Greb was no washed-up pug, even if he only had one good eye. He still had two good fists and they hammered Wilson for fifteen rounds, and lifted the world middleweight crown from his aching head. The *Times* reported, 'Greb completely baffled Wilson with a swirling attack which started in the first round and did not end until the bout ended. Greb won every round except the first and the last. When the final bell ended the hostilities, Wilson was a sorry sight. The bridge of his nose was cut from a blow in the second round, his mouth was bleeding, his lips were puffed and raw, he had a slight growth under his right eye, and his left was almost closed.'

At one stage of the fight, Greb's thumb accidentally got stuck in Wilson's eye. Referee Jack O'Sullivan pulled them apart to ask Greb what he thought he was doing. 'Gouging him in the eye,' he snorted. 'Can't you see?'

Southpaw Wilson described a different fight when interviewed by author Peter Heller for his book, *In This Corner.* 'We get into the ring there, for about three rounds I really hurt Greb in the stomach. He started puking in the first round. Around the third I think I started to tire till about the tenth. Then I came on around the eleventh, twelfth, thirteenth, fourteenth, fifteenth, I started plastering him all around the ring. The referee, Jack O'Sullivan, called it a draw. Paddy Mullins, who was an enemy of mine, had got to the commission and put two of his stooges in there as judges to take my title away. One of the stooges was Frankie Madden, who was a lightweight in the old days, and the other fellow was the gunman from Dodge City, Bat Masterson. He was the sporting editor of the *New York Telegraph*. And they put them in there. At the last minute they changed the judges.'

Yet from what is known of Wilson and Greb, any suspected chicanery would most likely have been in the champion's favour, rather then Greb's. My research failed to find any connection between Greb and underworld characters, whereas Wilson openly admitted palling around with Frank Costello, from being kids on the same street to starting out as a fighter. Wilson was later co-managed by Frankie Marlow, who was a close associate of mobster Bill Duffy and a pal of Al Capone. 'When I went to Chicago to fight there,' Wilson told Peter Heller, 'Frankie called Al Capone up. I knew him from Brooklyn before he went out there. He looked after me when I was up there for about a week. They were nice people.'

The records show that Harry Greb won a unanimous decision over Wilson to become middleweight champion of the world and by all accounts the Pittsburgh Windmill didn't need any help from dishonest officials.

Harry's wife, Mildred, had died shortly before the Wilson fight. She had been suffering from tuberculosis and, although Harry cut down his fight schedule and took her to warmer climes, her condition deteriorated. Mildred had been a chorus girl at George Jaffe's old Academy burlesque theatre in Liberty Avenue when Harry met her and they had a daughter, Dorothy, whom Harry adored. With his family looking after the child, Harry Greb went back to doing the thing he did best – fighting. He whipped Jimmy Darcy in Pittsburgh, dropped a decision to Tommy Loughran in Boston, and romped to newspaper decisions over Lou Bogash, Soldier Jones and Chuck Wiggins. On 3 December 1923 Greb gave Bryan Downey a crack at his title and beat him over ten rounds before the hometown folks in Pittsburgh, and just seven days later he climbed into the ring at Madison Square Garden to challenge Gene Tunney again for the American light-heavyweight title.

At the lunchtime weigh-in Tunney tipped the scales bang on the division limit, 175 pounds, with Greb coming in a little heavier than usual at 171½ pounds. That night, all of two hours before the first preliminary bout was due in the ring, New York's finest were having their hands full keeping the crowds in line at the ticket windows. In his Greb biography, James R Fair described a lighter moment before the drama of the battle to come: 'Joe Humphreys introduced the usual number of ring celebrities, of whom Battling Siki was far and away the most colourful. Smiling toothily like a child contemplating a lollipop, he was wearing brogans, skin-tight pants, tails and a topper and carrying a cane. After bowing all over the ring, he leaned against the ropes, slipped in a pool of blood from one of the pre-liminaries and started to tumble out of the ring. Irish Johnny Curtin, a good Jersey City bantamweight, grabbed him and pulled him back in. Greb and Tunney sat in their corners, bored with all the hoopla and itching to earn their night's pay. Obviously drunk, Siki went over to Tunney and tried to kiss him in the French manner. Tunney ducked. He tried it on Greb and Greb ducked. He was fifteen minutes en route to his seat, by which time he was barely a memory. Greb and Tunney had swung into action in their third fight, and when those two stalwarts started swinging everything else paled by comparision.'

Tunney had been out of the ring just over four months, but he had enjoyed his time up in the Maine woods and he had gone into his camp at Red Bank over in New Jersey refreshed and ready for action. His training had gone well and now he was looking forward to settling his argument with Greb. This was the rubber match, one win apiece, and may the better man win. In those early rounds Tunney remembered what Benny Leonard had impressed on him in the gym before the second fight with Greb. 'You ain't gonna hit Greb on the chin with a right hand! If you're gonna hit Greb with a right hand, the place to try to hit him is in the body.'

From the opening bell, as Greb rushed in with gloves flying, Tunney shot a stiff right hand to the body, then the left, getting his shoulder behind the punches, and he knew Greb felt them. He heard him grunt as he fell into a clinch. The New Yorker knew he had to keep Greb at a distance, keep his bullet head at a distance, keep those thumbs at a distance. One boxing writer described Greb's thumbs 'which, on their way to Tunney's eyes, resembled a leader duck in flight'.

In those early rounds, Greb's speed gave Tunney problems as he pivoted around the ring, but fortunately the quantity of his punches reduced the quality and Tunney was rarely hurt. His own punches were making a difference, however, and as the rounds passed, Greb lost some of his speed as those body shots raked his midsection.

Nat Fleischer reported the fifth round: 'Tunney hooked a left to the body and they clinched. Tunney drove a right to the face that sent Greb back on his heels and caused his mouth to bleed. Greb leaped in and they mixed at close quarters. Greb drove a right to the jaw, and Tunney countered with a right and left to the body. Tunney peppered Greb's body with rights and lefts at close quarters. Tunney hooked a left to the body and then jabbed a left to the face. Greb was wild with a right and left for the face. At close quarters, Tunney drove his right to the body. Tunney drove a right and left to the body as the bell ended the session.'

Tunney was more aggressive in this fight than he had been in their first two encounters, forcing the action, each attack spearheaded by those stamina-sapping body blows from either hand, and Harry Greb was forced to hang on grimly to call at least a temporary halt to the pounding of the heavier man's gloves. Blood ran from Greb's mouth as Tunney's left hooks found his face and he welcomed the bell that heralded sixty seconds' respite from those thudding fists.

'Tunney had lost most of his timidity, Greb never had any,' wrote Greb's biographer, James R Fair in *Give Him to the Angels*. 'For fifteen mean, fast rounds they whaled each other. Retreating only when common sense said they must, they literally leaned their heads against each other's chests and fought like jealous stallions. One New York newspaper referred to them as the new Tunney and the new Greb. It called Tunney new because, whereas he had been hesitant he was now almost audacious, and Greb new because he had fought one of his cleanest fights. The referee didn't call Greb for a single foul, though I detected some careless bobbing of the head and gouging of the thumb that were reminiscent of rougher nights.'

In the twelfth round, Tunney was hammering the body again, lefts and rights sinking in below the ribs and over the heart, and Greb clung like a drowning man to driftwood, wrestling Tunney across the ring into the ropes. As Tunney struggled to free himself from Greb's grip, he tumbled backward through the ropes and finished up sitting on the ring apron. In a rare moment of chivalry for him, Greb leaned through the ropes, placed his gloves under Tunney's head, and tried to lift him back into the ring. But he couldn't manage it and released Gene, leaving him to make his own way back through the strands. The bell had rung, but in the confusion and noise from the capacity crowd, neither Greb nor Tunney had heard it and they shaped up to resume the battle just as referee Lou Magnolia jumped between them.

'The fifteenth round was by far the most exciting of the contest,' reported Nat Fleischer, 'for both were striving to create a good impression at the finish. Greb, after the usual handshake, tore in like a Kansas cyclone and landed several good rights and lefts on Gene's head. Gene took them all with a cool attitude and came back with blows that were heavy enough to make Harry clinch at close quarters. Greb never got so sick of a man in his life as he did of Gene, and he couldn't see any comedy in those body blows which kept coming in. By centering a withering attack upon his opponent's mid-section as he had done in their second meeting, Tunney successfully defended his crown, and the result was in Gene's favour by a bigger margin than in the previous tilt.'

As he made his way out of the Garden that night, trainer Ray Arcel said to his companion, 'Tunney destroyed Greb.

He destroyed him. He really did. *Body punches.* He took Leonard's advice.'

Of course you couldn't destroy Harry Greb. Nobody ever did, not in 300-odd ring battles with some of the greatest fighters in boxing annals. He was never rendered unconscious, not by a gloved fist anyway, and after that third fifteen-rounder with Gene Tunney in Madison Square Garden, Greb still wasn't convinced that the man from Greenwich Village was his master. Which was why he jumped at the chance of another fight with the former marine. They linked up again in September 1924, nine months after the Garden fight, this time at the Olympic Arena in Cleveland. It was a ten-rounds No-Decision affair and this time Tunney had a seventeen pounds pull in the weights, coming in at 180 pounds to Greb's 163 pounds. Tunney was growing into a heavyweight, his dream of fighting Dempsey drawing nearer. But first there was this fellow Greb again.

This fight was more evenly contested than their last one, with first one then the other gaining an advantage. Greb stormed out at the opening bell and for two minutes swamped Tunney in a sea of leather that threatened to drown him. Then Tunney got behind his jab and steadied the middleweight champion with some solid body shots. At the bell Greb missed with a left and right to the head. Tunney had the upper hand in round two, waiting for Greb to come in and driving both hands to the body, then bringing him up short with jolting right and left hooks to the head. Round three and it was Greb making all the noise, sailing in with both gloves coming at Tunney from every angle, forcing Tunney to take evasive action along the ropes a couple of times. In the fourth the New Yorker targeted the body and slowed Greb with some savage punches, and Greb was glad to give ground after a thumping right under the heart.

The fifth round saw the Pittsburgh fighter again swarming all over Tunney, hurling lefts and rights to the head, while Gene carried his body attack on into the sixth round and at the bell the fight was still in the balance. Neither man surged to the front in the seventh, Greb missing more but still landing plenty as Tunney's more accurate blows continually found Greb's midsection. They were hammering away at the bell and referee Matt Hinkle had his hands full separating them. Greb flew at his man as the eighth opened and almost went through the ropes when a wild left swing missed the mark. Tunney won the round with those strength-sapping body punches and at the bell told Hinkle that Greb was butting him.

Round nine and back came Harry Greb, steaming into Tunney like a train into the station, rights to the body catching the bigger man and long lefts to the head giving him something to think about. In the tenth and final round the crowd went wild as both men clashed in mid-ring, Greb's gloves flying at Tunney with lefts, rights, hooks and swings, but Tunney was more than equal to the barrage, fighting his way off the ropes with searing body punches and of the two Greb seemed happier to hear the final bell. With the laws then operating in Ohio, a decision could not be rendered, other than the view of the ringside press, and most went along with the *New York Times* reporter, who saw it as a draw.

Tunney recalled in his 1941 autobiography, *Arms For Living,* 'Harry was bitter about one fight, our fourth. I won the decision, and this enraged him. He was sure he had beaten me, felt to the depth of his soul that he had been the victor. It was a newspaper decision affair of the period, sportswriters giving the verdict in their stories. Regis Welsh of the *Pittsburgh Post* was one of Greb's best friends. In his account of the battle, he gave the decision to me. He put my photo on the front page with the caption, "Too much for our boy." Greb never spoke to him again. They were enemies ever after. All the bitterness the battle had stirred in Greb was directed not against me, not against the antagonist who had been in there hitting him, but against his newspaper friend who had merely typed a few keys on a typewriter.

'He didn't resent the physical pain of being murdered, he resented losing unjustly, as he thought. His sense of right was touched, and his vanity. Greb was curiously secretive in pride, oddly vain. He was concerned about his looks. Strange that anyone so careful of his face should have selected prizefighting for a profession. When tough Harry Greb went to one of the roughhouse, slugging brawls for which he was famous, he took with him not merely his pugilistic equipment, trunks, bathrobe, ring shoes. Invariably he carried along a comb and brush, mirror, and, marvel at it, a powder puff! Going into the ferocious fracas, he always had his hair plastered down with stickum.'

They would meet in the ring one more time, on 27 March 1925, at the St Paul Auditorium, both guaranteed $6,500. Still growing, Tunney weighed 181½ pounds, with the middle-weight champion scaling 167½, a whopping fourteen pounds' advantage for the New Yorker. Gene Tunney was getting too big for Harry Greb! He was also getting too good for him. Once again Tunney used the formula that had proved successful in their previous three fights, the winning formula given to him that day in the gym by his stablemate, the great lightweight champion Benny Leonard. Attack the body, hard, with accurate blows from either hand – take the wind out of the Windmill's sails. Greb was a terrier in the opening rounds, worrying away at the bigger man, slamming lefts and rights to head and body, but Tunney stepped up a gear in the third round and fought Greb tooth and nail, from one side of the ring to the other.

Mid-West boxing authority and sports editor George A Barton was the referee that night. In his wonderful book, *My Lifetime In Sports,* he remembered, 'During the early part of the third round, Greb continued to hit Tunney freely with both fists. Harry tore into Gene after I had separated them from a brief clinch but Tunney, with lightning-like speed, countered with a vicious straight right to Greb's heart. The grin on Harry's face changed to a grimace of pain and Greb quickly grabbed Tunney in a clinch. Greb held on desperately, I had to shove him away from Gene.'

Nat Fleischer reported, 'Gene began to strut his stuff when the fourth round started. He punished Harry with terrific rips to the body, and in the fifth he caused the Pittsburgher to back up and take a whaling of an old-fashioned sort, dealing out smashes to the mid-section. Greb brought his elbows into play in the clinches which he made, and was cautioned by the referee.'

Barton went on to say, 'The action slowed down so much in the fifth round, due to Greb's repeatedly grabbing Tunney and hanging on tenaciously, that I went to Harry's corner after the round and ordered him to do less clinching and more fighting. "I'm doing the best I can, George," said Greb. "I think Tunney smashed a couple of my ribs. I've got to run and grab or he'll knock me out. I'll give it everything I've got in the next five rounds, but please don't stop the fight because I'm hurt." Greb's plea was so earnest that I decided to go along with him and permitted him to fight the last five rounds in his own way.'

Greb danced around the ring in rounds six and seven, trying to stay away from Tunney's crippling body shots, and his own work was not so effective. He was warned again for holding in the eighth. In the corner before sending his boy out for the ninth, Red Mason lit a fire under Greb, 'You're blowing it, son, you need these two rounds.' But Greb would never again see the day he could beat Gene Tunney and he was holding on when the final bell rang to end the fight, and one of the bitterest ring feuds of all time.

Barton again: 'A dramatic scene took place in one of the dressing rooms in the basement of the old St Paul Auditorium after Gene Tunney defeated Harry Greb in their fifth and final fight. The room was empty when I returned after handling the Tunney–Greb fight, but as I was changing into street clothes, Greb walked slowly into the room accompanied by his handlers. He squatted on a chair, leaned forward and put his head into his hands. For Greb, noted as a playboy as well as a great fighter, this was a strange attitude. Harry always dressed in a hurry after fights and hustled off to a nightclub for an evening of fun. Ten minutes elapsed and Greb still sat huddled over on his chair. I finished dressing and then asked him, "Anything wrong, Harry?" Harry replied it was just as he had told me in the ring. "I think Tunney busted a couple of ribs

above my heart," he said. "It hurts like hell." I was advising Red
Mason, Greb's manager, to summon a doctor after he and
Greb returned to their hotel when Tunney entered the dressing
room, walked over to his beaten opponent and patted him
affectionately on the shoulder. "Nice fight, Harry," said Gene.
"Let's do it again some time." Looking up, Greb managed a
smile as he replied, "No, Gene, not ever with you again. You've
become a helluva good fighter. Tonight you hurt me more than
I was ever hurt before and I'm lucky I was still around at the
end of ten rounds. You'd stop me for sure the next time. I'm
satisfied to call it quits as far as fighting you is concerned." A
medical examination the morning following the fight with
Tunney disclosed that Greb suffered two broken ribs over the
heart. I strongly suspected Tunney of easing up on Greb in the
last three rounds of the fight to permit Harry to stay the limit.
Several years later, Tunney admitted to me that during a
clinch in the seventh round, Greb had begged Gene not to
knock him out.'

When Harry Greb returned home to Pittsburgh a few days
after that last fight with Tunney, he told newsmen that Tunney
had carried him. 'He broke two of my ribs,' he said. 'He's
getting too big and too strong and hitting too hard. It's time for
somebody else to fight him for a change. Don't let no one tell
you Gene can't hit. He hit me so hard in the belly I couldn't
hardly breathe. He'll whip Dempsey. Maybe he'll knock
him out.'

10

Moving Up

Those five fights with Harry Greb were the making of Gene Tunney, and the New Yorker never failed to acknowledge the fact. 'To him I give credit for my rapid development from a novice to a champion,' Gene would tell newsmen. 'I learned a lot from Harry. I learned how to do as he did. It was he who taught me confidence, and I could see myself improve with each fight I had with him. The last time we fought, in St Paul, I could have knocked him out had I desired, but I liked him too much for what he had taught me, to do that.'

Being in the ring for one round with Greb was enough for most fighters. Tunney, having survived 65 rounds with the Pittsburgh Windmill, informed manager Billy Gibson that he was ready for anybody who stood between him and his ultimate goal, a crack at the world heavyweight title held by Jack Dempsey. Tunney even offered to fight Harry Wills, the Black Menace who was number one on everyone's list as Dempsey's next challenger. Wills didn't want Tunney, he wanted only Dempsey, and he had the backing of the powerful New York State Athletic Commission. But Tex Rickard, boxing's Barnum and leading promoter, had Dempsey, and there was no way he would promote a Dempsey–Wills match for the championship. After the violent aftermath of the 1910 fight between Jack Johnson and Jim Jeffries, Rickard made it clear that he would not promote another mixed match for the big title. He had another idea. With Gene Tunney already outgrowing the light-

95

heavyweight division, he would build up the handsome kid from Greenwich Village as the next challenger for Dempsey.

As 1924 came up on the calendar, Gibson took Tunney on the road, while Rickard set to work on a big fight for the summer months. In Grand Rapids, Michigan, Tunney went ten brisk rounds with Harry Foley in a No-Decision affair. A trip to Florida in January was always a good idea and Tunney knocked out Ray Thompson inside two rounds of their fight at West Palm Beach. Next stop was New Orleans to give local favourite Martin Burke a return match. Since their 1921 fight in New York, Burke had beaten guys like Fred Fulton, Jim Coffey and Young Bob Fitzsimmons, but he still couldn't beat Gene Tunney, who again took the decision, this time over fifteen rounds. Next Gibson lined up the clever Jimmy Delaney for a rematch in St Paul (Tunney had boxed him ten rounds in Chicago some ten months previously). But he couldn't do any better and the newspaper decisions all favoured Tunney. Then it was time to get back to Red Bank to start training for a big New York fight with Erminio Spalla of Italy, scheduled for 26 June at the Yankee Stadium in New York City.

Signor Spalla was no stranger to Gene Tunney. In the winter of 1921, when the New Yorker was training for the Battling Levinsky fight at Red Bank, he needed a good sparring partner; a rough and tough scrapper to give him a hard workout and sharpen his boxing. One of the trainers in camp suggested a big guy just over from Italy named Erminio Spalla, who was staying in Newark. Spalla was the heavyweight champion of Italy but had been knocked out by Tom Cowler in Berlin before sailing for New York. The Italian had just fought Jim Coffey twelve rounds in New York City, losing the decision to the man they called the Roscommon Giant. When Spalla was offered the sparring job with Tunney, he packed his bag and headed for Red Bank.

Actually he packed two bags, as Tunney recounted in his 1941 book, *Arms For Living*. 'He arrived with two small fold-over satchels, one of which he handled with loving care. He didn't speak much English, but his attitude toward the one satchel was eloquent. He tossed the other aside carelessly; it contained only his clothes. Then, with ceremony, he proceeded to open his treasure, and howled with anguish as he drew out some flat black pieces. In the satchel he had packed four big red seal phonograph records. What they had been you could tell by his lamentations in voluble Italian. Two Caruso records and two made by Titta Ruffo. The railroad porters had given them a rough bouncing around, and there they were, broken into large irregular pieces. Spalla was in despair. Music he had to have with his prizefighting. His great ambition was to sing baritone in opera, and he had brought the records along for study, vocal guidance. Caruso the all-time king of song, and Titta Ruffo the world's number one baritone of those years. There they were, all busted up.

'It looked as if Spalla might start right back for Newark. Needing a sparring partner so badly, I didn't want to lose the slugging music lover. I soothed Spalla, told him I'd replace the records. He virtually made me take an oath on it. Not so easy to procure the records in Red Bank, but I finally got them. Thereafter I had no reason to regret the trouble. Spalla played his four arias time and again. Moreover, he himself would sing. He had a resonant baritone voice, and made fight training seem like a series of song recitals. Spalla turned out to be an excellent sparring partner. The music lover was indeed a slam-bang scrapper in the ring, crude, no boxer, but a heavy and busy puncher, full of fight.

'There was one thing odd about him in training bouts. In the ring he'd wear a baseball catcher's chest protector. That got many a laugh and it looked as if Spalla might be shy of a punch, certainly as if he couldn't take it in the belly. But I found Spalla magnificently game. He feared no man's punch, and was plenty rugged around the middle. The reason for the chest protector was Spalla was afraid that constant training camp punching in the body would affect his abdominal muscles, for singing!'

Erminio Spalla returned to Italy to see his brother, Giuseppe, win his old title with a knockout of Mariano Barbaresi. Both the

Spalla brothers had been stopped by Tom Cowler in Berlin fights in 1920, and in January 1923 Erminio gained revenge when he hammered the English-born Cowler inside six rounds in Rome. He followed up by winning the vacant European heavyweight championship, beating Holland's Piet Van der Veek over twenty rounds in Milan. When an offer of a fight with Luis Angel Firpo in Buenos Aires came up early in 1924, the Italian grabbed the chance. It was just six months since the Wild Bull of the Pampas had blasted champion Jack Dempsey clean out of the ring in their sensational title fight in New York. Now he was trying to fight his way back to favour with an eye on those American dollars he so loved.

But Firpo didn't look so hot against Ermillo Spalla that sunny day in Buenos Aires. The Italian landed a long right swing behind the ear and Firpo crashed to the canvas. The hometown referee immediately stopped the fight and gave Signor Spalla a long lecture, threatening to disqualify him again if he continued to mistreat the local hero. By this time Firpo was back on his feet and when he knocked Spalla down in the fourteenth round, the referee quickly counted to ten and it was fiesta time! The publicity generated by that fight reached New York and Tex Rickard offered Spalla a fight with Gene Tunney at the Yankee Stadium on a show Rickard was promoting for Mrs William Randolph Hearst's Milk Fund.

In 1938 Erminio Spalla made a hit at La Scala Milan, singing Amonasro in Verdi's *Aida*. On that June evening in 1924 the Italian made a hit in New York City fighting Gene Tunney. 'During the first round,' reported Nat Fleischer, 'Spalla caught Tunney with a terrific right that crashed against the chin and Gene saw stars. It was the hardest blow the former Marine received in the entire fight. The full weight of the body went behind that punch and as Spalla scaled 195 pounds, it was a mighty hefty wallop.'

Tunney recalled, 'Signor Spalla fooled me. He hung my jaw on the end of a wild right swing at the beginning of the first round. It was a terrific punch and shook me up pretty badly. I no sooner realised I had been hit than another volley of blows came. Stunned again to the heels, I could not understand what was happening, so I feinted and moved around. I knew all about Spalla, or thought I did. Then, in his next rush I saw my mistake. I was trying to pull back from long swings which came one after the other, each reaching farther until finally one landed. I had received three terrific punches before discovering the error of my ways.

'About the time I had that figured out the bell rang. I went out and started feinting Spalla, but, instead of drawing my head back, I leaned forward and brought my head down. Spalla's swings flailed around the top of my cranium. That was the solution of the problem of the swinging Spalla. He kept launching haymakers that never landed, and the knockout was only a matter of time. He became disheartened. Referee Eddie Purdy stopped the match in the seventh round to save him from further punishment.'

In the second round Tunney's jabs found Spalla's eyes repeatedly and the Italian's right eye was soon puffed and the left eye closing. Spalla came out for the third round and mounted a furious attack, rushing at the American to land several right-handers to the body, but Tunney countered with rights and lefts to the body, just as he had done to Greb in their last three fights, and Spalla looked all in. A right hook to the jaw sent him back on his heels just before the bell rang. The fourth, fifth and sixth sessions saw Tunney at his best. He slammed his right to the body with frequency and peppered Spalla's face with a straight left that brought the blood from his nose and split his lips.

'This punishment caused Spalla to become infuriated,' reported Fleischer. 'He rushed pell-mell into Tunney only to be met with a fusillade of blows. His own punches went wild and those that didn't were either blocked or ducked. They got into a clinch and Spalla, refusing to let go the hold he had on his opponent, wrestled him to the floor. As the men arose, Referee Purdy stepped between them, held up Tunney's hand, and declared him the winner. There was a wild protest from Spalla's handlers who thought the foreigner had been disqualified for fouling, but the referee declared he had halted proceedings because the Italian was outclassed. Gene had displayed the kind of fighting fit for a champion.'

There was no rest for Tunney after this one for he was matched with Georges Carpentier a month later, on 24 July, at the Polo Grounds. This match was put together by Jimmy Johnston, the renowned 'Boy Bandit', on behalf of the Cromwell Athletic Club, and Johnston left no stone unturned drumming the fight up. A press release was given out stating, 'When Gene Tunney won the light-heavyweight championship of the AEF, it launched a feud with Georges Carpentier, which won't be ended until the night of 24 July 1924. Ever since Gene Tunney marched to the front ranks, Georges Carpentier has been trying to fight him. Deep down in his heart, Georges is positive he can whip Gene. There is deep resentment in his bosom against Tunney. It goes back to the time the Allied forces held a boxing tournament in Paris. A halo encircled Carpenter's brow, for he was revered in France as one of the country's greatest heroes and athletes. The boxing tournament finally reached the point where Tunney won the army title and there was talk of matching him with Georges. But the French-man was suddenly called back to the front on active service. Ever since, Tunney has accused Georges of running out on him and using the war as an excuse. Georges has been enraged, but this is his first opportunity to revenge himself on Tunney and his friends for circulating such propaganda.'

Ed Van Every, boxing writer for the *New York Evening World*, wrote, 'Though it is not generally known, Gene came near meeting Georges Carpentier while he was still abroad in the service. Gus Wilson, who acted as trainer for Georges, tells the story. "A match was proposed to Georges with the American champion," said Gus, "but Georges couldn't see the meeting at that time. He said he had fought long enough for nothing." Some five years later Carpentier was to meet Tunney. Georges got a lot of money for that fight, while Gene got only $6,800 for his end.'

The finances for that fight were thrashed out at a meeting in the Claridge Hotel in New York City. There was Billy Gibson on behalf of Tunney, Carpentier and his volatile manager Francois Descamps, Jack Curley as agent and interpreter for the Frenchmen, and Jimmy Johnston. Curley put his cards on the table, stating that Carpentier wanted a $50,000 guarantee. Johnston looked shocked.

'It's impossible to pay that much,' he protested. 'The fight won't be such a sensation.'

'It'll be a $200,000 gate easily,' countered Curley.

'How about Tunney, he'll have to be taken care of, too,' Johnston pleaded, 'and fifty thousand dollars is impossible.' Curley and Descamps wouldn't budge; it was fifty grand or no fight! Billy Gibson finally broke the deadlock by suggesting Johnston pay Tunney 55 per cent of the gate and they would pay the guarantee demanded by Carpentier. The proposition was put to Descamps and his fighter, and Curley nodded agreement, saying, 'They don't care who they get their money from, so long as they get it.'

Three weeks before Carpentier was due in the ring with Tunney, he and Descamps took a train from New York to Michigan City, where the Frenchman was to fight Tom Gibbons. It was an afternoon show at a local baseball park, a No-Decision affair that went the limit.

'He was not much bigger than me,' Carpentier described in his autobiography, *Carpentier by Himself*, 'but he was more massively built, a first class boxer, fighting at middle distance with short hooks delivered with both hands. However, he was not a very hard puncher. Neither of us succeeded in flooring the other and we shared the honours more or less equally. From the third round on I was handicapped by a sprained right ankle which gave me quite a deal of trouble, particularly after the match, and when we left for New York the next day I was hobbling along with the aid of a stick. Jack Curley was waiting for us at the station in New York when we arrived and he drove us straight out to his house at Great Neck, where he had a ring set up in his garden, and it was there I trained for my fight with Gene Tunney.'

A few days after the Gibbons–Carpentier fight, Mike Jacobs,

the Broadway ticket hustler, dropped into Johnston's office. 'I won't sell as many tickets as I figured on,' he said to the promoter. 'His fight with Gibbons ruined the Tunney match.'

Johnston called in Billy Gibson to tell him the box office was slow.

'Then we'll have to back the card up with some good prelims,' said Gibson.

Johnston shook his head. 'There was never a star bout helped by expensive prelims,' he said.

'I mean star preliminaries, big names,' said Gibson. 'How much did you figure on spending on the prelims in the first place?'

'About eight thousand dollars,' replied Johnston. Gibson stood up to leave. 'Spend sixteen and we'll pay the other half,' he said. 'Oh, yes, and I want some tickets to sell. About eight thousand dollars worth. If I don't pay you for the tickets before the fight, take it out of Tunney's share.'

George S Collins of the Cromwell Club was sitting in the office with Johnston and the promoter made sure Collins got everything that had transpired down on paper. He had dealt with Billy Gibson before. As the fight drew near, Johnston turned on his ballyhoo machine in a last effort to boost ticket sales. A big Broadway party was organised at Jack Curley's Great Neck home and newspaperman Hype Igoe reported, 'Georges, gracious, gallant, handsome, with a million-dollar smile, played waiter, Jack Curley acted as a bellhop, grapejuice tender, and man about the Curley lawn.' Among the celebrities there were Jane Cowl, beautiful stage star; Mrs Sam H Harris, wife of the theatrical producer; Mrs Oscar Hammerstein II; and Ziegfeld Theater star Miss Mary Eaton.

Johnston didn't forget the other half of his main attraction, staging an equally elaborate affair for Gene Tunney at the millionaire colony of Rumson, on the banks of the Shrewsbury River, with Mrs Harry McCormack acting as hostess. There were beautiful girls from the *Follies*, *Scandals* and *Vanities* shows on Broadway, and a handful of ex-pugs, among them heavyweight veteran Gunboat Smith. Johnston was surrounded by a group of newsmen, telling them, 'Tunney is a greater boxer than Corbett and a better hitter than Fitzsimmons.' Then, turning to Smith he said, 'Say, Gunner, how do you think Tunney would get along with either Corbett or Fitzsimmons, from what you know of the three men?'

The old Gunboat looked at Johnston as Jimmy winked at him, then said, 'Aw, Tunney, he's all right, but he wouldn't be able to hit either Corbett or Fitzsimmons with a horse whip!'

On fight day, the sports pages gave Tunney and Carpentier the big build-up. Gunboat Smith picked Carpentier to knock out Tunney, the Frenchman vowed to retire if he lost, and Tunney promised to knock his opponent all the way back to Paris. For the first time in his big fight career, Tunney was made favourite, at 8–5. A large wager of $25,000 had come from France to back Carpentier, and columnist Bugs Baer wrote, 'If Gene wins tonight, it will earn him a fight with Dempsey, which will be his own fault.'

At Carpentier's insistence, the match had been made at 175 pounds, the light-heavyweight limit, which Tunney hadn't made since his last title bout with Greb. He had weighed 183½ pounds for the Spalla fight and had had to work hard to shift those last few pounds, vowing never to do it again. No official statistics were released on this fight but the attendance was estimated at 30,000 with gate receipts totalling around $125,000. Polite applause greeted Joe Humphreys's introduction of, 'The pugilistic marvel of all Europe', while the crowd gave Tunney a tremendous ovation.

'It was a fight of thrills, sensations and heart throbs, such as had not been on view since the famous Firpo–Dempsey encounter,' wrote Nat Fleischer. 'Georges early began to shoot his vaunted right at Tunney. The weapon that had spelled defeat and oblivion for Joe Beckett, Bombardier Wells and many another British boxer, came whistling through the air time and again towards Tunney, but the Greenwich Village boy evaded it. But once the wallop landed in the opening round. Tunney caught it flush on the chin, but it failed even to shake him. Thereafter, Carpentier frequently struck Tunney with right-handers, sometimes shooting them straight from the shoulder, his gloved fist darting forward like a rattlesnake with fangs exposed and at other times circling in the air as a haymaking swing. But the wallop had lost its steam. Tunney did not kiss the canvas, as Carpentier had seen other foemen do and when the expected failed to happen, it must have borne in upon Carpentier's consciousness that he was carrying the standard of a lost cause.'

In the second round Tunney opened a cut over Carpentier's right eye and it bled for the rest of the contest. The Frenchman was feeling his age, thirty, and the wear and tear of a long career that started as a fourteen-year-old and saw him fight through every weight division from flyweight to heavyweight, and become light-heavyweight champion of the world. But after 104 ring battles, Gene Tunney was a fight too far.

'Tunney was a fine boxer,' Carpentier would recall, 'a big, well-built fellow with the head of an American clergyman, and his ring technique was very sound. I was impressed in particular by his defensive qualities and in that respect he reminded me of Jack Johnson. During our fight Tunney worried me a good deal with his long reach and he used a straight left in a very English style. Because of his defensive tactics I had to do a great deal of forcing. I certainly hit him often and sometimes heavily, but I also had to pocket his counters.'

'Slowly but surely the tide of defeat was setting in against the Frenchman,' wrote Fleischer, 'and all of it was preliminary to the hectic tenth round, when Carpentier reaped perhaps the greatest honour and acclaim in his career. The ninth rolled around and Georges staged a great rally that gave him the session on points. He was bent upon holding his momentary advantage as the tenth started. Like a flash, Georges leaped to midring and let go a nasty left to Tunney's face. It sent Gene's head back and must have aroused in the lethargic Greenwich Villager a spark of fighting instinct. He came back at Georges with a short, vicious left hook to the chin. This drove Carpentier's head between his shoulders and Tunney followed it instantly with an unbelievable short right chop to the jaw.

Carpentier hit the floor with a thud. The back of his head landed against the canvas and he stretched out. At the count of seven, Georges struggled to his feet and put his hands before him in a fighting pose. But he was so muddled that he was shadow boxing with the referee.

'Tunney was well to his left instead of in front of him. Carpentier suddenly caught sight of Gene and faced him. Tunney, scenting victory by a knockout punch, then began to rain blows upon Georges from every angle. Carpentier's gameness caught the fancy and fevered the imagination of the onlookers. Straw hats came hurling through the air from the stands. With less than half a minute to go, Tunney finally managed to connect with another left hook to the chin that dropped Carpentier for a count of five, and then again drove him to his haunches with a volley of blows that landed on various parts of the ex-poilu's anatomy. Carpentier was on his haunches, supporting himself by his hands placed against the floor, when the bell rang ending his interminable agony and sending him to the corner for the ministrations of his seconds.'

'Carpentier's showing in the tenth round was one of the finest exhibitions of sheer gameness I have ever witnessed,' recalled Tunney. 'He rose three times after being down and almost out. He shall have my eternal admiration for his showing of courage and gameness during that round. It was one of the greatest rounds of modern boxing second only to the first round of the Dempsey–Firpo fight.'

The gallant Frenchman reached deep down to the bottom of his soul and he found something that lifted him off his stool to face Tunney in round eleven. Carpentier attacked Tunney and the New Yorker appeared wary of the man who had a right hand good enough to shake a Dempsey. But the power was gone from the triphammer and by the thirteenth round Carpentier was running on fumes – his tank was empty.

Round fourteen saw the finish, as described by Fleischer: 'Cheered on by the thousands who were amazed by this heroic stand by the French gladiator, Carpentier tried to rally. He sprang forward, leaped at his adversary, attempted to curl over his famous right, but before it landed, Tunney countered for the body and Georges, unable to get out the path of Gene's delivery, took the punch that laid him low. The fist was driven with all of Gene's power, snap and leg leverage behind it, and it sank deep into the body.

'Carpentier sank, writhing with pain. He went down groaning to the canvas. He seemed to be in agony as the referee stooped down and began the count. His body was twisting and squirming but before the count could be completed, the bell sounded. Manager Descamps and Gus Wilson, Carpentier's seconds, jumped into the ring and yelled, "Foul!" Shrieking hysterically in mixed French and English, they tried desperately to have Referee Griffin award the fight to the Orchid Man, but to this gesture, the official paid no attention. As I viewed the fight, Gene sank a left into the pit of the stomach as the Frenchman rushed him towards the ropes. The punch, delivered with force, caught the Orchid Man squarely in the solar plexus and doubled him with pain. It was an exact duplicate of the blow that put out Corbett in his fight with Fitzsimmons.

'Andy Griffin, a cool and capable referee, insisted that the fight must go on, and on it went. The minute rest was over and the bell clanged for the start of the fifteenth round. Carpentier was lifted, then pushed out of his corner, though he barely could stand. The excitement was intense. Tunney himself stood near his corner uncertain what to do. He seemed scared for the first time in his ring career. With face contorted, Carpentier walked forward to meet his foe. The gallant Frenchman could hardly lift his hands to protect himself as Tunney, extremely loath to strike a man so defenceless, hesitated to go any further. He looked at the referee with a plea to halt the bout and the referee understood. He stepped in between them and sent Tunney to his corner. The bout was over. The light-heavyweight champion had climbed one step nearer his goal, the fight with Jack Dempsey.'

Carpentier's version of how the fight ended differed from Fleischer's, writing, 'I had to retire in the fourteenth round owing to a low punch which the referee did not recognise as a foul. A gesticulating Descamps sprang into the ring and almost debagged me to prove to the referee that the punch had landed below the belt, but it was no good. The blow had not floored me, but seeing me limping the referee stopped the fight and declared Tunney the winner. In all fairness I must say that if the fight had actually gone to the limit I should not have been ahead on points. I should have lost, not by much certainly, but enough. However the fight was in any case the usual no-decision bout.'

Carpentier did not retire in the fourteenth round, for as he admits a couple of sentences later, the referee stopped it. The blow did floor him, the bell saving him from a knockout. The fight was actually contracted for fifteen rounds to a decision, under the rules then in force in New York State. But Carpentier was right in one thing: he would have lost had the fight gone to the limit.

According to another contemporary account, 'Descamps, eyes blazing, leaped into the ring, attempting to rip off Carpentier's tights to show evidence of his injuries. Five policemen followed the manager, trying to restrain him. In the meantime the crowd swarmed the ringside and working press section, while special police and New York's finest battled to keep them back. Two showgirls evaded the police and jumped screaming into the ring. The ring was finally cleared by policemen and Griffin awarded Tunney the verdict on a technical knockout. Then did Descamps and Wilson declare, according to Bill McGeehan, "that they were not claiming foul from Tunney's punch, but Gene had kicked the Frenchman in the groin with his knee." But a dressing room examination by a physician did not reveal traces of a foul.'

Talking of the fight some time later, trainer Gus Wilson told boxing writer Ed Van Every that Tunney was a far more dangerous puncher than was generally credited. 'Gene may not be a deadly hitter, but he is a most punishing one,' declared Wilson. 'After that fight with Tunney, in which Carpentier was hit freely about the head, Georges didn't have cauliflower ears, he had elephant's ears. It's a fact his ears flopped downward just like an elephant's. Gene must have broken a lot of cords in both ears.'

Georges Carpentier couldn't beat Tunney in the ring, but he certainly whipped the New Yorker in the financial stakes. Tunney was mad as a hornet when his end of the fight came to a paltry three thousand-odd dollars, while the loser picked up his guaranteed fifty grand. Over manager Billy Gibson's protests, Jimmy Johnston stood firm. 'You bought eight thousand dollars worth of tickets and you told me you would pay half the cost of those expensive prelims, which amounted to sixteen thousand two hundred dollars, your share being eight thousand one hundred dollars. Gene's cheque is correct. You made a bargain, I'm keeping it!'

Reluctantly accepting the cheque, Tunney pointed a finger in Gibson's face, saying, 'You listen here to me, Gib. Don't ever, as long as you're associated with me, make any more promises or contracts or take any tickets and sign for them in my name. From this time on I do my own business!'

11

The Contender

Some called him Jimmie Bronson, others wrote about him as Jimmy Bronson, and his real surname wasn't even Bronson. It was Dougherty. But whatever they called him, all agreed that 'Bowtie' Bronson was a class act in the often-murky world of professional boxing.

In 1926 Ed Van Every, then boxing editor of the *New York Evening World*, wrote, 'Just a word about Jimmy Bronson and it is this: just to know this manager of boxers is to appreciate that there must be plenty of good in a game with which a man of his character could be so closely associated.'

In the late summer of 1918, Bronson arrived in Paris to work for the YMCA and was soon running the American Expeditionary Forces (AEF) boxing programme. He was a natural for the job, having been a fighter, referee and promoter between running a saloon in Joplin, Missouri.

'As director of boxing in the AEF,' he recalled many years later, 'I staged 2,075 bouts while refereeing more than a thousand of them myself. We had great shows, and the fighters were either name pros from the States or fellows who were to become topliners after the war. We had Joe Lynch, the bantamweight champion, and middleweight champion Mike O'Dowd. I groomed a lot of service fighters in Paris, including Gene Tunney, but my favourite at the time, and with our fighting men, was Bob Martin. Sergeant Bob weighed 210 pounds and stood six-three. General Jack Pershing put Bob Martin in my hands but Bob quit fighting following an automobile accident. I'll always say that Bob was the hardest hitter with a right the ring ever knew, but the only time he used his left was when he hung up his hat.

'As Martin's career was snuffed out, another former AEF fighter of mine was surging higher and higher. I mean Gene Tunney. I had continued friendly to Gene since the war but Gene had a manager, one of the best in Billy Gibson, and I had my own stable of fighters, guys like the Zivic brothers, Pete and Jack; Bobby Garcia, Allentown Johnny Leonard, and Jeff Smith. Gene, although champion, wasn't exactly a ball of fire overseas. During my work in charge of the service boxing abroad I had ample opportunity to study Gene's work as I refereed many of his AEF engagements, including the one with Ted Jamison that led to Tunney becoming AEF light-heavyweight champion. To tell the truth I wasn't impressed neither by his work then, nor by his various bouts professionally that I looked on up until the Jeff Smith affair. He was winning regularly and that was the best I could say for him. But what I saw him come through with against Jeff Smith gave me a big surprise.'

When Jeff Smith died in February 1962, *The Ring* magazine's Jersey Jones wrote, 'One of the most superb fighting machines and finest personalities this commentator has ever met up with died recently at the age of seventy. He was Jeff Smith, born in New York City but reared in Bayonne, New Jersey. Jeff was dubbed the "Globe Trotter" and he was probably the most travelled fighter of his generation. He estimated roughly that he must have covered close to 350,000 miles during his seventeen years of ring activity, which began as a lightweight in 1910 and ended as a middleweight in 1927. Jeff was a remarkable defensive boxer, adept at infighting, and an accurate two-handed puncher with a left hook his most potent weapon. Testifying to his superb boxing skill, Jeff, until he met Gene Tunney in New Orleans late in 1924, had lost only seven decisions in a busy career covering fourteen years, and so far as we know had never been knocked off his feet. What's more, Smith's ruggedly handsome features were virtually unmarked.'

Gene Tunney changed all that on a December night in 1924 in old New Orleans. He agreed to meet Smith over fifteen rounds but had so much respect for the ability of the veteran that he insisted on a No-Decision bout. This despite the fact that Tunney weighed a hefty 186 pounds to Smith's 154 pounds.

'I guess my main trouble up to then had been lack of proper confidence in myself,' Gene would later say. 'I didn't want to take chances. Jeff was a great boxer, but he was only a middle-weight, beyond the thirty-year mark, and a fading veteran with a long, active career behind him. I had every conceivable physical advantage over him; height, weight, reach, and youth. Yet I didn't have confidence in myself to gamble on a decision.'

Had there been an official decision rendered that night, it would have gone to the New Yorker. Smith gave a good account of himself in the early rounds, his vast experience and ring savvy standing him in good stead against the younger, heavier, stronger man. But as the rounds passed, so did Smith's hopes fade, Tunney coming on strong to hand out severe punishment to the veteran and flooring him twice in the later rounds. 'When I floored that wonderful veteran,' Tunney said later, 'my confidence knew no bounds, and from then on, I was sure no one could beat me.'

As he came out of the ring, Smith said to manager Jimmy Bronson, 'That fellow, Tunney, is a great fighter, he'll be the next champion, sure.' As a result of the head punches he received from Tunney's hammering fists, Smith began to suffer from double vision and that was the beginning of the end of a distinguished career.

Bronson would recall years later, 'Smith, who was under my management at the time, just missed being a champion. He had fought all over the world and was a really great boxer. But the way he was handled by Tunney just about had me stunned. Jeff always had been a defensive marvel but Gene crashed through at will. Smith was on the floor a couple of times and both his eyes were blackened. It went fifteen, but Tunney could have ended it at any time. We were all on the same train going north after the fight and Gene's manager, Billy Gibson, asked me what I thought of his man. I said, "Bill, Tunney is a greater fighter than even you realise." Gibson then asked me how I thought Gene would make out against Tom Gibbons. 'Tunney will surely knock Gibbons out," was my answer. It was then that it dawned on me that Gene Tunney had been tagged as an instrument of fate to bring about the defeat of Dempsey. I was watching for the thing to come to pass from then on.'

The fight with Smith closed out the year 1924. Tunney had averaged a fight a month and had not lost an official decision since Greb thrashed him in their first fight in May 1922, two and a half years and 26 contests ago. He was now a legitimate heavyweight, although he could still lay claim to the American light-heavyweight title since he had never been beaten for it. But he had vowed never to make the 175-pound limit again. In March 1925 he fought his last fight with Harry Greb, the one in which the Pittsburgh fighter suffered two broken ribs over the heart. After the fight Tunney walked into Greb's dressing room in the basement of the old St Paul Auditorum and, after they had kidded each other about fighting again, Greb said, 'There's something else I want to tell you. I know Jimmy DeForest is in St Paul trying to sign you to fight Tommy Gibbons but you've been holding off because you think you're not ready for him. I've fought Tommy twice and whipped him good the last time. Take my word for it, you'll lick Gibbons. Not only that, you're the guy to beat Dempsey. You've got the perfect style, the punches and the know-how to do it.'

'You're not kidding me and just trying to be nice, are you, Harry,' asked Tunney. 'Kidding, hell,' snorted Greb. 'I'll bet plenty of money on you to whip both Gibbons and Dempsey.'

Returning to New York, Tunney gave Billy Gibson the green light; get Tommy Gibbons! Tex Rickard wanted to match Gibbons against Dempsey in a re-run of their infamous 1923 title fight in Shelby, Montana, where the St Paul fighter had taken the champ through fifteen rounds, but the New York Commission was insisting that Dempsey fight Harry Wills if he fought in New York. Gibbons offered to fight Wills, but the

Black Menace and manager Paddy Mullins were holding out for a Dempsey fight.

'Well,' suggested Tunney. 'If Wills won't fight Gibbons, and he won't fight me, that ought to eliminate him. So how about Tom and me getting together, for the right to meet Dempsey?'

But Rickard still couldn't see Gene Tunney as a challenger for Dempsey and the boxing writers were of the same mind. So Billy Gibson called on matchmaker Jimmy DeForest, who was looking for a big fight for the Polo Grounds Athletic Club, and offered him Tunney if he could sign Gibbons. Terms were soon agreed with Eddie Kane, the St Paul fighter's manager, and Tunney versus Gibbons was announced for 5 June 1925, at the New York Polo Grounds, fifteen rounds or less.

Tom Gibbons grew up in the shadow of his brother, Mike, who was renowned in boxing annals as the St Paul Phantom. Mid-West newspaperman and referee George Barton said, 'No question about it, Mike Gibbons was just the greatest boxer who ever lived. One had to see Mike in action to fully appreciate his skill and understand why he was called the Phantom.' Mike, four years older than Tom, was a tough act to follow. The family remembered the two of them boxing an exhibition one time when they were both headliners. 'Let's dance around for the first couple of rounds,' said Mike, 'then in the third round I'll let you knock me down.'

'Sounds good, Mike,' said Tom. 'When do you get to knock me down?'

'Anytime I feel like it,' replied Mike. He was that good.

Tom Gibbons was good also. A clever middleweight, he was troubled by brittle hands so he carried a small rubber ball around with him, squeezing it first in one hand, then the other. As he grew he developed a punch, especially a left hook. In one two-year stretch Gibbons racked up 26 knockouts in 32 fights, and in 1923 he stood off heavyweight champion Jack Dempsey for fifteen rounds in the blistering heat of a Montana afternoon. When he signed to fight Gene Tunney, Tom Gibbons had lost only three official decisions and had never been knocked out in 105 pro fights.

★ ★ ★

Since 1872 the White Sulphur Springs Hotel had stood at the southern end of Saratoga Lake, nestling in the foothills of the Adirondacks some thirty miles north of Albany in New York State. Tom Luther bought the place in 1888 and it became a popular training camp for such fighters as Frank Moran, Jack Britton, Jack Dempsey, Luis Angel Firpo and, in 1925, Gene Tunney.

Jersey Jones, who covered the fight game for the *New York Globe* before joining Nat Fleischer on *The Ring* magazine, regularly handled publicity for the training camps of top ring names like Max Schmeling, Jack Sharkey, Sixto Escobar, Lou Ambers, Max Baer, Joe Louis and Henry Armstrong. In May 1925 Billy Gibson asked him to look after the press arrangements for Tunney at Saratoga Lake. The New Yorker was driving up to the camp and he picked Jones up at Gibson's office.

'What do you think of the fight?' Tunney asked when they were clear of the city.

'Candidly,' replied Jersey, 'I look for Gibbons to pin your ears back.'

'I guess a lot of folks think that,' admitted Tunney, 'but they're due for a shock. I can beat Gibbons. I wouldn't have asked for the match if I weren't sure of it. I'll tell you something else,' he added calmly. 'I can beat Wills, and I can beat Dempsey. Go ahead and sniff. I mean every word of it.'

Tunney would recall in his autobiography, 'I felt that the time had come when I was ready for Tom Gibbons. In my opinion Gibbons was the best fighter in America next to Dempsey. I had watched him, studied him, and I knew him. He was fast, clever, and could hit a terrific blow with an incredibly short movement of the arm. To Tom Gibbons, boxing was a science and he was a master of it. He was very methodical, however. I had seen Gibbons for the first time back in 1921 at the Pioneer Athletic Club on East Twenty-Fourth Street in New York. Tom's opponent that night was Paul Sampson with whom I had boxed a ten rounds no-decision bout a little earlier.

Above: Jack Dempsey beating Tom Gibbons (back to camera) in 1923. Gene Tunney beat them both.

Left: Gene Tunney – World Heavyweight Champion, 1926–8.

Below: Left to right – Jimmy Bronson (second), Billy Gibson (manager) and Lou Fink (trainer).

Above: Gene Tunney versus
Tom Heeney in Tunney's last
fight, New York City,
26 July 1928.

Left: Gene Tunney versus
Jack Dempsey. 'Battle of the
Long Count', Chicago,
22 September 1927.

Opposite: Harry Greb, the only
fighter to defeat Tunney in his
professional career.

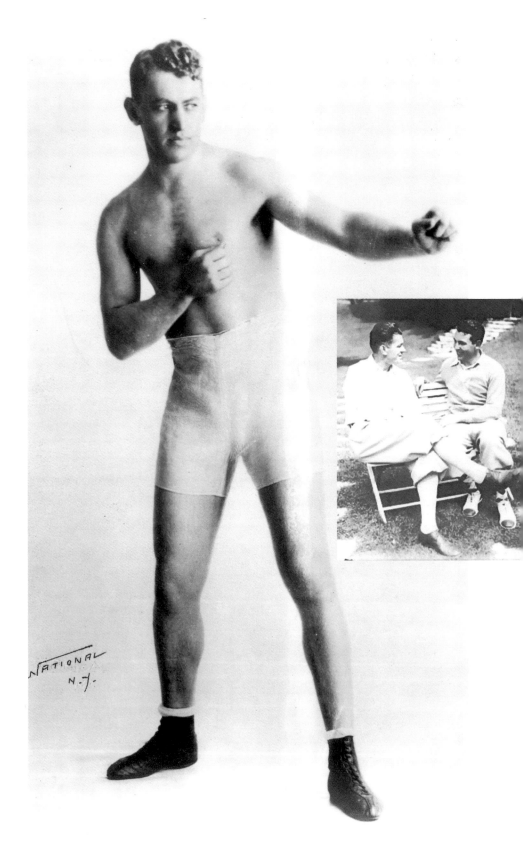

Above: Jack Dempsey – forever
linked with Tunney after their two
fights in 1926 and 1927.

Opposite, main photo: Battling
Levinsky (World Light-Heavyweight
Champion 1916–20). In 1922
Tunney beat Levinsky for the
American Light-Heavy Title.

Opposite, inset photo: Gene Tunney
(left) with his friend, Eddie Eagan,
who won the Olympic Light-
Heavyweight title in 1920.

Right: America's great promoter
Tex Rickard. He brought the
million-dollar gates to boxing.

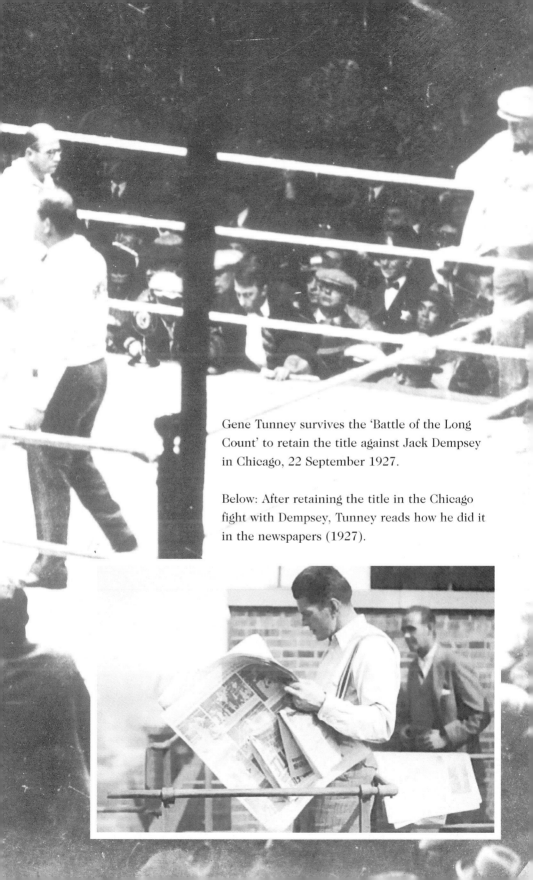

Gene Tunney survives the 'Battle of the Long Count' to retain the title against Jack Dempsey in Chicago, 22 September 1927.

Below: After retaining the title in the Chicago fight with Dempsey, Tunney reads how he did it in the newspapers (1927).

Above: Gene Tunney KOs Georges
Carpentier, New York City, 24 July 1924.

Left: Georges Carpentier.

'Gibbons, in dispatching Sampson, who was a pretty tough fighter, showed me the finest exhibition of effective boxing I have ever seen in the ring, though the contest lasted but a round and a half. Tom's unpretentious entrance into the ring, the completeness of his job, and his exit, reminded me of a first class journeyman carpenter arriving at one's home with his kit of tools, patching up the leak in the roof, and leaving. That was Tom Gibbons.'

In his own methodical way, Gene Tunney prepared for the day when he would face Tom Gibbons in a fight he would have to win if he was going to be a champion. When Tunney was training for his second fight with Harry Greb he hired Jock Malone as a sparring partner, knowing that Malone boxed regularly with Gibbons. He quizzed Malone on Gibbons, on his ring habits and his punches. Then when he trained for his fight with Carpentier he sent for Jimmy Delaney, knowing he had trained with Gibbons in preparation for Tom's match with the Frenchman, and added more vital information to his file on Tom Gibbons.

'We had been loafing at Luther's for nearly a week,' recalled Jersey Jones in a 1950 article in *The Ring*, 'and now, with Tunney about to start work, we were awaiting the arrival of his trainer Lou Fink and a couple of sparring partners he was bringing along with him from New York. "How much admission are you planning to charge the public for your workouts?" Luther asked. "Nothing," replied Tunney. When Uncle Tom, as he was known to the fight mob, seemed surprised, Gene hastened to explain. "When you charge admission," he said, "you're expected to give a show. I'm not here for that. I'm here to train for an important bout. When I work out, it won't be with the idea of entertaining the public with fancy boxing exhibitions, or by murdering my sparring partners. So there'll be no admission charged. If anybody wants to come in, he'll be welcomed, and he'll be free to leave without complaining that he didn't get his money's worth."'

Trainer Lou Fink had brought two good sparring partners to the camp, Bud Gorman and Paul Cavalier. Tunney had used

Gorman as a regular sparmate. He was a good boxer from Kenosha, Wisconsin, and a couple of months after working with Tunney he would upset Jack Sharkey. Cavalier was a promising heavyweight, standing six foot two tall and weighing 200 pounds, and he would lose only two of 120 fights. Neither man, however, had what Tunney was looking for in his preparation for Tom Gibbons.

'Who's the best left hooker you could suggest who'd be willing to come up here for a week or two?' Tunney asked Jones one day after his workout.

'The best one I know', said Jones, after pondering the question for a few moments, 'is Phil Krug, a middleweight out of Harrison, New Jersey. Phil is a fine boxer and uses a hook pretty much as Gibbons does. But he may not be available. He was operated on for appendicitis recently, and has been out of the hospital only a few weeks. It may be too risky for him to box with you.'

'Oh, I won't hit him,' said Tunney. 'I have big fellows for that. All I'll want Krug for is to keep pegging those left hooks at me, so I can concentrate on ways to handle them.'

Jersey Jones contacted Krug's manager, Billy McCarney, and within a couple of days Krug was in camp working with Tunney and making him look sick. 'Gene just couldn't seem to find a defence for the hooks Krug bounced off him,' recalled Jones. 'Phil would feint for Tunney's face, then rip one into the body. Or he'd feint for the body, and bang one off Gene's chin. But Gene, undaunted, continued to experiment with counter moves to check those hooks, and as the days progressed it became more and more evident that the Greenwich Villager was finding the right answers. By the end of the week, Phil said to Gene, "Guess I'm not of much use to you now. No matter what I try, or how I try it, you've got me stopped. If Gibbons hits you with that left hook, I'll be the most surprised guy in the ball park."'

A week before the fight, a large party of New York sportswriters made the trip from the city to watch Tunney go through his training routine, travelling on one of the New York

Central Railroad's luxury trains to Albany, where they were met by limousines for the rest of the journey to Saratoga Springs. Everything – transportation, meals, drinks – was paid for by Gene and manager Billy Gibson. And when they arrived at Luther's place by the lake, many of the scribes didn't even leave the bar to see Tunney's workout. Their stories in next day's papers even mocked Tunney's boxing ability and lack of personality.

Writer George Barton had travelled east to cover the fight for the *Minneapolis Tribune* and he had dinner one night with Tunney and trainer Lou Fink. 'George,' said the fighter, 'those New York smart alecs don't think I can fight, but they will look stupid after I defeat Gibbons in this fight and then Dempsey about a year from now. You are from the Twin Cities and I know you are very close to Mike and Tom Gibbons. I imagine you intend picking Tommy to beat me. Be smart, George, and pick me because I am certain I'll beat Gibbons. I expect Tommy to give me a bad time of it for six or seven rounds, but I'll start taking over in the eighth or ninth round. From that point on I'll give Tommy such a going over that I'll win the decision with plenty to spare. Don't be surprised if I knock Gibbons out between the twelfth and fifteenth rounds.'

The night before the big fight, Tunney moved into a hotel in the city, not far from Yankee Stadium. 'As this was an important battle,' he recalled, 'I naturally was wrought up to a high pitch. I foolishly took a cup of strong tea before going to bed. I had cut tea and coffee off my menu while training. Ordinarily it would have had no effect on me, but that night I didn't sleep a wink. I blamed it on the cup of tea.'

That June night in New York City was one of the hottest ever recorded, the temperature hitting 96 degrees and the stifling heat made worse by the big Klieg lights that had been installed over the ring for the movie cameras, which were filming the bout for posterity. Tunney's corner were prepared, Billy Gibson and Lou Brix bringing a washtub containing 24 towels wrapped around small chunks of ice. Two of these were used after each round, one on the back of the neck and the other on the head. A cold towel was also placed on each of Tunney's shoulders and crossing his chest. Of the 23,670 fans who paid $161,165 to get into the Polo Grounds that night, Gene Tunney was the coolest guy there!

At 10 p.m. referee Dick Nugent of Buffalo glanced at both corners then gave the timekeeper a signal. The bell rang, and Gene Tunney and Tom Gibbons stepped from their corners and moved across that hot canvas towards each other for a fight that would make or break one of them. Gibbons, at 34 the eldest of the two by seven years, came out fast and slammed his pet left hook into the stomach. Tunney closed with him and they exchanged short punches in Gibbons' corner. Breaking away, the New Yorker shot a stiff left to the face as Gibbons came back with another left hook to the body. The St Paul veteran jabbed a left and Tunney hit back with a left and right to the body.

In the second round, Tunney went for the body with both hands, with Gibbons boxing cagily, tying his opponent up inside. Then Gibbons lashed out with a short left to the jaw that made the New Yorker think he had better watch this old gaffer carefully. Both landed stiff rights to the head and they were mixing it up at the bell. In round three both men scored freely as they opened up with lefts and rights, Tunney concentrating on the body before banging one, two, three lefts to the face. Gibbons chopped two lefts to the head, then missed a sweeping left swing, grinning to himself. Then the grin disappeared and the hook smashed into Tunney's handsome face.

The Mid-Westerner boxed well in round four, with a left and right to the chin. Tunney forced him back to the ropes, then Gibbons smashed two stiff rights to the body before catching Tunney with a left to the face. A smashing right from Tunney got home and tested the Gibbons chin but at the bell the veteran was fighting back. The fifth round belonged to Tunney as he opened with a strong left and right to the chin, and Gibbons backed into the ropes. Tunney rushed at him and slammed in the leather before Gibbons could escape to the centre of the ring. At long range Tunney was superior, with his challenger doing better inside, scoring short hooks from either hand.

From ringside Nat Fleischer reported round six: 'Tunney rushed at Gibbons with a stiff left to the body. Another Tunney left to Gibbons' face partly closed his left eye. Tunney chopped Gibbons with short jolts to body and head. Tom lashed out wildly with a left and missed as Tunney ducked. Tunney landed a left to the body. Gibbons crossed over his right, cutting Gene's lip. Tunney shot a series of hard blows to Tom's mouth and Tom was bleeding as the round closed.'

In round seven a Tunney left to the body strayed low. Gibbons smiled and they shook hands briefly before battle was joined again. A stiff left to the head from Tunney then a right to the stomach, and more strong jabs sent Gibbons' head bobbing back, Tunney's strength now the deciding factor as he forced the other back around the ring. Gibbons finished the session with a sharp right to the chin that said, 'I'm still here, Gene!' But the New Yorker was stepping up a gear as round eight opened, jabbing strongly to the veteran's face, then throwing a heavy left hook into the body and Gibbons missed with a left as he backed off. Tunney smashed three punches to the body, but Gibbons shocked him and brought a roar from the crowd as he landed two terrific rights to the head, and Tunney looked shaken as he headed for his corner.

Gibbons followed up his attack as they came out for the ninth and his left hook twice thudded into Tunney's face, then two rights brought the blood from Tunney's mouth. The New Yorker fought back and got home a hard left, and Tom's left eye was damaged by the end of the round. In the tenth round, the pace and the sweltering heat began to take their toll on the man from the Mid-West. He boxed carefully, protecting his eye, but Tunney sensed his opponent weakening and opened up with strong punches. A hard left to the chin, then another, had Gibbons backing away. As the veteran reached the ropes Tunney crashed in short lefts and rights to the head, and Gibbons was glad to hear the bell.

Recalling the fight in his autobiography *A Man Must Fight*,

Tunney wrote, 'Gibbons never suspected I had had him in a test tube for over three years. To have his feints and leads blocked was baffling to him. He could not understand how he was being beaten to the punch. Not only was he baffled, but his seconds, newspapermen, and the ringsiders all shared his confusion. Gibbons had a keen fighting brain and realised he was being whipped at every department of the game. Even his famous double feint and slip in with a terrific left hook to the liver or chin, was foiled every time. I knew after the second feint that Tommy would advance his left foot, slip in with his head down, and try landing that awful jolt with his left. Before the left could get started I would drop a short right in on his forehead or left eye and then step back out of danger.'

The end came in round twelve. Fleischer reported, 'Tunney landed two lefts to the body as Gibbons covered. Tunney backed Gibbons around the ring and floored him with a right to the chin. Gibbons went down on hands and knees. He lay, propped up on one elbow, like the "Dying Gladiator." At seven he arose and with trembling legs spread wide apart, tottered backwards towards his own corner, only to have Gene, scenting victory by the knockout route, leap upon him unmercifully. Tunney rushed him, crashing over another right. Gibbons fell in his own corner. At the count of seven he strove vainly to raise himself to his feet. The referee counted the doleful decimal and the bout was over. Tunney outpunched and outguessed Gibbons all the way. He showed not the slightest fear of Tom's punch or cleverness. Gibbons had a good excuse for his failure to do better. His wife, mother of two children, was seriously ill in a Chicago hospital, and Tom entered the ring in a highly nervous state. Yet it is doubtful if Gibbons, at his peak, would have done much better against the Tunney who was at his peak that night.'

12

Honour Among Thieves

Writing of Tunney's success, Ed Van Every, of the *New York Evening World*, reported, 'Following his victory over Gibbons, who was reputed to be the cleverest heavyweight boxer that had ever graced the ring with the possible exception of Jim Corbett, there were the usual "inside" stories as to how poor Gibbons had been under great mental strain and how he had made a great mistake training down by the hot sands of Coney Island, though this was closer to the seashore than Tunney's camp at Saratoga Springs. And anyway, Tom had taken a dive when he found the going too hot. In other words they tried to rob Tunney of the credit of being the first man to knock out the clever Gibbons.

'Gibbons was finished in a spot so close to me that I could have reached out from my place in the press stand and touched the fallen man with my hands. I, for one, can testify, that there have been fewer knockouts more decisively delivered. The smash on the chin that Gibbons took was a fearful thing. It was a short punch, but driven in with such a snap and drive of the shoulders I knew it was over as soon as the blow landed. Ten minutes later I saw Gibbons back in his dressing room and he was still gibbering unintelligently and his eyes were vacant and dull.'

'I could have earned in excess of $100,000 after Tunney knocked me out,' Gibbons recalled for sportswriter George Barton, 'because there was such a demand for heavyweights during the boom era in the twenties. I decided, instead, to retire due to the serious illness of my wife, Helen, who became ill while I was training for my match with Tunney. I was also influenced by the fact that my brother Mike had lost the sight in his right eye as a result of being thumbed. I deemed it wise to quit the ring with two good eyes which meant more to me than a million dollars.'

Barton would write, 'After being paid his largest purse, $110,000 for his fight with Gene Tunney in New York in 1925, Gibbons built a Catholic Church at a cost of $50,000 and gave it to the little town of Osakis in Northern Minnesota where Tommy has maintained a summer home since 1915.'

Tunney's crushing knockout defeat of Gibbons, something heavyweight champ Jack Dempsey had been unable to accomplish in fifteen rounds two years earlier, sent Tunney's rating surging on the 'Sock Exchange'. Dempsey, engaged in a series of exhibition matches in Germany, cabled congratulations to the Greenwich Villager and Tex Rickard finally began thinking that this guy Tunney might just be a good fighter after all. Good enough, even, to match with Dempsey!

A month after the Gibbons fight, Tunney was in Kansas City to meet 'Italian' Jack Herman, a veteran trial horse for aspiring young heavyweights. Herman was no match for the new contender and was knocked out inside two rounds. A few months later Tunney used Herman as one of his sparring partners in some exhibition bouts and the veteran earned his keep as he came in for some heavy body punishment. About that time Tunney's manager, Billy Gibson, was developing a young heavyweight from Mount Vernon named Johnny Grosso, who was becoming a local sensation in the New York clubs. After seeing the way Tunney handled Herman, Gibson figured Herman's scalp would be a good one to hang on Grosso's belt. They met at the Columbus Club in New York and Herman ruined Gibson's protégé, climbing off the canvas to knock Grosso down fifteen times for a seventh-round knockout.

In knocking out Gibbons, Tunney had injured the first metacarpal of his left hand, and when it was still troubling him after the Herman blowout in Kansas City, he went to see a doctor. The local physician examined Tunney's throat and attributed the soreness to diseased tonsils, advising they be removed. Returning to New York, Tunney went to see Dr Bob Shea, who confirmed the diagnosis, and the offending tonsils were removed. To recuperate, Tunney took a holiday trip with his old friend, Bill McCabe, around New York State. McCabe, who had known the fighter from their days in France with the AEF, was an agent to the superintendent of state prisons and he and Tunney visited several penal institutions during the course of their travels. While at Danemora an urgent message was received from Tex Rickard asking for a conference in New York as soon as possible. Rickard had been unable to contact Billy Gibson and he wanted to talk about a Dempsey–Tunney fight for the championship. A meeting was hastily arranged at the home of Tunney's friend, Jimmy Eagleton, at 252 West 14th Street in New York, attended by Tunney, McCabe, Rickard and Eagleton.

As Rickard shook hands with Tunney, he said, 'Gene, I want to match you to fight Dempsey.' As Tunney replied that a Dempsey fight was his dearest wish, the promoter said he had repeatedly telephoned Gibson's office after the Gibbons fight, to no avail. 'Billy owes me some money,' said Rickard, 'and he probably thinks I have been calling to ask for it. To hell with the seventeen thousand dollars, what I want is his consent to have you box Jack Dempsey.'

Before he took his leave, Rickard surprised Tunney by asking, 'How much do you think it will cost you to live a year after you become champion?' Somewhat taken aback, Tunney managed to reply, 'Oh, ten or twelve thousand dollars a year would certainly be all I could find use for.' Rickard laughed and said, 'Seventy or eighty thousand dollars will not pay your bills!'

A few days later, Tunney was back in his training camp at Saratoga Springs when Rickard arrived to inform Tunney and Gibson that the New York Commission was standing firm behind Harry Wills and if Tunney wished to challenge Dempsey he would first have to remove the Black Panther from the equation. Tunney readily agreed to meet Wills and Rickard offered a purse of $150,000. 'Make it $200,000,' said Gibson, 'and the fight is on.' Rickard immediately agreed and went back to New York to get the ball rolling. It didn't roll very far. When Tunney arrived in New York to sign the contracts, Harry Wills failed to turn up, even though Rickard had offered him the same purse as Tunney. When the Wills fight went out of the window, Tunney, anxious to keep busy, took a September bout with Bartley Madden in Minneapolis.

A good journeyman heavyweight, Madden was no stranger to Gene Tunney. When Tunney had resumed his professional career after returning from France, he had started training with the instructor at the City Athletic Club on West 54th Street, Jack Denning. After a while Denning found he couldn't give Tunney enough of his attention owing to his other duties and brought in a fighter named Bartley Madden to work with Gene. They trained together for several months and now, six years later, they were to meet in a genuine match.

Madden was not a big man, standing five foot ten and a half tall and weighing 189 pounds, a fair boxer lacking a power punch. But he was as tough as old boots and had never been knocked out in almost one hundred bouts. Madden started fighting in his native Galway in 1910 and arrived in America a couple of years later. He was soon swapping punches with men like Harry Greb, Bill Brennan, Billy Miske, Battling Levinsky, Tommy Gibbons and Fred Fulton. The giant Harry Wills had punched Madden all over the ring for fifteen rounds without being able to put him on the floor, and now Madden was to fight Gene Tunney, the new contender for the heavyweight title.

'Tunney', reported Fleischer, 'showed better form than when he last fought. His lightning-like left worked with precision and he displayed increased power in his blows. The end came after a little more than two minutes of fighting in the third round, when Tunney backed Madden into a corner, gained his opening with a left jab and then crossed a crushing right to Madden's jaw. Madden landed on his back and wasn't able to get up until nine counts had been sounded over him when he feebly arose. No sooner had he done so than he met a short left hook that again sprawled him on the boards, face downward. The old war-horse tried to rise, but at the count of ten he was still in a horizontal position.'

Tunney would recall, 'Bartley was very tough, and had as game a fighting heart as was ever put in a man. Strict training always bored him. He went into many fights completely untrained, but on getting in he fought until he fell. He flew at me in the first round just as he used to at the City Athletic Club, back in 1919, when I was a youngster just discharged from service. Madden never thought of quitting as a means of extricating himself from a desperate situation.'

Of the finish, Tunney would say, 'The left hook that knocked Madden out in the third round, after he had got up from a count of nine, was the best that I have ever delivered. Lou Fink, my faithful trainer, who was with me in all important matches, contends that I never hit as good a blow before or since.'

Recalling the rumours that circulated following Tunney's knockout of Tom Gibbons, Ed Van Every wrote in the *New York Evening World*, 'In the same way they tried to take credit away from Gene following his knockout of Bartley Madden. Bartley had never been knocked out before. He had fought Fred Fulton and other good heavyweights in their prime and none of them could do anything with this rugged Irishman. He had taken the best that Harry Wills and Jack Renault could hand out in 1924. The Negro heavyweight had punched and roughed Bartley around until Wills had fought himself into such a state of dizziness that he didn't know his way to his own corner on at least three occasions. And at the end of the fifteen rounds, it cannot be said that Madden appeared in special danger of going down. But when he was later knocked out by Gene Tunney, why then it was a case of Madden laying down.'

When Madden returned to New York he was upset by the rumours, telling newsmen, 'I never have faked a fight in my life. Tunney beat me squarely. Do I look as though I had gone through a pink tea party? Here, look at my eyes, my nose, my lips and forehead. Was I not battered, maltreated, to say the least?'

Madden did indeed look as though he had been hit by a truck. His homely face was a mass of bruises and swollen to twice its natural size. He had earned his $5,000 blood money. Nat Fleischer would write, 'That fight was fought on the level. Tunney, who had been coming along like a house afire, simply proved too much for the worn-out veteran. There was absolutely no reason for casting aspersions on that fight.'

There was a reason, as later claimed by Tunney. A couple of months before the fight, Madden had fired his manager. This gentleman then became associated with Paddy Mullins, who was in charge of the Harry Wills muscles. Well aware of Tunney's growing stature as a contender for the title, Mullins and his associates also knew that anything they could do to discredit Tunney would help to keep their tiger in the frame for the big one. On the day of the Tunney–Madden fight, Madden's former pilot told a sportswriter he knew that the fight was in the bag – it was fixed for Tunney to win by a knockout. With an eye on increasing the circulation figures of the newspaper concerned, the story was published.

Tunney had no doubts as to the source of the allegations. 'The dismissed manager of Madden,' he stated, 'chagrined because Madden had been matched for an important fight in which he was not to get his managerial cut, gave vent to the malice of his nature. He forgot the previous fights in which Madden was battered around by larger and more skilful opponents; fights in which he shared in everything but the beatings. This is the brand of ingratitude that is so peculiarly a part of a good many managers.'

To further support their smear campaign, the newspaper set up a committee, which paid all expenses for promoter Jack Reddy, referee George Barton, the chairman of the Minnesota

State Boxing Commission, and several reporters who had covered the fight for their papers, to travel to New York and present their evidence. When the committee didn't hear what they wanted to hear, they accused everyone of being a party to the alleged fraud. The story was too outlandish for other papers to touch, but when Tunney took copies of the published allegations to his lawyer, he was told that intimation and innuendo had carefully circumvented the libel laws.

Paul Gallico, renowned sports columnist for the *New York Daily News*, would later write, 'There were accusations rife at the time that, on his way to the top, Tunney had engaged in several fixed fights, notably with characters by the names of Italian Jack Herman and Bartley Madden. A newspaper actually printed a story to the effect that Herman had gone into the tank for Tunney. I remember asking Gene, point-blank, if they were true or false. He replied, "Oh, come on, Paul! Why should I have to bother to fix ones like that? If I can't knock out all the Italian Jack Hermans there are, one after the other, I'd never put on another glove."

'The logic of this was irrefutable, and what is more, from the physical point of view it had to be true. The fact was that neither Gibson nor Tunney could have bought their way through such competition as Erminio Spalla, Harry Greb, Georges Carpentier, or Tommy Gibbons. Tunney fought his way to the top through the toughest opposition available with no more protection than he was able to provide himself with, using his two hands, his own skill, dexterity, and courage. There was not then, nor is there now, any sense in imagining that the ex-Marine would pursue the most difficult antagonists to establish his right as Dempsey's challenger, beat them or knock them out, and then hire unheard-of or inferior artists to quit to him.'

In November 1925, Gibson booked Tunney into Cleveland's Public Auditorium for a twelve-round bout with local favourite Johnny Risko. They called Risko 'the Rubber Man' and 'the Cleveland Baker Boy' and he would give the heavy bag in any gym a run for its money when it came to absorbing punches. In a professional career covering some sixteen years Risko would only be stopped three times, and he fought a veritable Who's Who of boxing that included twelve fighters who were, would become, or had been world champions. Short for a heavyweight and a bit on the tubby side, Risko was neither a puncher nor a clever boxer, but he would give you a fight and seventy per cent of him was all heart. Gene Tunney would vouch for that.

'In my own experience,' he told Wilbur Wood, sports editor of the *New York Sun,* 'the most courageous man I ever fought was Johnny Risko of Cleveland. I will never forget my twelve-rounder with him in 1925. Without boasting I think I can say that I could box rings around Risko and hit him almost at will, whereas he could not penetrate my defence. I battered him badly from the start and tried everything I knew to knock him out because my hands grew sore early from landing on him. Yet he never gave me a moment's rest, coming after me all the way. In the last few seconds of the twelfth round he was trying just as hard as he was at the start, even though he must have realised he had no chance at all. That, to my mind, is ring courage of the highest degree.'

Tunney had gone into the ring against Risko with a damaged right hand, injured the week before the fight, and he suffered a dislocated knuckle on his left hand in an early round when Risko blocked a punch with his elbow. Tunney was further handicapped when a low left hook to the groin left a huge black and blue bruise and semi-paralysed his left leg, hindering his ring movement.

'Each of Gene's fists was swollen when he drew off the gloves in his dressing room,' reported Nat Fleischer. 'In view of the condition of his hands, it was surprising that Tunney had punished Risko as he did, for he hurt this man of rawhide and iron more than any ten men had previously done. Even Risko admitted that to the newspapermen after the fight. He compelled Risko's knees to sag at least twenty times, snapped his mouth open by knocking all the wind out of him time and again and in the fifth round, he dropped Johnny to one knee with a right cross, followed immediately by a right uppercut.

'He battered poor Johnny's face until he peered through mere slits, punched him so that thick blood came from Risko's mouth and when the big Baker Boy's hand went instinctively to his face to wipe the crimson from his lips, Tunney sunk a left hook into his stomach that seemed to pierce John's very flesh. Risko fought gamely, as he always did. He was aggressive so long as his physical resources could permit him to be and then, when Tunney's body bombardment robbed him of much of his strength, he took his punishment courageously.'

Covering the fight for the *Cleveland Press*, Joe Williams wrote, 'They paid Johnny Risko $3,000 for meeting Gene Tunney last night, and he stopped 3,000 punches. Can anyone imagine what would have happened to Johnny Risko if he'd been paid $10,000?'

Tunney remembered the fight in his autobiography: 'One of the most pleasant experiences of my career came to me that night. I met James J Corbett and talked with him after the fight. Jim was playing in a local theatre and came down to the auditorium to see the match with Risko. He had never seen me box before. I felt because of my sore hands he did not see me at my best. At this suggestion, to my surprise Jim said, "If you had had Dempsey in there tonight you would have knocked him out." I said I did not think so and did not understand his reasoning. He explained. "When you hit this fellow Risko and had him all but out, which occurred in every round, he'd wrap his arms about his face and cover up, leaving you no opening in which to place a finishing punch. Now, if you hit Dempsey a blow like any of those and hurt him, he will not cover up. He doesn't know how. In rushing in, he'd leave an opening so that you could get in the finishing shot. When you fight Dempsey, fight him exactly as you fought Risko tonight and you'll surely win."' Corbett and Tunney would soon meet again.

★   ★   ★

In his biography of Grantland Rice, William Harper wrote, 'As a pioneer of American sportswriting, Rice helped establish and dignify the profession, sitting shoulder to shoulder in press boxes around the nation with the likes of Ring Lardner, Damon Runyon, Heywood Broun, and Red Smith. Besides being a first-rate reporter, Rice was also a columnist, poet, magazine and book writer, and film producer.'

In 1925 Rice was making pictures for Sportlight Films and hit on the idea of getting the old champion Jim Corbett to box a three-round exhibition with the new contender from New York City, Gene Tunney. Corbett's autobiography, *The Roar of the Crowd*, had been published that year and he was in the news again. He was somewhat reluctant, however, when Rice approached him with his idea, but eventually agreed. Gene Tunney was delighted at the chance of boxing with his former boxing idol and appeared promptly for the bout, which was to be held on top of the Putnam Building in Manhattan.

When Corbett arrived and saw Tunney attired in a new pair of trunks, he took one look and said to Rice, 'I'd like to wear long, white trousers. I had a pair of good-looking legs in the old days but they don't look so good now. I'm nearly sixty and they are kinda shrivelled.' Then Corbett and the contender from Greenwich Village boxed three two-minute rounds as the cameras captured this rather unique meeting of old and new.

'Tunney was on the defensive,' recalled Rice years later. 'Corbett was brilliant. He feinted with his left, then punched with his left. A left feint, a left hook, a right feint, a left jab, a right feint, a right cross. He still had bewildering speed! He mixed up his punches better than practically any fighter I've seen since, with the possible exception of Ray Robinson. After the exhibition, Tunney turned to me. "I honestly think he is better than Benny Leonard. It was the greatest thing I've ever seen in the ring. I learned plenty," he said. At fifty-nine Corbett was still the master.'

13

The Promoter

Tunney spent that winter in Florida. To help cover expenses he accepted a fight with Dan O'Dowd at St Petersburg, a few days after Christmas. It would be just over six years since Tunney had boxed O'Dowd in his first contest after getting out of uniform, and the tough, game Boston fighter had made Tunney go for the full eight rounds. This time, O'Down was down for the full count in round two.

Grantland Rice recalled playing golf with Tunney and Tommy Armour on a Miami course: 'Gene would hit his drive, toss aside his club, and run down the fairway throwing phantom punches, left and right hooks, and muttering, "Dempsey . . . Dempsey . . . Dempsey." "He's obsessed," observed Armour. "His brain knows nothing but Dempsey. I believe Jack could hit him with an axe and Gene wouldn't feel it. I don't know if Dempsey has slipped, but I'll have a good chunk down on Tunney when that fight arrives."'

As the world welcomed 1926, the signs were that the Dempsey–Tunney fight would indeed arrive that year. Tunney received a cable from Tex Rickard stating that Dempsey had signed for the fight and offering a purse of $150,000, with an option of fifteen per cent and $175,000 should the gate hit a million. Like a good manager, Billy Gibson burned up the wires between Miami and New York, to no avail. Rickard wouldn't budge on his offer, so Tunney packed Gibson off to New York to have the necessary contracts drawn up.

Tunney trained faithfully in the Florida sunshine and was tempted by an offer of $50,000 from a local promoter to box Young Stribling. Tunney contacted Rickard and informed him of the proposition, whereupon Rickard agreed to the match. At that time Stribling, the Georgia Peach, had packed in over 150 fights even though he had just turned 21. There were some good names on his record: guys like Tommy Loughran, Johnny Risko, Paul Berlenbach and Mike McTigue; but there were a lot of names such as Battling Mishound, Rabbit Palmer, Fearless Ferns and Sailor Martin, many of which were pseudonyms for the Stribling family chauffeur. No wonder Rickard gave his blessing to the match.

Billy Gibson opened negotiations with the promoter and received a $5,000 advance on signing the contract. Not bothering to tell Tunney about the binder, Gibson promptly invested the five grand at a local racetrack, where his knowledge of fighters was soon proved to be far superior to what he knew of thoroughbred racehorses. Gibson was further upset when the fight promoters failed to come up with the rest of Tunney's purse and the contest was called off. Tunney then learned of the five grand Gibson had received when the promoters asked for it to be returned. The manager claimed that since the promoters had failed to fulfil their obligations, the binder was forfeit. But he was eventually persuaded to repay the money.

Tunney returned to New York and went to see Rickard with Gibson. There was a good offer on the table from the Pathé Moving Picture Company for Tunney to star in a serial called *The Fighting Marine*. Rickard thought it a good idea; it would keep Tunney's name before the public until he was ready to announce the Dempsey fight. Just when that might be was still far from settled. The New York State Athletic Commission had suspended Dempsey's licence until he signed for the fight with Harry Wills, its challenger since Dempsey had beaten Firpo in his last title defence in September 1923. Furthermore, the commission announced that any promoter attempting to do business with the banned champion would have their licence suspended. Tex Rickard needed some political clout if he was to score a knockout over the Solons of Sock in Gotham City.

Eager to help the situation, Tunney and his friend, Jimmy Eagleton, went to see James Riordan, a close associate and friend of New York Governor Alfred E Smith. Riordan, unable to be of assistance, suggested Tim Mara might be the man to swing things with the commission. Timothy J Mara was a bookmaker and sports promoter whose main interests were in horse racing and football, where he was known as 'Big Tim', though he had been known to get his feet wet in the fight game. He said he was sure he could get a favourable hearing with the commissioners and promised to do what he could.

Tunney particularly wanted the Dempsey fight to take place in New York, for several reasons. First, of course, he was a New Yorker and would be the first city-born fighter to win the heavyweight title in a gloved contest should he be successful. It was also in his favour to box under the rules of the New York Commission as the contest would be over fifteen rounds to a decision. Rickard's proposal to have the fight in New Jersey would mean twelve rounds with no decision being rendered. Tunney was confident he could outbox the champion and win the decision. But if he failed to knock Dempsey out in a No-Decision match, even if he punched Dempsey silly in every round, the title would stay with Dempsey if he was still standing after twelve rounds. Rickard was also well aware that a contest to a decision had far greater box-office appeal than a No-Decision match.

With Hollywood beckoning, Tunney set off for California along with Billy Gibson. He was going into uniform again as 'the Fighting Marine'. As Grantland Rice recalled in his autobiography, *The Tumult and the Shouting*, 'He didn't allow the greasepaint and glitter to interrupt his training or, more important, his thinking. Each afternoon he'd work at the Hollywood Athletic Club where sports columnist Harry Grayson got to know him. An ex-Marine himself, Harry spent a lot of time with Tunney. The more he saw him, the better he liked him. Six months before the fight, Grayson picked Tunney to beat Dempsey. He never recanted. Matter of fact, Grayson was the only fight writer in America to go overboard on Tunney. We all thought he was crazy.'

Back in New York, Rickard announced that he had matched Gene Tunney against Jack Dempsey for the world heavyweight championship, and Big Tim Mara suddenly decided it was time he got a piece of the action. He contacted Tunney and Gibson in California, stating that he wanted 25 per cent of Tunney's earnings should he manage to swing the fight for New York and should he become champion. Tunney countered with an offer of ten per cent. When Mara refused the offer, Gibson thought they had better go along with his demands, but Tunney did refuse to sign the contracts that did not contain the stipulation that Mara would benefit only if the fight was staged in New York.

When Tunney returned from California, he called on Rickard who advised him to start training for his fight with Dempsey. 'Commissioners Farley and Brower are against Commissioner Muldoon in voting to bring the fight to New York,' he said. 'If Brower does not change his mind in a week, I am going to Chicago to arrange for a site there.'

Muldoon's refusal to back a Dempsey–Wills fight for the heavyweight title would cost him his position as Chairman of the New York State Athletic Commission, a post he had held since 1923. William Muldoon was born in Belfast, New York, in 1845, and fought for the North in the Civil War. A physical-fitness fanatic, he boxed and wrestled as amateur and professional, was a policeman, ran a saloon, and trained such great champions as John L Sullivan, Kid McCoy and Jack Dempsey ('the Nonpareil'). Soon after the Walker Law legalised boxing in the state of New York in 1920, Muldoon was appointed to the commission, ruling with an iron hand. In 1926, when Tex Rickard was trying to stage the Dempsey–Tunney fight in New York, Muldoon gave his backing. He remembered the violent aftermath of the Jack Johnson–James J Jeffries fight in 1910 and was opposed to mixed matches for the world title, refusing to give his support to Harry Wills in his challenge to Dempsey. Unfortunately, Muldoon's fellow commissioners, George E Brower, a Brooklyn attorney of note, and businessman James A

Farley, threw their weight behind a Wills match, and forced the suspension of Dempsey's New York licence until he agreed to meet Wills.

Tunney set up his training camp at Tom Luther's White Sulphur Springs Hotel at Saratoga and Rickard travelled to Chicago, where he was given to understand the fight would be most welcome. However, before he could sign anything, he received a cable from Commissioner George Brower to the effect that he was now willing to go along with Muldoon in backing the fight for New York, no doubt influenced by several groups of businessmen with an eye on the revenue the contest would generate for the city. This left Farley out on a limb so he announced that, having done all he could to uphold the commission rulings, he was washing his hands of the whole affair.

Celebrations were premature, however: there was another stumbling block in the form of the Licensing Committee, chaired by Colonel John J Phelan. This committee duly sat in New York, and Tunney and Dempsey were called to the city from their respective training camps. Tunney was given his licence, but Phelan refused Dempsey's application on the grounds that he had refused to fight Wills. George Brower immediately challenged this decision on the premise that Phelan had acted illegally in refusing the licence for a contest already sanctioned by the Athletic Commission. On Brower's advice, Rickard had his lawyers apply for an injunction, but before this could be served, the promoter was visited in his office at Madison Square Garden by a party of gentlemen from Philadelphia. It was the year of the Sesquicentennial celebrations in the City of Brotherly Love, and representatives of Mayor Kendrick, Governor Pinchot and the Chairman of the Pennsylvania Boxing Commission were ready to guarantee Rickard all the support he needed if he would take the fight to Philadelphia. Rickard immediately telephoned Commissioner Muldoon, who advised him to accept the offer. Three hours later everything was signed, sealed and ready for delivery. The world heavyweight championship fight between Jack Dempsey and his challenger, Gene Tunney, would take place at the

Sesquicentennial Stadium in Philadelphia, on 23 September 1926. Tex Rickard was about to promote a boxing contest that would draw the largest paying crowd in the history of sports up to that time.

★　★　★

Boxing writer Hype Igoe would recall Tex Rickard as, 'the last of the quaint picturesque Westerners, cowboy, gold hunter, gambler, promoter, a man with so great a personality that he attracted attention wherever he went. The greatest showman on earth, a fellow who could sell anything. He was a cowboy, and a mighty good one, because he lived in a cowboy country where men are fearless daredevils who would take a chance at anything just for the fun of doing it. Gold hunter, because he lived among a rough and ready, daring crowd whose every move was one of prospecting along one line or another. Gambler, because he lived among the men whose day and night dream was the hope that they could run one of their shoestrings into a million dollars. Promoter, well, because that might have been an accident of chance, or possibly an opportunity.'

George Lewis 'Tex' Rickard was born in Clay County, Missouri, some ten miles from Kansas City, on 2 January 1871, one of six children born to Robert Woods Rickard and his wife, Lucretta Josephine. Clay County was a bloody strip of land along the Kansas border, the stamping ground of Jesse and Frank James and the Younger brothers, and as a boy Tex could remember bullets flying and the thunder of hoofbeats. It was not a healthy place to raise a family and the Rickards moved to Cambridge, a small town in Texas, then to Henrietta. Tex was in the third grade when his father died and he quit school to help his mother, getting his first job with local rancher Jim Curtis for ten bucks a month. He worked as a horse wrangler and graduated to trail driver.

While taking a herd across a river one day, Tex was knocked from his horse when a steer went berserk. Injured in the ensuing stampede, he was nursed back to health by Dr Bettick. Leona, the daughter of the household, took a fancy to the handsome young cowboy and they were married in 1894. Leona persuaded Tex to put up for town marshal and he got the job. Then tragedy struck. The following year, Leona presented Tex with a son, but both she and the baby died shortly afterwards. With nothing to live for, Tex left town and headed for Alaska. Gold had been discovered.

'Partners Tex Rickard and Will Slack were among the first to rush to the Klondyke [sic] when gold was discovered,' wrote author Bill Kelly, 'reaching Alaska in the winter of 1895. They spent the winter in Juneau playing poker, waiting for the thaw, and in April pushed on to Chilkoot Pass. Tex described the journey as the coldest and most difficult task of his entire life. Slack turned back but Tex pressed on for Circle City, a town that boasted twenty-nine saloons, gambling halls, and brothels. He was broke when he landed a job in a gambling joint owned by Sam Bonnifield, the Yukon's greatest and most famous poker player. Tex learned from Sam, and when Bonnifield bought the finest casino in town, he gave his old place to Tex Rickard.'

Unfortunately Rickard, like his clientele, couldn't resist a gamble, and in a short while he had lost everything and was back working for Bonnifield again. Over the next few years, Rickard made and lost several fortunes while moving around Alaska. At one time he chopped wood for river steamers at $15 a day, another time he ran his own saloon and cleared $1,000 a day at the gambling tables. By 1905 he had moved to warmer climes in Goldfield, south-western Nevada, where he built the Northern Hotel with Kid Highly and Jim Morrison. There was a sixty-foot mahogany bar over which six barrels of whisky were sold every day. Keeping a watchful eye over the fourteen gaming tables was the celebrated Wyatt Earp.

Al Meyers, who had discovered and named the town, was drinking at the Northern one day and he asked Rickard what he thought they could do to celebrate Labour Day, a national holiday. On a visit to New York, Rickard had seen a fight between Terry McGovern and Jimmy Britt. Although not too impressed with the event, he sold Meyers on staging a rematch between the two and set about organising what would be his first big fight. He fired off a cable to Joe Humphreys in New

York offering a purse of $30,000 for McGovern to fight Britt in Goldfield. Humphreys, who was associated in the management of McGovern, had never heard of this guy Tex Rickard and he sure as hell had never heard of Goldfield, Nevada. Humphreys tossed the telegram into the wastebasket and forgot all about it.

Undismayed, Rickard looked around for another big fight. The world lightweight championship was in dispute at that time, with both Joe Gans and Battling Nelson claiming the title. The brilliant Gans, now a veteran of fifteen years in the ring, was champion from 1902 until giving the title up in 1904 to fight Joe Walcott for the welterweight crown. Walcott boxed a draw and many still considered him the lightweight titleholder. Nelson had beaten Jimmy Britt in a fight billed for the white lightweight title, and as far as he was concerned he was the lightweight champion of the world and not Joe Gans. When Tex Rickard offered a purse of $30,000 for a fight in Goldfield, Nelson agreed to meet Gans, although he insisted on two-thirds of the purse for a fight to the finish and on wearing five-ounce gloves, with both fighters to weigh not more than 133 pounds at twelve noon, 1.30 p.m., and at 3 p.m. ringside. The Dane and manager Billy Nolan knew that Gans would struggle to make the weight. He did, but he fought magnificently against the rugged, brawling Nelson who left the rulebook in the corner by the water bucket! In the 42nd round, Gans crumpled to the hot canvas from a low punch and referee George Siler declared Gans the winner and lightweight champion of the world.

It had been a great fight under the Nevada sun that September day in 1906, especially for the town of Goldfield, and for a fellow named Tex Rickard. A statement was issued by the Goldfield Athletic Club revealing an attendance of 7,285, paying $69,715 at the gate. 'There were about 500 entered without paying admissions, including newspaper men, deputies and special officers, making a total of almost 8,000 people in attendance. There were about 1,500 women in attendance from all parts of the world.' The statement was signed by G L Rickard, President.

Although delighted with his success, Rickard didn't see boxing as his calling and spent a few years travelling around the

West buying up coal mine leases for a man named Ryan. He
was in Duluth one day, bargaining with a mine owner, when the
talk got around to boxing. 'You should sign up Jim Jeffries and
Jack Johnson, help Jeff get his old title back,' the man said to
Rickard. When he mentioned the idea to a friend, Tom Cole,
Rickard was surprised when Cole told him to bid for the fight
and top any other bid by $20,000. Accepting the challenge, the
promoter travelled to Pittsburgh, where Johnson was appearing
in vaudeville. Meeting Johnson's white wife first, Rickard
promised her a fur coat if she would persuade her husband to
sign with him. Then he visited Johnson in his dressing room at
the theatre and put $2,500 in new bills on the table in front of
him. The cash looked good to the world heavyweight
champion, who was broke. He shook hands with Rickard, then
told him that a bid of $100,000 was going to be made for the
fight with Jeffries. 'If you put in a bid for $101,000, you'll get it
sure,' said Johnson.

Rickard then went to New York, where he talked with Jack
Gleason, a one-time actor and playwright who had the inside
track over Jeffries. Rickard closed the deal to promote the fight
with Gleason in San Francisco and set about building a suitable
arena. He had spent $35,000 when Governor James N Gillett
pulled the plug, bowing to pressure from social and religious
groups to ban the fight from the city. Rickard immediately
shifted the operation to Reno; he knew people in Nevada and
they knew him by now. An arena was built and on a blazing July
day in 1910, with Rickard himself acting as referee, Johnson
toyed with the old champ before knocking him out in the
fifteenth round. A crowd of 15,760 paid $270,775 and Rickard
sold the film rights for $101,000. But the result of the fight
triggered off race riots, with eleven people reported killed, and
Congress was so upset by the aftermath that it passed
legislation banning the interstate transmission of fight films,
which actually remained federal law for the next 38 years.

Still not hooked on boxing, Rickard set off for South America
to become a cattle rancher, investing $400,000 in a huge spread
in Gran Chaco, Paraguay, stocking it with 50,000 head of cattle.

It would be 1915 before he returned to New York with his
second wife, Edith Mae. When Rickard was introduced to Jess
Willard, the giant Kansan who had just beaten Jack Johnson in
Cuba to become world heavyweight champion, the showman
stirred in him and he knew he had to promote this big fellow.
Renting Madison Square Garden for $15,000, Rickard staged a
fight between Willard and Frank Moran. Moran called his big
right hand Mary Ann, but she ran out on him that March night
in 1916 and Willard won easily. Rickard was delighted with the
turnout, which included many socialites mingling with the
regular fight crowd, and he cleared $42,000 from the gate
receipts of $152,000, the largest return for an indoor attraction
up to that time. 'I'm satisfied that the fight was a success,' he
told reporters afterwards, 'that the public has no kick, and you
newspaper fellows can't say anything terrible about me.'

Just over three years later, Rickard signed a young sensation
called Jack Dempsey to batter his giant champion into oblivion
inside three brutal rounds in a wooden arena the promoter had
built at Maumee Bay, just outside Toledo. Rickard dropped
money on this one, with the crowd totalling less than twenty
thousand, but he had the greatest attraction in the fight game:
a two-fisted slugger who would draw five million-dollar gates
over the next eight years and make Tex Rickard a very happy,
and very rich, man. One of those fights was with a giant from
South America named Luis Angel Firpo.

In the January 1931 issue of *The Ring* magazine, Hype Igoe
wrote, 'Tex was a great judge of boxing. I never knew a man
who was quicker to sense a great match, to foresee the dramatic
possibilities of a proposed bout than Tex Rickard. I happened
to be in Tex's office the day that Luis Firpo entered and Tex
first laid eyes on the Argentine. Luis had just collected $125 for
a fight in Jersey City with Sailor Maxsted. He had knocked
Maxsted kicking like a sea crab and Tex had sent for Luis. It
was that sense of the dramatic that had appealed to Tex, the big
fellow possessing a wallop. Firpo had sold himself as soon as
Tex laid his peepers on him. Tex's cold, discerning eyes were
drinking in Firpo's shaggy frame like rare wine. I saw Tex

mentally whip a tape measure all over Firpo. When Luis left, up spoke Tex. "God, what a man! Hype, he and Dempsey will make the greatest fight you ever seed." He slapped me on the back and laughed. I never saw Tex so happy as then. That was picking them. That was *knowing* fighters and fights.'

That September night in 1923, Rickard was right on the money. A huge crowd of 88,228 paid over a million bucks to see Dempsey knock out Firpo in what is still called one of the most sensational heavyweight title fights ever, with Dempsey sent hurtling out of the ring in the first round by Firpo's massive fist. Dempsey crawled back and flattened the giant in the second round. In all Dempsey knocked Firpo down nine times. He only got up eight times.

'Dempsey was the cornerstone of Tex Rickard's monument, Madison Square Garden,' wrote Igoe, 'yet Tex wouldn't change his mind about the prowess of Jack and Jim Jeffries. He loved Dempsey, but Jim was Rickard's idol. Dempsey made ten million dollars for Tex and his organisation, and Tex would admit that there never was a more colourful fighter in the game than Dempsey, but when it came to fighting, that was a horse of another colour with Tex. To him, the greatest of all the heavyweights was his friend Jim Jeffries, and no amount of argument could alter that opinion.'

President of the Madison Square Garden Corporation, Rickard was the driving force behind the building of the new Garden on Eighth Avenue, between 49th and 50th Streets. It opened in November 1925 with a six-day bicycle race and would become the most famous sports arena in the world. Sadly for Tex, his wife Edith Mae died of a heart ailment that October, just before the official opening of what would become known as The House That Tex Built. The New York Rangers ice hockey team was named after Rickard as a word play on Texas Rangers. Rickard could not have flourished without rich backers. He once boasted he had been perfumed by the smell of four hundred millionaires – 'My nice people,' as he called them.

14

The Man Behind the Gloves

The fight mob never quite knew what to make of Gene Tunney. 'It was argued that I was a synthetic fighter,' he would recall in a magazine article. 'That was true. They said I lacked the killer instinct, which was also true. I found no joy in knocking people unconscious or battering their faces. The lust for battle and massacre was missing. I had a notion that the killer instinct was really founded in fear, that the killer of the ring raged with ruthless brutality because deep down he was afraid. Synthetic fighter, not a killer! There was a kind of angry resentment in the accusation. People might have reasoned that, to have arrived at the position of challenger, I must have won some fights. They might have noted that, while the champion had failed to flatten Tom Gibbons, I had knocked him out. The prizefight "experts" were almost unanimous in not giving me a chance.'

Nat Fleischer, publisher and editor of *The Ring* magazine, recognised that, 'In Tunney, the boxing world had found a new type of fighter, one far different from all the rest, including the amiable Corbett. His studiouness and determination are what enabled him to rise to the heights. A man with an abundance of confidence, a fighter without fear, a self-made man, a model for the American youth, that was Tunney. But call it fastidiousness or what you will, there was something in Tunney's nature that revolted against the jovial shoulder slap of the blatant politician, the familiarities of the millionaire bootlegger, and the coarse congratulations of underworld leaders and their henchmen.

'If popularity depended upon such favours and such men, Gene wanted none of it. Tunney knew the seamy side of life. He learned the inside of things thoroughly during hard years spent struggling upward toward the goal of his profession. He could not avoid contact with sinister persons whom he despised, but neither could he bring himself to their level of boisterous comradeship. He was, in a sense, with the gang. He was certainly never of it.'

The sportswriters of the roaring twenties were spoilt for choice when tapping out their daily columns. Jack Dempsey (the Manassa Mauler) and Harry Greb (the Pittsburgh Windmill); baseball king Babe Ruth (the Sultan of Swat); golfing greats Walter Hagen and Bobby Jones; the graceful Suzanne Lenglen in tennis; the Flying Finn Paavo Nurmi burning up the track; Johnny Weissmuller moving through the water like a torpedo on his way to Olympic records and Hollywood stardom as Tarzan. 'Who the hell is this guy, Gene Tooney?' they would ask. He was a guy who became the whipping boy of the American press because of his refusal to allow the newspapers to exploit his personal life, and that of his family.

'Gene was perpetually duelling with the Fourth Estate,' wrote Ed Fitzgerald in a 1950 article for *Sport* magazine. 'Keenly aware that he owed his contender status to no one but himself, Tunney refused to jump through hoops for the boys with the pencils and portable typewriters. He told them precisely what he thought they ought to know. And no more. They got statements from him only when he was good and ready to issue them. The whole boxing world laughed along with the Dempsey retinue when Brian Bell, a sportswriter for the Associated Press, encountered Tunney at his camp reading Samuel Butler's classic novel, *The Way of All Flesh*. To say the least this was unusual conduct for a prizefighter, and Bell made the most of it.

'He got even more colourful copy when he discussed Gene's literary interests with the studious battler and got from Gene the statement that he admired the works of William Shakespeare. When Bell's story broke, one of Dempsey's followers couldn't restrain himself. He ran to his hero, clutching the newspaper. "Hey, champ!" he yelled. "It's in the bag! The sonofabitch is up there reading a book!"'

'There seems to be an inclination to point fun at Gene's scholarly demeanour,' said Dr Fred Van Vliet, who had known Tunney since he was a boy growing up in Greenwich Village, 'but this is as real a part of the boy as his success in pugilism. He was an inveterate reader as far back as I know him, which is quite some years. My library, which was a much larger collection of books than it is at present, my library had a sort of fascination for the boy and I guess he must have browsed through practically every book in my possession. Books on ancient Greek and Roman history seemed to hit his fancy hardest and these he would read over and over again.'

As a thirteen-year-old at St Veronica's Parochial School, young James Joseph Tunney was already well acquainted with the works of Shakespeare, acting in several plays, among them *The Merchant of Venice*. He would study his lines over and over, and could recite the speeches of Portia, Antonio and Shylock with ease. He also played the Prince in the court scene in *Romeo and Juliet*. As a young marine getting ready to embark with his company bound for the war in France, he noticed the fellow next to him was packing two volumes of Shakespeare into his kit bag. Tunney knew he was the company clerk, a quiet and intelligent man who had been a lawyer in civilian life. 'Now my respect for him went up many notches,' recalled Tunney. 'He must be educated indeed to be taking two volumes of Shakespeare to carry on his back on the long marches we would have in France.'

Landing at Brest after a rough crossing, Tunney was dressing for inspection when, to his horror, he realised his tunic was missing. It was too late to do anything but report his loss and he drew extra guard duty as a consequence. He subsequently learned that the company clerk had suffered terribly with seasickness, ruined his own uniform, and 'borrowed' Tunney's.

Feeling guilty when hearing of his comrade's punishment, the clerk apologised and offered him anything he fancied. The young New Yorker asked for one of the Shakespeare volumes. 'He retained *Julius Caesar* and gave me *A Winter's Tale*,' remembered Tunney. 'He knew what he was about, as anyone who knows Shakespeare will attest. Having the book, I tried to read it but couldn't make any sense of it. I kept on trying. I always had a stubborn streak, and figured the book must mean something. But it didn't, so far as I could make out. I went to the company clerk. He had given me the book and it might mean something to him. It did, and he proceeded to explain. He coached me, led me through *A Winter's Tale* which turned out to be interesting. I finally got the meter, not as intelligently as I wanted but enough to know what was going on.'

In the years he spent punching his way to the position of challenger for Dempsey's title, Gene Tunney's love of literature filled many a tedious hour in training camps and on long train journeys to and from fights. Besides, he couldn't play pinochle! In *Arms For Living*, Tunney explains, 'That moderately intricate card game was the perennial favourite among the people of pugilism, and a most characteristic training camp sight is the manager, the trainer, and their fighter for hours in a game of auction pinochle. In my training entourage, I had past masters of pinochle. My manager, Billy Gibson, was an indefatigable addict of bidding, melding, and counting points. And my trainer, Lou Fink, was reputed to be perhaps the best pinochle player in the country. He could bid like a pawnbroker, meld like a financier and squeeze the last point out of the play. They pushed the pasteboards incessantly in training camp, and on railroad trips to fights they played all night.

'The melancholy fact was I never could get interested in pinochle. So what was left for me? I had to fall back on books. It became part of my training routine to read during the five hours between the roadwork, breakfast sequence, and the ring stints in the afternoon. Books filled that hiatus. I found that literature provided me with the best occupation for passing the time restfully and keeping from worrying about the fight to come. Five hours of book work in a day of training, and I was training for bouts for most of the time the year round for ten years. Yes, I was able to do quite a bit toward catching up with my reading. I always had a genuine interest in books, or rather the ideas contained in them. I finished the works of Shakespeare from cover to cover. I particularly liked *Henry IV, Hamlet, The Merchant of Venice, Macbeth,* and *Othello.* By reading anthologies and collections, I became familiar with the works of many English, Irish, and American poets.

'I struggled through Gibbon's *Decline and Fall of the Roman Empire.* I have read Hendrik Willem Van Loon's *Story of Mankind,* and believe me, it's a lot easier than Gibbon. I have read much of Cooper, Dickens, Dumas, Victor Hugo, and Bulwer Lytton. I have read Samuel Butler's *The Way of All Flesh,* a book that had a tremendous influence on George Bernard Shaw. I am familiar with the works of Jack London, Sir Arthur Conan Doyle, Jeffrey Farnal, just as almost every man who likes a good story.'

'This bookworm quality,' wrote Ed Van Every, in a somewhat odd observation, 'it is my opinion, has had something of an effect on Gene's eyes. Although he has never admitted as much, quite possibly out of fear that it might bring to light something of a handicap to his pugilistic ambitions, it seems there is plain evidence of optical strain in Gene's gaze. Those remarkable eyes of a rather limpid blue seem especially sensitive to the sharp rays of the sun, as a study of most of his outdoor pictures will reveal. In fact there is a tendency to squint and in the examination of hundreds of his recent pictures I have found none that gives an excellent view of his eyes.'

'Tunney was something beyond the comprehension of the fight mob,' wrote Tim Cohane, sports editor of *Look Magazine,* in a 1956 story on Tunney. 'He compounded his pariahhood by behaving at times as if he deemed himself the original discoverer of culture. His dialogues often advanced on stilts, as when he dismissed an objectionable fellow from his training camp with the castigation, "You are full of self-approbation and deceit." Except for a few writers, notably W O McGeehan, who called him "The Golden Boy of the Golden Age," the sporting press did not take to Tunney.'

Paul Gallico, sports editor and columnist of the *New York Daily News*, would reveal, 'There was simply no logic to the reactions which the strange, contradictory personality of Tunney aroused in us. I cannot bring myself to deposit the blame far from the door of the Bard of Avon. All through Tunney's rise, one heard over and over the same theme, a bona fide pugilist ought not to be quoting *Hamlet* or caught browsing in a copy of Spengler's *Decline of the West* in the solitude of a bosky Adirondack dell where his training camps were pitched. There must be something phony about a fellow like that. Such behaviour was an offence to the entire industry, and the thing to do was to take this stainless knight down a peg or two. One way to accomplish this was to smear his character. Almost to a man, the boxing writers were arrayed against him, disliked him, and lost no opportunity to pillory him for his bookishness and present him in as bad a light as possible. Some of us, Westbrook Pegler of the *Chicago Tribune* and myself of the *Daily News*, took an almost perverse joy in hounding this character who, by every tenet and qualification, was the twin of Jack Armstrong, the All-American Boy.'

For his 1925 fight with Tom Gibbons at the Polo Grounds, Tunney trained at Uncle Tom Luther's place at Saratoga Lake. Jersey Jones handled publicity for the five weeks' stint, and later recalled the complex character of the contender. 'Seldom have we encountered any fighter as deadly serious in his training as was Gene. Tunney's main relaxation was reading. Gene didn't go in for cheap dime-novel trash. He preferred the more serious, cultured writings. One day, a gang of about ten New York newspapermen drove into camp to see that afternoon's workout. "Where's Tunney?" asked Stan Lomax, then with the *Bronx Home News*. We pointed to a cliff across the road from the hotel. "He's up there," we said, "nestling in the cool shade of the trees and reading a book."

'"A prizefighter reading a book?" Lomax grunted. "What's he reading?"

'"What,' we retorted, "would you expect a prizefighter to read? Shakespeare, naturally." It's remarkable at times what a flippant remark can produce. Tunney came in for so much good-natured joshing on the Bard of Avon that he began to take it seriously and actually made something of a Shakespearean scholar of himself. One reason Tunney never was too popular, personally, with the sports scribes was that he wouldn't be natural with them. In press interviews he made himself sound like a pompous corporation lawyer rather than a guy from the sidewalks of New York.

'We had ample opportunity, during that stretch at Saratoga Lake, to see both sides of Tunney. Entertaining neighbourhood pals from Greenwich Village one day, Gene was a genial host, completely relaxed and at ease, swapping yarns in the same language as his guests. A day or two later, a delegation of sportswriters dropped in for a workout. It had rained during the night and the ring canvas was damp and slippery. Sparring with Bud Gorman, Tunney skidded. Gene stopped boxing and strutted to the ropes. "Gentlemen," he solemnly addressed the assembled scribes, "the footing in this ring is atrocious."'

Jack Sharkey, the Boston heavyweight contender, paid a visit to Tunney's camp a couple of weeks after he started training for Dempsey. Talking to a newspaperman, Sharkey scratched his head and, looking somewhat bemused, said, 'I come from the city of culture, but that fellow has me licked with his easy flow of chatter. It don't sound natural to me, but ya gotta give him credit. He sure knows how to put on the dog!'

As the Tunney–Dempsey championship fight drew near, Tunney's penchant for polysyllabic language drew this comment from Jerry 'The Greek' Luvadis, one of Dempsey's trainers. 'Tunney will have an edge over Dempsey on account of them six-syllable words of his. Jack is strictly a two-syllable kind of guy.'

Jack Dempsey was strictly a two-fisted kind of guy too, and Gene Tunney was going to need more than a few big words if he was going to take the heavyweight crown off the man they called the Manassa Mauler.

15

Dempsey

As a sinewy teenager scuffling for a living around Utah and Colorado, William Harrison Dempsey worked at any job he could find. 'I could have made a life's work being a cowboy or a miner,' he would say. 'I was pretty good at both. I dug for everything you can dig for, from coal to gold to uranium.'

But it was when he threw his shovel away that young Dempsey really hit pay dirt with his hands. Calling himself Kid Blackie before changing his name to Jack Dempsey, he became a fighter and slugged his way to a million-dollar fortune as heavyweight champion of the world. His official boxing record shows that he knocked out fifty guys and most of them reckon he still had the shovel in his hands!

The road to riches started in a log cabin that now houses the Jack Dempsey Museum on Main Street in the Colorado town of Manassa, where Dempsey was born on 24 June 1895, one of eleven children of Hyrum and Celia Smoot Dempsey. The family came from Logan County, West Virginia, and moved west to Colorado after being converted to the Mormon religion by a missionary. The boy they named William Harrison, after the president, was of Irish and Cherokee blood, with a Jewish strain from his father's great-grandmother who was called Rachel Solomon.

The Dempseys moved around a lot; Montrose and Steamboat Springs in Colorado, Provo in Utah, and Salt Lake City. Celia ran a cheap hash house in Montrose that catered for the workers building the huge Gunnison Tunnel, and young Jack recalled washing dishes there when he was eleven. 'I guess I was a boy for only two years of my life,' he'd say. A year later they were living in Provo, where Jack, or Harry as he was known at home, attended Lakeview Elementary School, quitting in the eighth grade. He shined shoes, picked crops and unloaded beets at a sugar refinery for ten cents a ton, before going on the road, taking jobs where he could and riding the rods of freight trains, a cheap and dangerous way of getting from place to place. 'You're only a few inches from the roadbed,' he remembered, 'and if you fall asleep and fall off, you die. I often bet my life that the train would stop and let me off before I shook and shivered my way to my death beneath the wheels.'

The kid wanted to be a fighter, like his older brothers, Johnny and Bernie. It was Bernie who made him chew pine tar gum to strengthen his jaw, and soak his hands and face in brine to toughen the skin against cuts. Using Salt Lake City as his base, and calling himself Kid Blackie, Dempsey started fighting at Peter Jackson's saloon-gymnasium on Commercial Street, where Hardy Downey was promoting fights. Promised a purse of $2.50 to fight One-Punch Hancock, he duly knocked out his man with one punch! Downey wouldn't pay him until he fought Hancock's big brother, so he flattened him also.

'I learned as a kid,' Dempsey would say, 'that no fighter has everything. Hit a fellow on the chin and if he doesn't blink, hit him in the belly. It is as simple as that.' He studied other fighters whenever he got the chance. Sparring in a Reno gym with a good black fighter, Anamas Campbell, he let himself be punched around, and when Campbell agreed to fight him, knocked him out inside three rounds. 'I knew this white boy was kidding me in the gym,' said Campbell, rubbing his chin as he came out of the ring. 'I should never have fought him.'

Bernie had been fighting as Jack Dempsey, after the middleweight champion, Jack Dempsey, the Nonpareil. Taking a fight in Cripple Creek, Bernie had second thoughts and asked his brother to take his place. So Kid Blackie became Jack Dempsey, knocked his man out, but lost an argument with the promoter who refused to pay him, claiming he had been duped. Bernie hung up his gloves and there was only one Jack Dempsey after that. He climbed off the deck to fight a draw with Jack Downey, and in Salt Lake City, Two-Round Gillian failed to live up to his name, being blasted out in just one round!

By the summer of 1916, Dempsey felt ready to try his luck in the east. Together with his friend Jack Price, he took a train bound for New York City, where they rented a cheap room not far from the Polo Grounds. When the money ran out, they slept in the park. Price finally booked Dempsey a fight with Andre Anderson, a heavyweight who outweighed him by fifty pounds. It was a ten-rounds No-Decision bout at the Fairmont Athletic Club, and after Anderson had bounced Dempsey off the canvas a couple of times he got tired, and Dempsey finished strong over the last few rounds. A boxing writer named Damon Runyon gave the newcomer the decision in his report for the New York *American.* Jack Price got fed up with hanging around New York and bought a train ticket back home, using the money he got from selling Dempsey's contract to John 'The Barber' Reisler, a Broadway gambler.

John the Barber was one of those brave managers and promptly matched Dempsey with the formidable Sam Langford. When Dempsey got over the shock, he told Reisler, 'Nothing doing. I won't fight Langford. He'd kill me!' The man from the West also vetoed Gunboat Smith, finally going in with a black giant named John Lester Johnson at the Harlem Sporting Club. Dempsey stayed the limit with Johnson, despite three broken ribs, and some of the boxing writers gave him a draw. Next day, Dempsey was on his way back to Salt Lake City. He worked as sparring partner to Carl Morris after his ribs healed and married Maxine Cates, a sometime prostitute and piano player in a Commercial Street saloon. They were together for only a couple of months and divorced several years later, but not before Maxine had claimed Dempsey had lived off her immoral earnings.

In February 1917 Dempsey challenged Fireman Jim Flynn in Murray, Utah, and was knocked out inside two minutes of round one, Bernie throwing the towel in after seeing his brother on the deck four times. 'He'd have killed you with another punch,' Bernie consoled Jack as they headed for the dressing room. It was the only time Jack Dempsey failed to go the distance in a professional career of eighty fights. He worked as a lumberjack for a spell, and was catching hot rivets in a Seattle shipyard when his mother wired him to say Bruce, a younger brother, had been stabbed to death. He got home too late for the funeral and was still there when a letter arrived from manager and promoter Jack 'Doc' Kearns, asking if he still wanted to be a fighter.

Kearns had been in the Klondike gold rush, worked in saloons, was a fighter, a wrestler and a gambler. He hit the jackpot when he got a rough, tough kid named Jack Dempsey for $5 and a train ticket. Kearns knew how to move a fighter, and after a win and a couple of draws with a fat ex-sailor named Willie Meehan, he took Dempsey on the ferry across the bay from Oakland to San Francisco for a fight with Gunboat Smith. The old Gunner had missed none of the good ones and his right hand would take your head off if he caught you right. He bombed Dempsey in the second round and the kid fought on automatic pilot the rest of the fight, winning the decision. He didn't know he had won until Kearns told him going home on the ferry! Kearns also told him he was going to be the heavyweight champion of the world. It took them 22 months and 27 fights, 22 by knockout.

A year after Flynn had stopped him, Dempsey knocked his old adversary out in one round. He beat big Carl Morris, who had abused him as a sparring partner, three times, the last time on a first-round KO. 'He was the only fellow I wanted to murder,' growled Dempsey. 'I knew the bum wouldn't get up.' He knocked out Bill Brennan and had the better of Billy Miske in two No-Decision bouts.

In the summer of 1918 Mike Collins was pushing the claims of his tiger, Fred Fulton, for a title shot at Jess Willard. At six foot six Fulton was as big as the champion, though not as heavy. When the fight didn't happen, Collins offered Dempsey a fight with his contender. Kearns snapped it up and the fight was signed for Harrison, New Jersey, in the ballpark. A crowd of ten thousand turned up and most of them didn't even see the fight. Dempsey turned loose a blistering barrage of punches, and Fulton was down and out in eighteen seconds of the opening round!

'We got $9,000 for eighteen seconds work,' recalled Dempsey in his autobiography. 'After the fight I was mobbed by enthusiastic fans, for the first time in my life. They tore at everything, just wanting to take a little piece of me home. One friend, who had bought a high-priced ticket, told me after the fight that the minute he saw Fulton go down he had rushed outside and managed to sell his ticket for twice what he paid for it, to an anxious fan at the end of the line waiting to get into the park!'

With America joining in the war in Europe, both Dempsey and Kearns had registered for the draft but had been deferred as Kearns was supporting his mother and Dempsey was supporting his family as well as Maxine. Dempsey boxed in benefits for the Red Cross, helped sell war bonds, and readily agreed to do a photo shoot in a Philadelphia shipyard to aid recruitment. They posed him in a pair of overalls over his street clothes, stuck a riveter's gun in his hands and snapped some photos. Next morning in the newspaper there was the photo of Dempsey, dressed in overalls and holding a riveting gun, with his neatly pressed trousers and his shiny patent leather suede-topped shoes 'sticking out like sore thumbs,' as Dempsey put it. He was disturbed by the photos, which were wrongly alleged to show him working in a shipyard and doing his bit for the war effort. He told Kearns of his concern. 'Listen, kid,' snorted Kearns, 'What're you worried about? You're making a big deal out of nothing!'

After the Fulton blowout, Kearns kept Dempsey busy as he chased a title fight for his meal ticket. Dempsey knocked out guys like Terry Keller and Jack Moran, Kid Harris and Kid Henry, Big Jack Hickey and Eddie Smith just to cover expenses. The few name fighters who agreed to meet him fared no better than the others. Battling Levinsky was world light-heavyweight champion when Dempsey put him away inside three rounds, contenders Porky Flynn and Carl Morris were both blasted out in the first round, while vetern Gunboat Smith was sunk without trace in round two.

Kearns was making headway with promoter Tex Rickard, who had already signed world heavyweight champion Jess Willard to a $100,000 guarantee to defend his title. Rickard remembered Kearns from their days in the Klondike when Kearns had worked in Rickard's Northern Bar saloon weighing gold for him. Kearns used to thicken his hair with Vaseline and every now and then would rub his hands through his hair, leaving gold dust that he washed out when he got back to his room. Rickard didn't trust Kearns then and he certainly didn't trust him now, in 1919, when he was pushing this kid Dempsey for a crack at the champ. Besides, Rickard thought Dempsey was too little to fight Willard, who towered six foot six and a quarter and outweighed Jack by some fifty pounds. And if he did agree to the match, Dempsey could expect no more than $20,000, maybe $25,000 at most. Kearns blew his top, yelling at the promoter, 'Listen, Rickard, this isn't just an ordinary fight. I'm pitting the kid here against Jess Willard, and that ought to be worth at least fifty grand! Jack's string of knockouts makes him a pretty good draw, so don't sell him short.'

They kicked it around for a while, Rickard offering $25,000, Kearns asking for $30,000, and they finally settled for a compromise, $27,500. Now all Rickard had to do was find a suitable site, promote the fight, and find a backer with a spare hundred grand in his back pocket!

Kearns contacted a member of the Toledo Athletic Club in Ohio who was willing to put up the cash for the fight, so long as the state governor okayed the bout. Kearns and Rickard made tracks for Toledo, convinced Governor James Cox that the fight would bring prosperity and publicity, and even got the hundred grand from a guy named Frank Flournoy. Back in New York, Rickard called in the press and announced that Jess Willard would defend the title against Jack Dempsey in Toledo, Ohio, on Independence Day, 4 July 1919.

Rickard built a huge wooden arena on the shores of Maumee Bay and on fight day a crowd of 19,650 paid $452,224 to see a massacre in the sun. 'I weighed in at 187 pounds', recalled Dempsey, 'and Jess Willard at 245, almost sixty pounds and five inches separated us. Jess was like a mountain; he was even bigger close up, in those blue trunks of his. I ignored him and he sneered. He was the 5 to 4 favourite and was pretty damn cocksure. He even had the nerve to approach Doc for legal immunity in case he killed me.'

In that dramatic, thrill-packed first round it looked as though Jess Willard would be the one to be killed. Waiting for his chance, Dempsey suddenly unleashed a vicious left hook that smashed against Willard's head and the giant crashed to the canvas, a look of shock and amazement on his face. Struggling to his feet Willard was immediately hit with a storm of leather that drove him back into the ropes and down to the canvas again. Gamely he hauled himself up by the ropes and Dempsey, standing behind him, launched another attack, a final left hook toppling the champion for the third time. The referee prevented Dempsey from another rearguard attack but he couldn't stop him hitting Willard again, and nothing could stop Willard from hitting the floor again. The crowd was screaming as the giant was destroyed before their unbelieving eyes, his face already a bloody mask, his legs barely able to carry his body away from this snarling, vicious man they called the Manassa Mauler.

Willard went down for the fourth time and when he got up, Dempsey had circled behind him. The unseen punches ripped into his face and body, and the canvas came up and hit him hard again. If nothing else, Jess Willard was as game as a pebble and he somehow kept hauling himself back to his feet to face his tormentor. He was down for the seventh time in the round when referee Ollie Pecord counted him out, unaware in the bedlam that surrounded the ring that the round had already ended when the bell had rung.

Doc Kearns was beside himself. He had bet $10,000 at odds of 10–1 that Dempsey would win in the first round, and as he leaped through the ropes into the ring he was already spending the hundred grand! He told Dempsey to leave the ring, and Jack was almost in his dressing room when frantic calls drew him back. The round had ended during the final count but a rope holding the canvas down had fouled the bell, muffling the sound. The fight was still on! Bad news for Dempsey and for Kearns, even worse for poor Jess Willard. As the second round got under way, Dempsey would recall, 'Willard was a sorry sight. His face was swollen and bruised. His right eye stared at me glassily. I pelted him with more blows, including a hard left to his eye, partially shutting it. He was becoming bloodier and he spat out a tooth. He was staggering with his tremendous arms outstretched as if to keep me at a distance.'

'When the third and last round began,' reported Nat Fleischer from ringside, 'Jess looked like one being butchered. He was an object of pity. Blind, mouth cut, legs tottering, he presented an appearance never before seen in a heavyweight championship bout. He could scarcely see his opponent, yet was willing to stand up despite his loss of blood and weakness. Yet, strange as it might seem, Willard, desperate, came through with a rally that was difficult to believe. He jarred Dempsey with several powerful lefts to the mouth, and for a time it seemed that the tide would turn. It looked as if Dempsey, in his eagerness to score a knockout, had spent all his energy. He had shot his bolt. The bell proved sweet music to both.'

In his autobiography, Dempsey revealed, 'I couldn't wait for this massacre to end. I was sapped both mentally and physically. I looked at Willard again. I couldn't seem to take my eyes off him. He was a broken man now, he had nothing left. Willard and his seconds called the referee over and told him that Willard wouldn't make it out for the fourth. Ike O'Neal and Walter Monaghan then threw in the blood-spattered towel. I won. I won. My God, I won! I made it! *I was the new champion!*'

Now he could live like a champion, this wild kid who had fought for his life in hobo jungles, who had risked his life riding under trains because he couldn't afford to ride inside them, who had lived on the free lunches they gave you in saloons when you bought a nickel beer. Now Dempsey was the heavyweight champion of the world, and they toasted him in Hollywood and along Broadway. Pathé Pictures paid him a thousand dollars a week to appear in action-filled shorts, and he palled around with the likes of Wallace Reid, Douglas Fairbanks and Charlie Chaplin in Los Angeles; in New York he enjoyed the high life in clubs such as Texas Guinan's and the Cotton Club in Harlem.

It wasn't all roses, however. In March 1920 Dempsey appeared in United States District Court in San Francisco to answer charges of draft evasion. His former wife, Maxine, had written a letter to a newspaper maintaining that Jack's claim to have supported her and members of his family in those final days of the war had been false; she had in fact been supporting Jack on her immoral earnings. The newspapers printed that celebrated photograph again, showing Jack in the shipyard, and allegations of 'slacker' were hung on him. The judge threw out the case and Dempsey was cleared of all charges, but the stigma followed him for some time.

Kearns reckoned it was time his champion got back to work and matched him with old opponent Billy Miske at Benton Harbour, Michigan. Miske was suffering from Bright's disease, which eventually took his life in January 1924, and Dempsey knew the $25,000 purse would help Billy and his family. That September day in 1920 the champion didn't know whether to carry Miske along or knock him out. The record shows Dempsey did what he did best: KO, round three! Three months later he had a tougher assignment facing another former victim, Bill Brennan, in the old Madison Square Garden.

A capacity crowd of 15,000 screamed themselves hoarse as Brennan staggered the champion with a terrific right uppercut in round two. By the fifth Dempsey was back in the fight and in the eighth a tremendous right hand nearly took Brennan's head off. In the tenth a booming right from Brennan ripped Dempsey's left ear almost from his head and Doc Kearns was having fits in the corner, yelling, 'You gotta knock this bum out, Jack!' In round twelve the champion did just what the doctor ordered and flattened Brennan for the full count.

New York Daily News sports editor Paul Gallico wrote, 'Dempsey was a picture book fighter. By all the sons of Mars, he looked the part. He had dark eyes, blue-black hair, and the most beautifully proportioned body ever seen in any ring. He had the wide but sharply sloping shoulders of the puncher, a slim waist, and fine symmetrical legs. His weaving, shuffling style of approach was drama in itself and suggested the stalking of a jungle animal. He had a smouldering truculence on his face and hatred in his eyes. His gorge lay close to the surface. He was utterly without mercy or pity, asked no quarter, gave none. He would do anything he could get away with, fair or foul, to win.' Gallico knew what he was talking about, from experience. As a cub reporter he visited Dempsey's training camp at Saratoga Lake, where the champ was getting ready for his fight with Luis Angel Firpo in 1923. Gallico thought it would be a good idea for a column to spar with the champion, so Doc Kearns set it up, winked at Dempsey and rang the bell. The next thing Gallico knew, they were picking him off the canvas. He had his story, but it was some time later before he was up to writing it!

The press played up the slacker angle when Rickard matched Dempsey with French war hero Georges Carpentier in what would be boxing's first million-dollar gate at Jersey City in 1921. Carpentier was hardly a light-heavyweight, even if he did throw a straight right that was good enough to cream the best heavyweights in Europe. He jolted Dempsey with it in the second round but was knocked out two rounds later.

Dempsey didn't have a serious fight for two years, loafing through exhibition bouts for pocket money and touring Europe with friends. In the summer of 1923 a group of civic leaders and businessmen in the Montana town of Shelby thought it would be a good idea to host a world championship fight. It wasn't. They raised $200,000 and Doc Kearns grabbed it with both hands. Dempsey fought Tom Gibbons on a broiling Independence Day and won easily, though Gibbons was still defying him at the end of fifteen rounds. As the town went bust, Kearns collected a further $72,000 and took the next train out of there. The banks closed their doors in what became known as the Rape of Shelby.

Dempsey hadn't been at his best against Gibbons, but it was a good job he was in shape for Firpo when they clashed at the Polo Grounds in New York. That September night, Tex Rickard had his second million-dollar gate as a crowd of 82,000 paid $1,188,603 to see what they still call the most sensational heavyweight title bout of all time. The shaggy Argentine giant sent Dempsey flying through the ropes in a riotous first round that saw Firpo himself smashed to the canvas seven times. Pushed back into the ring, Dempsey got his act together in round two and knocked Firpo out. Dempsey 's purse for the fight came to a little more than half a million dollars and he collected it himself from Rickard, much to the annoyance of Doc Kearns. It would be their last fight together and this time Dempsey paid Kearns off, deducting what the manager owed him. It was the end of the line for Jack Dempsey and Doc Kearns, and from then on they talked to each other through their lawyers.

The champion was by that time living in Los Angeles, where he met and married Estelle Taylor, a beautiful movie star. Estelle didn't like Kearns and she didn't like her husband being a fighter. The champ had his nose remodelled and they did a play on Broadway, with Taylor getting $300 a week and Dempsey pulling down $1,000. Estelle didn't like that either, but she stuck it out for the six-week run of the play. Dempsey did a tour of burlesque houses, offering $1,000 to anyone who stayed three rounds with him. He toured with a circus at $2,500 a week and in Hollywood made several movie serials, even starring with his wife in a feature film called *Manhattan Madness*. He didn't fight.

There was an attempt made to match Dempsey with big Harry Wills and they signed for a promoter named Floyd Fitzsimmons. Wills received a down payment of $50,000 but when Dempsey's money was not forthcoming, he finished up with a cheque for $25,000, which bounced when he tried to cash it. Tex Rickard told Dempsey to forget Wills; he had a new guy for Dempsey to fight, a former marine named Gene Tunney. Dempsey didn't think Tunney, or any other contender for that matter, was strong enough to fight him or draw a decent gate. He himself picked Paul Berlenbach, a strong puncher who had just lost the light-heavyweight title, but Rickard was adamant. It was Gene Tunney or nobody. So Jack Dempsey agreed to defend his title for the first time in three years against New York's own Gene Tunney.

16

Mind and Muscle

The year 1926 would see the 150th anniversary of the signing
of the Declaration of Independence, and the civic leaders of
Philadelphia proudly celebrated the event by hosting the
Sesquicentennial Exposition, built on 450 acres on the south
side of the City of Brotherly Love. With thirty nations par-
ticipating, it had been five years in the planning and it was
expected to draw some fifty million visitors over the six
months it was open, from 31 May to 1 December 1926. Sadly,
the event was starved of funding by the federal government
and by the state, and it closed with a loss of $5 million. It was
reckoned that the overall attendance throughout the six
months was nearer ten million rather than the fifty million
that had been expected. One contributing factor was the lousy
weather – it rained for 107 of the 184 days the event was open.
And it was on one of those rainy nights that Gene Tunney
fought Jack Dempsey for the heavyweight championship of
the world in the huge Sesquicentennial Stadium, the only
permanent structure built for the exposition at a cost of
$3 million.

It had taken them five years to bring this lavish spectacle to
the city of Philadelphia, just about the same time it had taken
Gene Tunney to bring his dream to reality – the fight with the
legendary Dempsey. In 1921, after the Dempsey–Carpentier
fight, Tunney had hired Larry Williams to work out with him at
Red Bank. Williams had been Dempsey's chief sparring partner

for the Carpentier fight, and the New Yorker recalled, 'Larry was a smart, fast, good-hitting heavyweight who at the beginning used to say about me, "Good, game boy!" In 1923, Larry said, "He's as hard to hit as Battling Levinsky and hits faster than Dempsey. In another year he will surely lick the champion." Whenever I heard of a fellow who had boxed with Dempsey, I tried to engage him as a sparring partner. In this way I got a good deal of information. I had seen the Dempsey fights with Brennan, Carpentier, and Firpo and studied at length the moving pictures of each. In the Brennan fight, though Dempsey showed a lack of skill, he was fast and tireless. But his lack of boxing skill interested me.

'In the Carpentier fight when the light Frenchman clouted him on the cheekbone with a long right hand punch in the second round, he was dazed. He swayed for a moment like a sapling in a stiff wind. I saw that Dempsey was not invincible. In the Firpo fight, as he rushed out of his corner in the first round with a left hook that started when he left his chair, I saw that in excitement he was an open target. Though the Firpo fight was three years after the Brennan fight, I saw no improvement in his technique. He was not the kind of fellow, I reasoned, who interested himself in skill. He depended on his wallop. Most all good hitters do!'

Tunney had started his training at Uncle Tom Luther's place at Saratoga Lake, but when the champion arrived in the east from his California home, Luther told Gene that Dempsey had made previous arrangements with him. Tunney moved out and went to the Adirondack camp of a former marine buddy, William Osborne, at Speculator in New York State, about forty miles west of Saratoga. Tunney's camp was pitched near a small river amid gorgeous scenery. He never did like training in the city gymnasiums, as his friend Jimmy Bronson recalled, 'The only mark that Tunney ever got, a damaged ear, was received in a gymnasium workout. Tunney disliked headgear. It didn't fit in with his idea of training. Many things didn't fit in with his training ideas. Most of the fighters enjoy the atmosphere of the gyms. To Gene, the smell itself was repugnant. He knew what he wanted, and he didn't precisely want gymnasiums.

'Once he sent an emissary to tell Lou Stillman, the owner of the noted New York City gymnasium where most fighters train, that he had to have the use of his gym at a certain time. Stillman is an extremely independent citizen who has his own ideas as to when his equipment will be available. Lou refused the demand indignantly. Tunney did not train at Stillman's. It wasn't that he wanted to tell Stillman how to run his business. He knew better than that. But Tunney also knew how he must run his business, the business of his own training. If the other man would not accommodate his wishes, the single-centered Tunney went elsewhere.'

While Tunney was training at Speculator, he was asked by Rickard to come into the city for a reception by the Mayor of Philadelphia and the Sesquicentennial Committee. Newsreel cameras recorded every minute and reporters bombarded Tunney with questions about the forthcoming battle. He smiled confidently and said, 'If he stands up and fights, I will knock him out in two or three rounds.' It made a banner headline for the papers next day.

With three weeks to go, Tunney moved into a new camp that had been prepared for him in Stroudsburg, Pennsylvania, a typical small American town about sixty miles from New York City, nestling between the Pocono Mountains and the Blue Ridge Mountains. The challenger was housed in the clubhouse on the grounds of the Glen Brook Country Club, just a short walk to a newly erected wooden platform supporting a punch bag and, a few yards away, a boxing ring in the shade of a big tree.

'I think I have been favoured with as nearly an ideal place as it is possible for a man to train in,' Tunney told Ed Van Every of the *New York Evening World*. 'In Lou Fink I am working with a trainer of experience and judgement and with sparring partners such as Bud Gorman and Osk Till, whom it is a pleasure to be associated with. I expect to be joined by Billy Vidabeck, Harold Mays, Jimmy Delaney and others soon, and

I am not only certain I will be in the best possible condition, but I am almost certain that I will beat Dempsey.'

With a couple of weeks to go to the fight, Tunney was ready to chew nails and spit rust! His roadwork, four or five miles, was done only on the days he didn't box. But he still went through the arduous daily exercises to strengthen his hands, and only a few newspapermen were privileged to see these morning workouts. Van Every was one of the few.

'That Tunney's hands are not impervious to damage is no secret,' he wrote in his daily column. 'It is not the wrists, as has been generally believed that really give Gene trouble, it is the knuckles that have gone bad so often. A special form of exercise for building the hands and reinforcing the knuckles has been adopted by the challenger. Gene starts off in "knuckle exercise" by placing himself about four feet from the wall of his room and then, tensed on his toe tips, he places his clenched fist knuckle out and puts forward the full pressure of his weight on his hands as he works his body backward and forward on his extended arms.

'What follows is considerably harder upon the leg and arm muscles, but more particularly on the knuckles and fingers. For now, Tunney extends himself face downward on the floor, and from this position he raises his rigid body many times on the flat of his knuckles and the tips of his toes. Then after a time he opens his fist until as he raises himself his weight is being lifted on his toes and finger tips. It is far harder work than would appear from the ease of practice with which Gene manages the business. It has produced a sort of bony callousness to the covering of the knuckles on Tunney's fists. I also witnessed the secret boxing practice. Oscar Till is the only one permitted in the room with Gene at the time, with the possible exception of Lou Fink, his trainer, and Bill Gibson, his manager. Till is the fastest boxer in the camp. He is the Sid Terris of the middleweights in the matter of legwork and makes a shifting target far from easy to shoot at. He is as elusive as a shadow as he flits in and out. During these morning sessions Tunney practices the various blows with which he expects to bring about the defeat of Dempsey, but in the main aims to perfect his timing in the delivery of his punches.'

Those three weeks at Stroudsburg saw the sleepy little town besieged by thousands of people as they flocked to see the young upstart who figured he could defeat the great Dempsey. The lush green grass of the Glen Brook Country Club disappeared underfoot as crowds of five to six thousand gathered around the outdoor ring and bag platform, while others peered precariously from the branches of the adjacent trees. The nearby roads were lined with cars.

'Where did they all come from?' Tunney would query as he waved a friendly response to the cheers that greeted his appearance for the daily workout. He worked on the light bag first, beating a rapid, rhythmic tattoo, his gloved fists and the bag seeming as one in the afternoon sunshine. Then he moved to the heavy bag and, with Lou Fink holding on, smashed in the punches that he hoped would bring him the title. Fink was always glad when that session ended. 'The jarring always gives me a headache,' he would say.

Former opponent Jimmy Delaney was the first to box with Tunney, the St Paul light-heavyweight moving smartly around the ring, his fast punches sometimes breaking through Tunney's guard. One powerful right hit Tunney flush in the pit of the stomach but the title challenger showed no discomfort. In the second round Tunney's left-hand work was accurate and impressive. Heavyweight Harold Mays worked with Tunney next and he roughed his boss up more than somewhat without causing any distress. The sparring ended, Jack De Mave, who had worked with Tunney for his fight with Tom Gibbons, said to a reporter, 'He's sure toughened up since I worked with him last.' On the other side of the training ring, Jimmy Delaney was talking to Big Tim Mara, who had come up from the city with a large party of New Yorkers. 'It's hard to believe how this boy has come along in both his boxing and the strength of his hitting,' said the fighter who had twice gone ten rounds with Tunney in No-Decision bouts. 'He's sharpshooting now, and it's shooting that hurts.' Big Tim, who had already backed

Tunney to win a considerable amount, said, 'I think the betting public will realise the falsity of the odds, and it is my opinion that there will be a great shrinkage in 2 and 2½ to 1 in the betting in favour of the champion.'

Tunney's old friend, Bill McCabe, was in camp and Ed Van Every recalled an amusing incident for his paper, the *New York Evening World*. 'One morning, two days before the big fight, McCabe was playing golf, or rather I should say playing at golf, with Gene. Bill has never had much experience in that popular game. And there was Gene taking great pains to perfect his friend's stance, his grip, his swing, just as though that was the most important business in the world. "You never saw the beat of it," related McCabe, "and I kept telling myself, this is the lad who is going to fight the great Jack Dempsey. Well, I may be worried about it, but he certainly isn't." During the play, the ball rolled down a treacherous little gully and McCabe started down to recover it. But Gene stopped him and went down for the ball himself with the remark that Bill might turn an ankle. "Can you imagine it?" queried McCabe. "Him with a two million dollar fight a little more than a day off, and he's worried about MY ankle!"'

One thing that did worry Tunney was a telephone call he received from manager Billy Gibson saying that Rickard wanted to change his contract, giving him a straight $200,000 as his end of the purse. When Tunney refused to go along with it, Gibson put Rickard on the line. The promoter pleaded extra expenses for seating and various other items and Tunney finally agreed to accept the offer. Bill Carey, who would become president of Madison Square Garden, would later tell him that he was in the room with Rickard at the time and was shocked by his misrepresentation of the figures he had given Tunney over the phone. 'My contention was that I should have received $283,648, representing 17½ per cent, instead of the $200,000 that was given me,' wrote Tunney in his autobiography.

Tunney boxed four rounds in his final workout before breaking camp; two rounds each with Jimmy Delaney and Harold Mays. Ed Van Every reported, 'There was a spasm of toe-to-toe mixing in the second round of the set-to with Delaney that is not likely to be improved upon much next Thursday night. For a few seconds they smashed away with both hands without let up. Delaney is a fast puncher, but Tunney's blows were faster and harder, though Gene was not putting his full weight in his blows very often.'

Fight manager Jimmy Dime was among the onlookers and was impressed, commenting, 'This man has a great chance. He is a far bigger and more powerful youth than I realised, and he is a much stiffer puncher with that right hand when he wants to cut loose. He knows how to hit with that right. I've always liked right-hand punchers, and this boy gets a lot of shoulder in his right when he wants to. I have not seen Dempsey, but he will need to be close to his real self. Tunney has a great chance.'

Former featherweight champion Abe Attell was also impressed by the challenger. A shrewd judge of boxing who backed his opinion with his money, he told reporters, 'It will go to ten rounds, but the last half of the distance will be terrible rounds for Dempsey.'

Tunney's pal from his days in France, Jimmy Bronson, had been invited to join the camp as chief second in those closing days. 'It is a surprising thing to me the way Tunney has improved right under my eyes,' said Bronson on that last day as workmen began dismantling the ring. 'Few people appreciate into what a wonderful physical fighting machine this man has perfected himself. It is a mechanical perfection and lacks the colour of the great natural fighting instinct that is so pronounced in the case of Dempsey, but a perfectly geared machine is an effective one. Tunney's mental control is something to marvel at.'

Bud Gorman had been chief sparring partner for Tunney before leaving camp for his own fight with German heavyweight champion Franz Diener. Gorman had come out a winner and was back to see Tunney's final workout. 'Gene will win sure as you are a foot high,' he told Van Every. 'This camp is going to turn out two champions. You know I am now the champion of Germany and Thursday night Gene will be champion of the world.'

★ ★ ★

Meanwhile, at his training camp at Atlantic City, the reigning champion of the world was not looking too impressive as he prepared for the sixth defence of his title. There were reasons, as Dempsey explained in his 1977 autobiography. 'Doc Kearns came to me one afternoon to inform me that he was still legally my manager and that he was working to set up a match with Harry Wills. I told him that I was a free agent and that I didn't need him taking his cut any more. The only way I'd keep him on a percentage would be if he agreed to take 33%. "Listen, Doc, it's either 33% or nothing. What's it gonna be?" He took nothing. From this point on, Doc Kearns fought against me twice as hard as he had fought for me. I tried to ignore him, but everywhere I turned I'd either be slapped with a subpoena or some strange lawyer would approach me with a deal. Crank calls woke us up during the night and my bank accounts were frozen.

'Word reached me that Doc had said he was, "licking me for Gene Tunney," figuring I'd be a wreck by fight time. He sued me for hundreds of thousands of dollars and even got a writ of attachment on the Rolls while Estelle was driving it in Atlantic City. She was forced to get out and walk back to camp, and by the time she got there she was out for Doc's blood. This didn't help our marriage. Estelle was now complaining that she was feeling the brunt of my mistakes. By the time of the Tunney fight, Doc had served me with no less than seven injunctions.'

By the time Dempsey had moved from Uncle Tom Luther's place at Saratoga, he was suffering from dermatitis, brought on by nervous strain, and his skin was beginning to crack. Rickard even suggested postponing the fight but the champ wouldn't hear of it. Too many tickets had already been sold and, besides, Dempsey was sure he could beat Gene Tunney seven days a week. Just listen to the sportswriters, they know what they are talking about. Almost to a man they were picking Dempsey to knock Tunney out in a few rounds. 'It will last,' wrote one knowing scribe, 'until Dempsey gets from his corner to hit Tunney, who will be too frightened to leave his chair, a matter of some fractions of a second.'

There were some dissenting voices. Harry Greb, who had just retired, let it be known that Dempsey had offered him a thousand dollars a day to get him in shape for the Tunney fight. 'I turned him down,' said Greb, 'I would feel like a burglar takin' Jack's money. Nobody can get him in good enough condition to whip Gene.'

Dempsey had better luck when he approached Tommy Loughran, a brilliant young light-heavyweight from Philadelphia who would eventually become champion of his division. Though not yet 24, Loughran had been a money fighter for seven years and had already boxed Greb several times, as well as Gene Tunney. 'Jack asked me to come down to the training camp at Atlantic City and work with him,' Loughran recalled. 'He knew I could do a lot of the things he would have to expect against Tunney and I was a lot younger than either of them. The first day we boxed, I could see Jack's reflexes were gone, his judgement of distance shot. As a matter of fact, as soon as the bookies got word of the workout they knocked the odds down on Dempsey from 3½ to 1 to 2 to 1. If they'd asked me, I would have told them to make Tunney favourite. But Jack was my friend and I suggested he cancel all public training and work six rounds a day with me in private. He was about to do it but Tex Rickard said, "That's out, secret workout, bah! The public would think there's something wrong with Dempsey. It would kill the ticket sale."'

So the champion trained in public and the crowds rolled up to see him at $1.10 a pop, which added about thirty to fifty thousand dollars to the kitty. And the press were there every day, recording every punch. Ed Van Every filed this report for the *New York Evening World*: 'Tommy Loughran was the first to face the champion in the boxing session. He started off by left-handing Jack with accuracy. This was not surprising since Tommy fires a nifty left and is very shifty when it comes to footwork. It was plain to see that Jack was pulling his punches.

Where he did not look so good was when Dempsey cornered Loughran and the fact that the champion was beaten to the punch with frequency and the fact that Tommy worked his way out with no special damage.

'Loughran took quite a thumping around the body, but had plenty of success with a right uppercut to the head. It was plain that Dempsey was practicing a left hook for his counter. The champion's timing, however, was not so good. Martin Burke in two rounds took a rough pummeling. He was bleeding from the nose before his time was up. Jack crossed two long rights to his jaw. Burke was not seriously shaken up at any time and when he stood up and traded with the champion he gave a good account of himself. For the last round of boxing Benny Kruger, announced as the light-heavyweight champion of Germany, was offered as a sacrifice. Kruger was no more than a middleweight and knew very little or nothing about boxing. If he was sent in to make Dempsey look good it didn't work out that way. Jack started off by smashing a heavy left hook to the jaw and it was soon apparent that Dempsey could hit this opponent as he pleased. The champion gave the German boxer quite a mauling but didn't seem to hurt him much.'

Among the onlookers unimpressed by this final session was Joe Dundee, the Baltimore welterweight who would become champion a few months later. 'Trying to look good at the expense of a mug doesn't get you anywhere,' said Dundee, loud enough for nearby reporters to hear, and note. Former undefeated lightweight champion Benny Leonard was another critic of the champion's training session. 'I can't understand it,' said Leonard. 'After what he showed me in other workouts, Jack certainly is a puzzle to me.'

Veteran Jack Skelly was on hand for the champ's workout. Skelly had made his own bit of ring history when he challenged George Dixon for the world featherweight title back in September 1892, the day before Corbett knocked out John L Sullivan in New Orleans. It was Skelly's first professional fight and he was knocked out by Dixon, who also went home with all the money. Commenting on Dempsey's form, Skelly said, 'To my point of view, the champion's main danger is that he can be held off with a left and he is a sucker for a right uppercut. Where you can detect Dempsey's loss in stamina is by watching his hands. He was starting to drop them a bit after his punches, that was where Dempsey was great at his best. Then when he cut loose with his wallops he always brought his hands back well up and with plenty of snap. Now, as he pulls them back to strike, they drag a little.' Then he added, 'But I don't think Dempsey's title is in the least danger as far as Tunney is concerned.'

'I'll never forget my parting with the champion that afternoon,' wrote Ed Van Every.

'"As we shook hands he said, "It looks to me like you are going to pick Tunney." "It looks that way, Jack," I admitted. "You're wrong," smiled the champion with very quiet conviction as he looked me in the eye. "And yet," and a peculiar smile lit his face, "who knows?"'

17

To Philadelphia in the Morning

That last day in camp Gene Tunney didn't run on the road, work in the gym, or even talk about the fight. With two old friends of his, Bill McCabe and Reggie Worthington, he went over to the Shawnee Country Club and played eighteen holes of golf on the championship course. Later, as the trio headed back to the clubhouse, Tunney was one down to Worthington, having scored two over-fives, and he said to McCabe, 'I don't think anybody could say my mind wasn't on golf after a round like that.'

Returning to his quarters at the Glen Brook Country Club, Tunney enjoyed his evening meal, prepared as always by his chef, George Ransberry, then retired to his room. He would read a few chapters before dropping off to sleep, perchance to dream that on the morrow he would become heavyweight champion of the world. In the other room, Ransberry played pinochle with 'Pants' Lawrence, Tunney's Adirondack woodsman friend. Outside, as a breeze murmured through the trees, the moon played hide-and-seek behind dark clouds. On the morning of 23 September 1926, those clouds were blotting out the sun as Tunney awoke at eight o'clock and dressed.

'How's Gib? I mean how's his hay fever?' Tunney enquired of Jimmy Bronson, who had come into the little cottage.

Manager Billy Gibson was a summer sufferer but Bronson just smiled and said, 'Gene, he has other problems today. He's worried; he has to fight Dempsey tonight. How about a little breakfast?'

'In a little while,' said Tunney, 'George Ransberry knows I like to wake up a bit before putting even a little fruit in my stomach.'

Just over an hour later, Tunney emerged from the cottage to tell the small crowd of well-wishers gathered to see him off that he was going to fly to Philadelphia for his date with Dempsey; with destiny. There was a short silence, and then a cheer went up as Tunney climbed into a high-powered Duesenberg. At the wheel was racing car driver Wade Morton, who had finished fourth in the last Indianapolis 500 race. The roar of the engine split the morning air as they wheeled out on to the road for the five-mile drive to the Shawnee Country Club at Buckwood Inn, closely followed by a carload of pressmen on the scent of a big story. With a million-dollar fight only hours away, Gene Tunney was to make the 85-mile journey to Philadelphia in a small plane flown by ace stunt pilot Casey Jones! This was a year before Charles Lindbergh made the first non-stop solo flight across the Atlantic to Paris, a feat that inspired world-wide interest in aviation.

Arriving at the Buckwood Inn, Tunney jumped out of the car and shook hands with Reggie Worthington. 'Where's Casey?' he asked.

'Oh, he's out playing golf,' replied Worthington.

'Say, I might play a couple of holes myself before I leave,' said Tunney calmly. His friends thought otherwise and Jones was summoned from the course. He walked over to a nearby shed and a few minutes later taxied out in a blood-red Curtiss Oriole. On the third tee, Tunney and Morton climbed aboard the small plane and at 10.05 a.m. on that misty morning, they took off. Jones circled the course twice before heading eastward, flying along the silvery Delaware River that winds its way through the Pocono Mountains, and making a perfect landing at the Philadelphia Navy Yard less than an hour and a half later.

'Weren't you worried?' a newsman asked Tunney as he alighted from the plane.

'If I'd crashed, it wouldn't have mattered,' he replied. 'The longest life is very short. It's Rickard's show but it's my life, remember.'

Author Mel Heimer records in his book, *The Long Count*, 'On the morning of the bout, Rickard was standing in front of the Bellevue-Stratford Hotel in Philadelphia, talking with Billy Gibson, Gene's manager, and some sportswriters. Tex was leaning debonairly on his Malacca cane, pontificating, when one of the writers asked, "Hear the latest, Tex? We just got word that Tunney's flying into town for the weigh-in." "Goddamn that son-of-a-bitch!" Rickard said. "What's he trying to do to me?" Whereupon W O McGeehan, the New York writer, raised an eyebrow and said, 'To you? What about himself?"'

Top sportswriter Grantland Rice would later give his version of what happened, writing, 'Casey Jones, the airplane stunt flyer and instructor, had flown his little biplane up to Stroudsburg and landed it on the golf course the morning of the fight, after Gibson had left. Casey could smell out a promotion stunt quicker than the next man. Gene had never been in a plane. Jones convinced him that it would be far easier and quicker, too, to fly down the Delaware River to Philly, a distance of only 70 or 80 miles, than it would be to drive. To prove his point, Casey would take Gene for a five-minute trial hop. Tunney, in fine mental fettle, agreed, climbed aboard and they were off into the wide blue yonder.

'Once they were airborne, however, the golf course and all surrounding terrain were immediately socked in. Jones couldn't land. He took a compass heading for Philadelphia and drilled into a fog bank. "I could have reached over that open cockpit and touched the Delaware Water Gap with either hand," said Tunney later. "It was that close! It took us about and hour and twenty minutes to cover eighty miles. I think we came by way of California." Tunney had been airsick. After the weigh-in, he hid out in a friend's apartment, ordered a steak, and went to sleep. The steak burned up. "We had a spare," said Gene. "I stayed awake until that one was on the platter, ate, then dozed off for several hours. I felt okay."'

According to Tunney, however, the flight to Philadelphia had been planned in advance. In *A Man Must Fight* he wrote, 'Weeks before the match, I made arrangements through Wade Morton, automobile race driver, to have Casey Jones, best known pilot of that time, come to Stroudsburg on the morning of the contest to fly me down to Philadelphia. I had decided to fly rather than take a train or automobile, for the definite effect its psychology would have on my opponent. I denied this, however. This flight very nearly proved a boomerang. Jones, in an article subsequently published in an aviation magazine, said that, in flying across the Poconos, he was lost in a dense fog the first hour, and I was airsick all the way.

'Our plane was met at the Naval Flying Field at 1.30 p.m. by a motor car. I was driven to the office of the Boxing Commission, still airsick. Chairman Frank Weiner of the Boxing Commission weighed me. The scales balanced at 186½ pounds. I went to a private home where I ate and rested until time to leave for the arena. Frank Weiner went direct to the late Jules Mastbaum's house, where many sportsmen had foregathered. Among them was a friend of mine. Commissioner Weiner said, "I have just weighed Gene Tunney. I never saw anybody so scared. He is as white as a sheet. I hope he doesn't die from fright between now and ring time." This friend of mine, Bernard F Gimbel, asked Weiner if he were sure Tunney's whiteness came from fright or illness, to which Weiner replied, "I tell you he is scared to death!" "We will see tonight," said Bernard.'

Tunney stayed in the two-story annex to the Spruce Hotel, at the corner of Spruce and 13th Street in Philadelphia. He would not let the suspicious members of his party make a change, saying, 'Why worry? I'll win, but if I don't the number 13 won't make any difference.'

But something did upset the challenger that afternoon as he rested. Billy Gibson woke him. With Tunney's manager was

Max 'Boo Boo' Hoff and another man who was later understood to be Hoff's lawyer. Gibson, sensing Tunney's anger at being disturbed, said, 'It is very important that you witness a paper to make sure we get our dough.' When Tunney found out that the document concerned only Gibson and Hoff, he witnessed the paper and made to see them out of the room. 'This one, too,' urged Hoff's lawyer, producing another paper. Tunney may have been drowsy but he was not daft. A quick inspection of the document showed it to be a long-term contract between Gibson and Tunney. He handed the paper back to Gibson without signing it and ordered the three men out of the room.

'This experience with Gibson so infuriated me', wrote Tunney in his autobiography, 'that, after we had settled the financial affairs of the night, I told him that he was no longer my manager. I could not reconcile loyalty to me with his actions that afternoon. However, months later, after hearing in full his side of the case from mutual friends, I changed my mind about Billy's intentions. For some time before the match he had been irresponsible. This was later confirmed by diagnosis and the testimony of two famous neurologists before a court which declared Billy mentally incompetent.'

So who was this guy Max 'Boo Boo' Hoff and what did he have to do with Gibson and Tunney? The Philadelphia crime family was organised by Salvatore Sabella, who ran operations from 1911 to 1927, but Hoff controlled city-wide bootlegging operations during Prohibition and was recognised as the real power of the local underworld. In the words of one journalist, 'Hoff had the appearance of a candy store owner, not the part bon vivant, part ruthless gangster the papers often portrayed.' A *New York Times* reporter wrote that Hoff 'was often arrested but never jailed, often accused but never convicted'.

According to magazine writer Parry Desmond, 'Hoff was a major East Coast bootlegger, racketeer, and nightclub and speakeasy owner in the 1920s and 1930s. He also was reputed to be Al Capone's Philadelphia connection. Hoff claimed that his vast income was the result of managing boxers and boxing promotions. But he and Billy Gibson had not been on speaking terms for several years because when Hoff was promoting at Shetzline Park in South Philly, Gibson had reneged on a verbal agreement to have his then world lightweight champion Benny Leonard fight on a Hoff promotion.'

Paul Gallico recalled the period in his book, *The Golden People*, writing, 'When one went to fight in another city, say Detroit, Pittsburgh or St Louis, there was always some local thug who let it be known that he was the power and could fix it for you to win or lose, depending on whether or not you paid. It might be nothing but wind, but who could afford to take a chance? The manager paid. If his boy won, the gangster got the credit, if he lost the manager was usually too scared to ask for his money back.

'In that decade not even the good name of James Joseph Tunney could escape the accusation that he had "protection" in the first Dempsey fight in the shape of a character called Max 'Boo Boo' Hoff, Philadelphia underworld boss, dabbler in prizefight promotions, and alleged proprietor of an imposing string of *maisons de joie*. The situation was ripe for just such kind of gossip. Tunney's manager was an old-line, old-time Irishman, Billy Gibson, a veteran of the bad old days, when managers were not above taking out some kind of an insurance policy in a strange city.'

The story going the rounds was that Abe Attell, ex-champ and known gambler who had been involved in the infamous 'Black Sox' baseball scandal of 1919, had come back from Tunney's camp claiming that Gibson was broke and needed $20,000 to pay their expenses. Max Hoff had advanced Gibson the twenty grand on the promise of 20 per cent of Tunney's championship earnings, should he win the title. He did take out a $350,000 lawsuit against Tunney, insisting that he had a strong case, but would later drop the suit without negotiating a settlement with Tunney's lawyers. It was also reported that when Tunney had witnessed the document between Gibson and Hoff, he had signed 'Eugene Joseph Tunney' rather than his real name of James Joseph Tunney.

Referring to the 1926 fight with Tunney in his 1959 autobiography, Jack Dempsey claimed, 'You couldn't hold a big fight in those days without doing some kind of business with the mob in charge of the town. The mob fixed that fight. It was a crazy kind of fix, because neither fighter knew anything about it. A few days before the fight, one of Hoff's gorillas came to Billy Gibson, Tunney's manager, and asked him how Tunney felt about the fight. "My boy has trained hard and thinks he can win," Billy said. The guy looked at Gibson, sizing him up, I guess, and said, "Would you like to be sure?" Billy said anybody would like to be sure.

'Out of that talk came a plan, or a fix, based on what you might call a calculated risk. It was a cinch, they figured, that sometime during the fight I'd hit Tunney low. If I hit him low and he showed signs of being in distress, or if he went down, the fight was to be stopped long enough for Tunney to be examined. Then an official would announce that I had fouled Tunney and Gene was the new heavyweight champion of the world. The story was that the mob had reached the officials.'

Dempsey had weighed in at 1.30 p.m. on the afternoon of the fight in an upstairs room of his home in West Atlantic City, by special dispensation of the Pennsylvania Commission and under the supervision of Commissioners Harvey J Boyle and Harry Farrell, together with Dr J Hall Lilly of Philadelphia. The champion hit 190 pounds.

'Dr Lilly's medical examination', reported Nat Fleischer, 'showed the titleholder to be in perfect physical condition and ready for the fight. A conspicuous feature of this examination was the fact that Dempsey's pulse rate registered 72, a condition which was said by Dr Lilly and Philadelphia Jack O'Brien, experienced in such affairs, to be remarkable under circumstances where the pulse beat should have been registered at the lowest, 74. Dempsey's heart was described as normal, his lungs, normal, his kidneys, perfectly normal, nervous reflex, normal, position of heart, fifth interspace, respiration, normal, temperature, normal, and pulse, 72.

'On the day of the fight I was one of two scribes permitted to remain in the sanctum of the Pennsylvania Commission for the medical examination of Tunney. Upon entering the office of Commissioner Weiner, Gene extended his hand to me. His hand was cold, clammy, and bore every physical indication of one who was extremely nervous of the outcome of his coming battle. Of course, Gene had just arrived from his airplane trip from Stroudsburg, and this might have accounted for his general appearance, but whatever the reason, Gene certainly fooled me as he did hundreds of others who placed Dempsey head and heels over the former Marine.'

After his weigh-in and medical, Dempsey took the train to Philadelphia with trainer Jerry 'The Greek' Luvadis. Long-time bodyguard Mike Trent should have been with them but was nowhere to be found. 'When we pulled into the Broad Street Station in Philly,' recalled Dempsey, 'I knew something was wrong, but I couldn't put my finger on it. I felt funny and queasy. Jerry was all over me, not knowing what to do. By the time the train had stopped, I felt my legs had turned to rubber. Jerry leaped off the train and ran to where manager Gene Normile was waiting with a hired car. "Mr Normile, you better call the fight off!" he said excitedly.

'"For Chrissakes, why? What's the matter?" "Look, over there!" said Jerry, pointing. Normile turned in time to see me brace myself against a door. My eyes were shut and I felt fuzzy. It didn't register when he called me, nor did I recognise him. Normile was worried. "What's the matter, Jack? What is it, kid?" I opened my eyes and grinned weakly. "It's nothin' I can't lick. Just a funny feeling's all. Here. And here." I pointed to my belly and my head. We headed for the stadium, stopping several times so I could jump out and vomit my guts out. I was experiencing sickening heat waves and wondered how many more times I could be sick. I was empty inside and I ached. We finally pulled up to the Stadium where Jerry and Normile helped me out of the car and held me up. I couldn't stop from retching as I walked. I managed to make it up the steps to the dressing room, but I couldn't take off my street shoes for fear of falling down. In the dressing room a letter was handed to me, a beautiful letter filled with love and encouragement from Estelle, sent to me through Louella Parsons.'

Over in Tunney's dressing room, the New Yorker was stripped and ready for the ring, making small talk with Jimmy Bronson and trainer Lou Fink, when Commissioner Frank Weiner and Tommy Reilly, the referee, visited him. When Reilly asked Tunney if he had read the rules of the Pennsylvania Commission, the challenger replied that he had, adding, 'I understand that the rabbit and kidney blows are barred. Is that right?' When Reilly nodded confirmation, Tunney asked, 'How many times are you going to warn the man who uses either of these foul blows before you disqualify him?' Somewhat taken aback, Reilly raised his voice. 'This ain't gonna be no pink tea,' he said. 'This is gonna be a fight for the championship of the world.' Tunney looked at him calmly, then said, 'So I have read in the papers. But since you have come in to discuss the rules, I would like to know all about them, and just what you consider a foul or fair blow. It makes no difference to me if we go in without gloves, just so I know beforehand.'

By this time Reilly was becoming agitated and, sticking a finger in Tunney's face, he growled, 'Listen, I want you to understand that I don't want squawks from the loser when this fight is over.' Tunney had his counterpunch ready. 'Go over and tell that to Dempsey,' he said quietly. 'He will be more interested in what the loser has to say than I.' As Weiner and Reilly left the room, Bronson and Fink burst out laughing.

'I never dared lecture,' Bronson would recall of that tense moment before Tunney went out to face Dempsey. 'Gene had a mind of his own. But in the dressing room the night of the fight, I sensed he wanted to hear from me. "Gene, I think there are just a couple of vital things," I said. "For one, stay away from that left hook of Dempsey's. And, most important, get home the first punch of the fight. The first, the very first. God Almighty will be taking your right hand and landing it on Dempsey's chin if you do what I say. It may break your hand but it will be the story." Gene had listened. Gene had absorbed. I knew he would heed me.'

Tunney had actually been practising that very punch for over a year. 'I knew that Dempsey, when we met, would do his utmost to knock me out in a punch,' he would tell Ed Van Every. 'And, fourteen months ago, the thought occurred to me that the best possible way of treating Jack to a surprise would be by reversing the process, by my knocking him out in a punch. I figured that by meeting his rush with a rush, and putting all I had into a single punch, I could knock him out with the first blow of the fight. Study of Jack Dempsey's tactics as he rushed from his corner soon convinced me that a straight right-hander, timed to the instant and delivered with all the beef and spirit I possessed, was the ticket, so I began practicing that punch. I practiced it against punching bags, with sparring partners; I bombarded the empty air with it in shadow boxing. I even let it loose at odd moments, as when I was waiting for my turn to tee up a golf ball. Months ago I had it worked out to the utmost perfection of timing and accuracy.'

That September night in 1926, as Gene Tunney waited in the dressing room under the stands at the Sequicentennial Stadium, he was as ready as any fighter ever was for his big moment, the fight for the championship of the world. When the commission inspector knocked on the dressing room door to tell them it was time, they shook hands all round; Tunney, manager Gibson, trainer Lou Fink and chief second Jimmy Bronson. Before they went through the door, Tunney halted and said, 'Stop! This is what you want me to do, Gib, isn't it?' he said to his manager, then shot a right hand past Gibson's chin that was only a couple of inches off the mark, a blow of terrific speed and power.

'Yes,' said Gibson weakly, as he stepped back. 'That will do the trick.'

'Watch me,' said Tunney calmly. 'Let's go.'

18

Ya Gotta Pick Dempsey!

Harry Greb had known it for eighteen months, ever since that last fight with Tunney in St Paul. 'Gene, I've fought you for the last time,' he told Tunney in the dressing room after the New Yorker had beaten him for the fourth time in five fights. 'You're too rough. Go and get Dempsey. You'll beat him. You're the next world's heavyweight champion.'

Back in New York, Greb dropped in to the press room at Madison Square Garden to tell the assembled reporters and sportswriters there, 'That fellow is far better than you scribes believe. Make no mistake about that, he'll whip Dempsey.'

Wilbur Wood, respected boxing writer for the *New York Sun*, reported, 'One afternoon some days before the fight, I was walking down the boardwalk when I ran into my old friend Greb, who was getting ready for an eye operation. One of Harry's eyes was very bad, but it turned out that he could see much more with one eye than most of us could with two. "Who are you picking?" said Greb, a bit ungrammatically, it is true. "How can you pick anyone but Dempsey?" came back this writer, question for question. "Jack will knock him out."

'Greb let out a loud snort of disgust. "You guys are all alike," he exclaimed. "You can't see anything but Dempsey.

Say, you want to get a rep for being smart? Pick Tunney, and you can't miss."

'It was my turn to snort. "Now I know you are punch-drunk," I said. "You sure are batty. What are you trying to do, kid somebody?" "You're the one that's doing the kidding and you're kidding yourself," Greb came back. "Please listen to me. Don't make a fool of yourself. Dempsey will be lucky to win a round. I know because I've worked with Dempsey and I have boxed Tunney. Tunney has just the stuff to beat Dempsey and do it all the way. If Dempsey beats him it will be an accident." Of course I didn't listen to those wise words. I went out on a limb for Dempsey.'

Mickey Walker had lost his welterweight title and had been working as a lumberjack in Nova Scotia, getting ready for a comeback. 'My fight wasn't until October,' he recalled, 'but I came back in September. I wanted to see the fight between Dempsey and Gene Tunney in Philadelphia. Even though Kearns and Dempsey had broken up, Doc had never lost his admiration for Jack as a fighter. He was sure Dempsey would win and he and I bet $25,000 on Jack against Bernard Gimbel, the department store magnate. Gimbel is a great friend of Tunney's and he had as much faith in Gene as we did in Jack. In fact we offered Gimbel six-to-one odds but he insisted on an even bet.

'We figured we had a sucker's money. The odds on Dempsey ranged from four-to-one to seven-to-one. The only knowledge-able fight man I knew who was smart enough to take the short end was Harry Greb, who put ten thousand dollars on Tunney. Greb had inside knowledge of their styles. He had worked out with Jack in gyms and had fought Gene five times, beating him only once. Harry came to me before the fight. "Mickey," he said, "bet on Tunney. He's going to beat Dempsey. He has real boxing ability, he has the tools, he's classy, a much better fighter than anybody imagines." Like almost everybody else, I didn't believe him.'

As zero hour approached, the odds on Dempsey were coming down. British journalist Trevor Wignall was a regular

trans-Atlantic traveller in those days and he was in town to see
Dempsey fight Tunney. 'Philadelphia itself was the hottest spot
in all America for a couple of days before the fight,' he wrote in
his book, *Almost Yesterday.*' It was jammed with gamblers and
gangsters and bad men of every conceivable kind. In some of
the main streets shops had been leased for betting purposes, but
what I could not understand was why all the big money was on
Tunney. I met Abe Attell, the old rival of Jim Driscoll, one
morning, and he told me that if I wanted to put myself right for
life I would sell everything I possessed and gamble the proceeds
on the former marine. Another night, while I was sitting around
with a bunch of newspapermen, the most notorious gambler of
his period entered in search of a drink, and casually announced
that he had just laid a bet of one hundred thousand dollars
on Tunney. I was completely mystified, but very naturally
the yarn soon got going that Dempsey had agreed to throw
away his title.'

There were a few writers bold enough to pick Tunney to
upset the odds, among them Harry Grayson and Ed Van Every.
Manager 'Dumb' Dan Morgan recalled, 'Grayson can talk for
hours about how Gene planned that particular fight. "Gene had
every movement figured out weeks in advance,' said Harry.
"He knew he was going to knock much of the will to win out of
Jack with that first right-hand smash to the head, and I'll bet he
practiced the punch a hundred thousand times."'

Ed Van Every, veteran sportswriter and boxing editor of the
New York Evening World, wrote on the eve of the fight, 'Gene
Tunney has an excellent chance of defeating Jack Dempsey. So
real are his chances that they have impressed me with the
likelihood that a new heavyweight king of the fistic world is due
to be crowned in Philadelphia tomorrow night . . . To pick
against Dempsey is no easy matter. As you look over this
beautiful figure of a fighting man you cannot do otherwise than
concede, Jack Dempsey looks as good as he ever was, and in
some ways, even better than that. But just the same, I don't
think he actually is.

'Dempsey has fought but twice in five years. He couldn't

catch Tom Gibbons in fifteen rounds at Shelby. And two months and ten days later he came close to defeat at the fists of the powerful, but ponderous and rather inexperienced giant, Luis Firpo. Plainly Jack Dempsey wasn't at his best after a two years lay-off. And all the showy work in the world in the training camp does not convince me that Dempsey has not deteriorated a whole lot more after another lay-off, and this time of three years duration. Even those who concede these points, however, scoff at the idea of the champion succumbing to such a challenger as Gene Tunney. "If Dempsey is only forty per cent of his old self then he will have enough left to beat an opponent such as Tunney," they say.' But Van Every would not be swayed in his judgement.

'As terrific a hitter as Dempsey undoubtedly is,' he wrote, 'I expect to see Tunney survive three or four rounds fraught with the most fearful punishment for the challenger. And from then to the end I expect stamina, the result of the clean living of the challenger, to make his superior skill and straight punching count for a decisive advantage. The contest will probably go the ten round distance and Tunney will gain the decision.'

In his 1996 book *When Dempsey Fought Tunney*, Bruce J Evensen, an associate professor in the Department of Communication at DePaul University, Chicago, writes, 'Our generation might consider Babe Ruth the most extraordinary sports celebrity of the 1920s, but jazz-age circulation managers knew better. Jack Dempsey meant a fifty-per cent leap in readership in the weeks before and in the days following his title defences. He was good copy whether divorcing, marrying, acting in films, appearing in vaudeville, or standing trial for evading the draft. That was why these managers named him the century's "greatest stimulus to circulation." At the *New York Times* office on Times Square, three stenographers from the State Law Reporting Company worked in relays to provide a verbatim record of NBC's nationwide broadcast of the event . . . Eight hundred correspondents covered the fight under headlines that had not been seen since the signing of the armistice. Tex Rickard had "never seen so many people claiming to be reporters" and seeking passes to a championship fight. After accommodating the first three hundred of them, several hundred more from smaller cities and towns and foreign duchies too small to have papers were encouraged to "find seats as best as you can" in the stands. More than two million words would be filed on the fight, a record for any sports event in the nation's history, on more than one hundred wires installed by Western Union.'

Grantland Rice of the *New York Tribune* recalled, 'Two days before the fight, the sports section of the *Sunday Tribune* went ten solid pages. The *Tribune's* owner-publisher Ogden Reid was amazed. As the paper was going to bed Saturday night, Reid exclaimed, "Grant, you're making the *Tribune* more of a sports paper than anything else. At this rate, we're becoming ALL sports, and damn the rest of the world!" "You could do worse," I replied, trying to manage a straight face. Matter of fact, that weekend was one of the greatest in sports. George Von Elm defeated Bobby Jones for the Amateur golf crown at Baltusrol. Rene Lacoste defeated Big Bill Tilden in the National tennis finals at Forest Hills. The crush on Philadelphia was under way, with 25-dollar tickets being gobbled up at anywhere from 100–175 dollars each, and Rickard threatening to call the fight off, so great were Dempsey's legal complications.'

In an article on the front page of the *New York World* Gertrude Lynahan estimated that some twenty-five thousand women would attend the fight, heralding, 'the era of the two-fisted woman'. On the sports pages, commenting on Dempsey's weight of 190 pounds, fight expert Hype Igoe wrote, 'Dempsey is lighter than expected. Did he work it off or did Jack Kearns worry it off?'

'Paul Gallico of the *New York Daily News* arrived early for the big event,' recorded Bruce J Evensen in his book, *When Dempsey Fought Tunney*. 'Like others who had seen Dempsey's lacklustre training, it crossed his mind that Tunney might "hand the experts the greatest shock of their careers by winning." But his personal antipathy towards Tunney and the strength of Dempsey's man-killer reputation, which he had helped to create, put him in Dempsey's corner. "Every person I spoke to prayed fervently that Dempsey would knock his block off. Tunney's strutting, his blowing, his vain parading have aroused a longing in the breasts of many to see his still form stretched beneath the white lamps."'

Arriving in Philadelphia, baseball legend Babe Ruth simply said he expected his pal Dempsey, 'to murder the bum!' Harry 'Slug' Heilmann, Detroit's American League batting champion saw Tunney lasting, 'four rounds tops before Dempsey finishes him'. Even New York Judge E C Smith, hoping to see his hometown hero win, feared, 'Dempsey will be too much for him.'

A rather literate observation on the fight came from an unlikely source, one of Jack Dempsey's sparring partners, Bill Tate. As Nat Fleischer recalled in his *Black Dynamite* series, 'When Jack Dempsey was in his prime, he had more sparring mates than any heavyweight fighter since Jim Jeffries' time. The reason for his large entourage was that few of those who trained with the Manassa Mauler were able to continue after one round of workout during a training session. There was only one fighter who could stand the gaff, Big Bill Tate, 6-foot, 6¼ inch giant from Montgomery, Alabama, probably the first Negro boxer in history who was a college graduate with a degree.'

Big Bill had been Dempsey's chief sparmate for his title-winning fight with Jess Willard, and Fleischer recalled a humorous aspect of their training. 'Tate chalked up about fifty polka dots in the ring and he would stand on one of them then shift to another as occasion demanded, his idea being that he could hop around from one to the other and not only bewilder Jack, but could also make Dempsey work for speed in that manner. After Dempsey had missed several times, he cornered Tate and then demanded that he stick to one dot until a punch was fired before he shifted to the other. But the shifty Tate made him miss so often that Jack ordered all polka dots removed from the floor of the ring.'

Tate had also trained with Dempsey for the Tunney fight, at Saratoga Springs and at Atlantic City, and on the morning of the contest he told a reporter in Philadelphia, 'I don't see how Tunney has a chance unless he decides at some crucial moment in the fight to read a stanza of Tennyson, and Jack so far forgets himself as to stand and listen. But if Jack doesn't listen, I'm afraid Tunney will wake up to realise that he has been reading a poem by Shakespeare or Kipling or one of those big writing fellows. And I'm a-thinking that the title of that poem will be, "A Fool There Was."'

In his book *The Long Count* author Mel Heimer set the scene. 'Tex Rickard liked to say, when impressed, "I ain't never seed anything like it," and that was the way it was when fight night arrived. The confusion was almost total. Seventy thousand in the big crowd had come from the greater New York area, many of them by car, and the parking spaces weren't big enough and were far away from the arena. Fake tickets had been counterfeited, of course, and there were sporadic arguments and fistfights over who belonged where.

'Everybody Who Was Anybody was there; Secretary of the Treasury Andrew W Mellon, a half-dozen governors, countless mayors and Congressmen, Charles M Schwab, Percy Rockefeller, Vincent Astor, Jimmy Walker, William Randolph Hearst and Joseph Pulitzer, Anthony J Drexel Biddle, Jr., W Averell Harriman, Harry Payne Whitney, George and Joseph Widener. From show business, Tom Mix came into Philadelphia with his own special train and a party of five hundred. Charlie Chaplin, Norma Talmadge and Florenz Ziegfeld were also in the stands. Samuel Vauclain was on hand; the head of the Baldwin Locomotive Works was, in effect, the night's top bidder, since he had bought $27,000 worth of tickets for friends and associates. Peggy Hopkins Joyce sat in the third row, almost demure in a black dress and coat, except for a small bouquet of orchids, which would sag and collapse in the wet of the night, pinned to her lapel. Gertrude Ederle, who momentarily had replaced Marilyn Miller in the hearts of Americans, was with the moon-faced lawyer, Dudley Field Malone. Jack Kearns was flitting here and there, not bothering to confirm or deny the reports that he had bet $50,000 on

Dempsey, his old meal ticket, despite the lawsuits he had flung at the champion.

'Four thousand of Philadelphia's city policemen were on duty in and around the Sesquicentennial Stadium, in addition to the small army of ushers and special police, keeping order and breaking up heated discussions. The thirty-four arc lights over the ring threw a glare over the spectators, who looked a little washed out and waxen, even the show people. There were four hundred or more newsmen clustered around the ringside (if you paid $27.50 for a ringside seat, the chances were that you were sixty rows back) and long before the main event they had started filing the two million words that would go out on the telegraph wires and set a record of its kind for sports event coverage. The words would continue to go out sputteringly late that night as the downpour soaked the wires and shortcircuited many of them, including the entire special layout installed by the *New York Times*.'

As rain clouds gathered over the huge stadium, a record crowd of 120,757 had paid $1,895,733 into the coffers, boxing's (and Rickard's) third $1 million gate, and all three featuring the Manassa Mauler himself, Jack Dempsey. Ticket scalpers made a fortune. Mike Jacobs was a more or less legitimate ticket broker and he was in town from New York, doing business as usual. On the day of the fight, Jacobs had a visit from Max 'Boo Boo' Hoff. The Philly mob guy was desperate for 25 ringside seats to take care of some friends in the city and in Pennsylvania politics. Jacobs told him the entire ringside section was sold out, but 'Boo Boo' wasn't listening. 'I gotta have them!' he insisted, and pulling out a roll that would have choked a horse, peeled off 25 $1,000 bills, and handed them to Jacobs. The crafty Jacobs promptly rearranged the ringside seating plan, marked in chairs, moved people who wouldn't gripe too much, handed the 25 tickets to Hoff, and shoved the twenty-five grand in his pocket. As 'Boo Boo' was about to leave, clutching the pasteboards, Jacobs said, 'Just a minute. You forgot to pay me for the tickets. They're fifty bucks each.' And Hoff paid!

Broadway columnist Damon Runyon had a rather unique way of picking a winning fighter, as related by author Jimmy Breslin in his biography of Runyon. 'A week before the fight, Runyon leaned against the ring at Tunney's training camp and listened hard. He had a theory that when a fighter was in the best condition, he groaned like an old cow when he threw a punch. As Tunney punched, Runyon heard only the squeak of his shoes on the ring canvas. No other sound. When Tunney threw a punch, it made a great deal of sound as it landed on the sparring partner's nose. Runyon heard no grunt. Before the fight, he told this to Jimmy Walker at a party in Walker's private railroad car on the tracks alongside the Philadelphia Stadium. "I was going to make a good bet on Gene," said Walker, Mayor of New York City. "He's one of the neighbour's children." Runyon insisted he remain clear of betting.'

At ring time you had to put down eleven bucks to win five if you fancied Dempsey, and you could have four, five, six to one if Tunney was your man.

Ya gotta pick Dempsey!

19

Battle in the Rain

The sun didn't shine on the city of Philadelphia that September day in 1926. There was some rain in the morning but it held off for most of the day and evening as the crowds began gathering in the huge Sesquicentennial Stadium for the world heavy-weight championship fight between Jack Dempsey and Gene Tunney. Promoter Tex Rickard glanced nervously at the leaden skies before heading for Dempsey's dressing room. 'Jack, for God's sake, hurry up,' he said anxiously, as the champion prepared for the ring. 'It is going to rain any minute and here we have all these people in.'

Dempsey merely grunted, then said, 'Don't worry about that rain, Tex. This guy ain't goin' over two rounds, anyway.'

As the last of the preliminary bouts ended, a light rain began to fall. Announcer Joe Griffo, prompted by Rickard, bellowed into his microphone, 'Keep your seats, please, keep your seats. The fight will go on.' There was a great wave of movement over the arena as people stood and struggled into raincoats, while others improvised with newspapers and programmes. Griffo introduced the referee, fifty-year-old Tommy 'Pop' Reilly of Philadelphia, a small balding guy in white sweater and trousers. The two judges, Mike Bernstein of Wilkes-Barre, Pennsylvania, and Frank Brown of Pittsburgh, were announced to the crowd.

Then a thunderous cheer rippled through the stadium as Gene Tunney was seen climbing through the ropes, smiling, dressed in a scarlet-trimmed blue robe with the insignia of the

191

US Marine Corps in gold on the back. With him were manager Billy Gibson, chief second Jimmy Bronson, and trainers Lou Fink and Lou Brix. A few minutes later Dempsey pushed his way through the ropes, wearing a white sweater with a white towel around his neck. There was a mixture of boos and cheers from the crowd, and when Griffo introduced him, more boos cascaded around the ring, prompting one reporter to observe, 'If ever a yet undefeated heavyweight champion, favoured to retain his crown, received such a reception, nobody at ringside could recall it.' With Dempsey were manager Gene Normile, in white cap and sweater, trainer Gus Wilson, chief second Philadelphia Jack O'Brien, and Jerry the Greek, carrying Dempsey's old black-and-white checked bathrobe over his arm.

'Hello, Champion,' Tunney greeted Dempsey.

'Hello, Gene,' Dempsey replied.

'May the better man win,' added Tunney.

'Yeh, yeh,' muttered Dempsey as he went to his corner.

'It had been provided by the Boxing Commission that the bandages which they were to furnish were to be put on in the ring,' recalled Tunney. 'Jack hurriedly wound his bandages on his hands and waited for me to finish with mine. I deliberately delayed the bandaging as long as possible, sometimes re-winding several strands. I kidded with his seconds, Philadelphia Jack O'Brien and Gus Wilson, who were watching my bandaging. "Too bad, Jack," I said, "that you're seconding a loser tonight." "Yeah?" replied O'Brien, not quite comprehending. Dempsey had kept me waiting. I did not mind. But I knew that he would resent this waiting. He seemed to.'

'Tunney insisted on wrapping his own hands,' reported George A Barton at ringside for the *Minneapolis Tribune*. 'I, along with the other newspapermen, marvelled at Gene's calmness as he sat on his stool wrapping the bandages on his fists with no outward indication of nervousness. There never was a more confident challenger for the world's heavyweight championship. The bandaging complete, Gene gazed around the ringside, smiling and nodding to friends as his seconds adjusted the gloves.

'Spotting me as I sat in the second row of the working press near his corner, Tunney gave me a friendly smile and then raised his right fist to his lips and kissed it, a reminder that he intended to land the first blow of the fight with his right hand.' In those last few minutes, Dempsey recalled, 'Tunney was just a boxer I kept telling myself. I'd move in through those light punches and flatten him as soon as I caught him. Who the hell was Tunney? Sure, I knew he was a Marine. So did the crowd. There were boos for me. The gamblers had a long memory. They made me the favourite.'

'Not by the wildest stretch of imagination,' wrote Nat Fleischer, 'taking into consideration the records of the contestants and their workouts in camp, could one have picked Tunney to defeat the champion. From all outward appearances before the contest, during the weighing-in, and during the appearance of the fighters in the ring for the start of the Battle of the Sesqui, Dempsey still was every inch the giant killer. He looked like the mauler who had manhandled the tall Jess Willard, who had pummeled into submission Billy Miske, Bill Brennan, Georges Carpentier and Luis Firpo.'

At the opening bell, Dempsey came out like the Manassa Mauler of old, a scowl on his sunburned face, and his rush took Tunney into his own corner. The champion rushed again and hammered a terrific left swing to the jaw, driving Tunney back to his corner, but as Dempsey came in Tunney sent a hard right to the jaw. Dempsey snarled and charged again, ripping a left to the body. This time, however, Tunney timed his rush and jammed a right hand into Dempsey's face that had everything on it. Luckily for the champion, his habit of fighting with his head down and his chin on his chest meant the blow caught him high rather than on the jaw. But it shook Dempsey back to his Colorado roots, and Tunney knew it.

'His knees sagged,' recalled Tunney in his autobiography, 'and in the short exchange that followed he was very unsteady and dazed. He later said that if I had followed up this advantage

I should have won the fight in the first round. I did follow up my advantage, but Jack had not been ten years in the ring for nothing. He covered.'

Ed Van Every, in his report for the *New York Evening World*, wrote, 'Tunney did not fall back from the menacing figure before him. Gene stepped in and met the charge with a short but sharp and powerfully driven right that found its mark on the jaw of the champion. And almost instantly there came a strange change over the features of Dempsey. The ferocious scowl that is so much a part of the real Jack Dempsey gave way to a look of tense determination. In that very first charge Jack must have realised that he was no longer the Dempsey of old and he was face to face with a youth who had no fear of him in his makeup.'

George Barton recollected, 'Tunney quickly convinced me he had planned his battle strategy perfectly as, true to his prediction, he met the champion in mid-ring and set Dempsey back on his heels with a power-packed straight right to the jaw. There was a thunder of applause from the crowd.'

'I shall never forget that blow,' recorded Trevor Wignall. 'It missed Dempsey's point by a fraction of an inch, but I saw his knees buckle, and I also saw the glaze in his eyes as he stumbled back towards the ropes. Any other man on earth would have fallen flat on his face, to be counted out, but somehow the Mauler stayed on his feet.'

'I came in with what I thought was my usual attack,' described Dempsey in his autobiography, 'weaving from side to side and throwing a left hook at Gene's jaw. But before it could even land, his own right counter blow took me on the side of the head with a force that staggered me. Here was my first fight against Bill Brennan, in reverse. Instead of my having landed the first blow against a formidable opponent, softening him up for the entire fight, Gene Tunney had handed it to me. All through the first round he outboxed me, landing a lot of good blows. I tried not to let him see how badly I had been shaken up. I was even able to fool a good many of the reporters at the ringside.'

'Here was something the vast majority of the spectators had not expected,' wrote James P Dawson, at ringside for the *New*

York Times. 'Tunney not only standing fearlessly before the bull-like rushes of Dempsey, the killer, but meeting this attack flat-footed and dealing out his blows with a marksman's accuracy and with staggering force, or dancing away and pecking at the charging human in front of him. The crowd was awed; some of it was distinctly shocked, but the greatest shock was experienced by Dempsey himself.'

As the bell summoned them for round two, Dempsey charged over to Tunney's corner and swung a heavy right to the head. Tunney rode the punch and moved into the centre of the ring, sending right and left to the jaw. Dempsey hit back with a long right to the body that drove Tunney back into his own corner, and the Mauler forced him along the ropes into another corner, landing blows to the head, bringing blood from Tunney's lip. The ex-marine fought back with two solid lefts to the champion's head and they clinched until Pop Reilly pulled them apart. Dempsey came back with a left and right to the body, then Tunney hammered short rights and lefts to the jaw. A tremendous right to the heart rocked the challenger but he was fighting back at the bell.

The crowd was in an uproar as the men went to their corners and, with the rain falling heavily now, nobody was leaving their seat. Round three and the champion came out slowly, then rushed at Tunney and launched a heavy right for the head. The blow missed and Tunney stepped in with sharp lefts and rights before Dempsey could regain his balance. A smashing right to the head halted Dempsey in his tracks and Tunney wrestled him to the ropes, then scored with rights and lefts to the jaw. Dempsey was spitting blood and his renovated nose was leaking claret as another marine assault bombarded the position he was defending. Two rights found Dempsey's jaw and the champion staggered, but Tunney was wild in his follow-up and the Mauler charged back at him with a long right to the head. Tunney didn't fall back, he went forward, and met Dempsey with a sizzling right uppercut and the champ looked happy to hear the bell above the roar of the crowd. 'After three rounds of the fight,' wrote Wilbur Wood in the *New York Sun,* 'I was wondering if what I saw really was happening.'

In the corner, Gus Wilson and Jerry the Greek lit a fire under their champion that even the heavily falling rain could not dampen. 'Dempsey's greatest exhibition of savageness came with the opening of the fourth round,' reported Dawson in the *New York Times.* 'The defending champion charged like an enraged bull and plunging across the ring, almost drove Tunney out of the ring near Gene's corner, with a swishing left hook to the jaw. Going in close Dempsey pounded the body and they wrestled across the ring to Dempsey's corner, where as they parted from close quarters Tunney wobbled weakly against the ropes. Here, it seemed, was the old Dempsey.

'He had Tunney in distress, or so it appeared. But it developed it was only a flash, a desperate effort by Dempsey to overawe his rival and instill in this pretender some respect for the monarch of the ring. Tunney didn't see it that way. He recovered his poise in a jiffy and began boxing. After a few stabs of his left Tunney opened a cut under Dempsey's right eye from which a crimson stream flowed and flecked the beautiful bronzed body which had been so liberally praised in song, story and picture. More, Tunney stepped in with a right to the jaw which staggered Dempsey and with a succession of left jabs and hooks and right crosses and swings he blinded Dempsey in a furious counter assault. Tunney had his rival navigating on unsteady legs and his face blood-smeared at the bell.'

Coming out for work in the fifth, Dempsey looked weary and he and Tunney fenced around in the centre of the ring before clinching. Whenever they wrestled at close quarters, it was Tunney who appeared the stronger, always shoving the champion back around the ring, up against the ropes, into corners. Tunney crashed a right to the head and Dempsey came back with a hard left into the body, then crossed a right to the jaw. Tunney's unerring left found Dempsey's right eye again and the blood ran freely down on to his chest. Dempsey's left eye was bruised and discoloured, but he still kept circling his challenger, looking for an opening for the left hook. He forced Tunney into a neutral corner and hammered lefts and rights to the head, but the New Yorker stood up well and fired his own guns at the Mauler. Dempsey was glad to grab his tormentor until the storm of leather abated.

Nature's storm had not abated, the rain increasing in its intensity, splashing on the canvas and forming little pools here and there. 'All I heard', Dempsey would recall, 'was the sound of the rain drowning out the clicking of typewriters and the roar of the crowd. The ropes and the canvas were soaked. I found myself blaming the wet ring, but it didn't seem to bother Gene's footwork. He glided around the ring like he was on ice. He jumped a lot, and backed up, and wherever I went, looking for him, he stuck that left of his in my face, keeping me off balance. I was wide open, looking for a big one.'

Dempsey landed a big one, twice in the sixth round. It was his pay-off punch, the left hook that had chopped down the giants Willard and Firpo until they could no longer go on, but that was then and this was now. It had been three long years since that sensational battle with the huge shaggy Argentino, three years of enjoying life, of marriage to his lovely movie star wife, Estelle, three years of Hollywood with a new nose job for his films. 'Don't fight too often,' promoter Rickard had cautioned his champion after the Firpo fight in September 1923. Now, after six rounds in the rain at Philadelphia, Jack Dempsey knew he hadn't fought often enough.

Where the champion's attacks were now sporadic as the pace began to tell on him, Tunney's work was constant, ongoing, moving in to score with his solid, hurting punches before moving out, away from danger. The last thing a puncher loses is his punch. Take no chances now, they cautioned Tunney in the corner. Not me, not now, Tunney reasoned as he waited for the bell to summon him for the seventh round. This was the dream coming true, the ending of the long journey he had started seven years ago on a boat on the Rhine, a champion in uniform wondering if he could ever beat this new guy, Jack Dempsey, who had just become world champion in the

Massacre of Toledo. 'Who knows, Gene,' his pals had said. 'Maybe someday.'

Well, that someday was now, Thursday 23 September 1926, and Gene Tunney was coming out for the seventh round at the Sesquicentennial Stadium and a record-breaking crowd was sitting out there in the darkness, ignoring the drenching rain and willing him on to victory over the feared killer of the ring, Jack Dempsey. Old timer Bill Brady, who had managed Gentleman Jim Corbett, remarked to a ringside neighbour, 'That Tunney boy reminds me so very much of Corbett when he fought John L Sullivan. It's a duplicate of that fight. Gene will win and win by a big margin.' In that seventh round, Dempsey came out stooped over, chin on his chest, throwing the long right to Tunney's body. They clinched and the referee pulled them apart.

Tunney landed two punches to the jaw as Dempsey came back at him and they wrestled to the ropes. Dempsey ripped a left to the head and Tunney was cut by the right eye. The sight of Tunney's blood spurred Dempsey to the attack and he rushed the New Yorker to the ropes, smashing lefts to the head, and Tunney was hanging on. A right to the jaw failed to stop the champion and he crashed heavy lefts and rights to the body before Tunney claimed him and wrestled his way back to the centre of the ring. A right to the jaw from Tunney, then another, to the side of the head, and Dempsey stalled, crouching, then launched a terrific left hook to the head of the challenger. They swapped vicious lefts and rights in a mighty exchange, then just before the bell a blow from Tunney landed on Dempsey's left eye and it was swelling shut as he went to his stool.

'With the rain,' recalled Tunney's chief second, Jimmy Bronson, 'the conditions in Philadelphia were working against a boxer and in favour of a puncher like Dempsey. Yet in the eighth round, Gene almost floored Jack with a left to the jaw.'

As the eighth opened, Dempsey was crowding in, taking two lefts to the face as he swung two hard lefts to the back of Tunney's head. Dempsey crouched, swayed, gloves waving slowly as he worked for an angle, a crack in the marine's defence, but he couldn't find one and while he was looking, Tunney crashed over a heavy right to the head. As Dempsey rushed in with a wild swing for the body, Tunney countered with his own and the punch stopped the champion in his tracks. Tunney sent a hard jab over, then another, forcing the Mauler back into his own corner and down there at the side of the ring Gus Wilson and Jerry the Greek were screaming for their champion to do something. They knew the title was slipping away, and in his heart Jack Dempsey knew it too.

'I kept plodding toward him, trying to land a telling blow,' recalled Dempsey, 'but Tunney refused to carry the fight to me, he let me do the attacking. That was sound ring strategy, he was well ahead and taking no chances of being knocked out. I was still trying to get home a blow that might save the title. I wasn't able to do it. The old legs wouldn't take me in there fast enough.'

'By the end of the eighth round,' reported George Barton, 'Jack's left eye was completely closed and his right eye badly swollen. He was unable to put up a defence against Tunney's rapier-like left hand and the equally accurate, but more jolting, right fist of the challenger . . . Dempsey was sorely lacking in speed of foot and hand. He floundered, missed many punches, and was practically helpless before Tunney's two-fisted attack. There was nothing wrong with Dempsey's great fighting heart. Despite the brutal punishment he absorbed every second of every round, the courageous and determined champion fought on and on with the ferocity of an English pit bulldog.'

Seated in the first row of the working press section were Doc Kearns, Mickey Walker, author Gene Fowler, and Mark Kelly, a Los Angeles newspaperman. Kearns and his Toy Bulldog, Mickey Walker, were becoming more and more depressed as the night wore on. They were drenched by the driving rain, their 25 grand bet on Dempsey was going down the drain along with the rain, and they hated seeing Dempsey being punched around up there in the ring.

'I felt sorry watching Dempsey blow his title,' said Walker. 'Tunney was giving him a boxing lesson. Kearns sat next to me and didn't utter a word as he watched, stone-faced. I knew that in his heart, Doc was sorry for Jack, too. I grew more and more nervous as the fight went on. I could see that Jack was not fighting Tunney right and I couldn't stand it any longer. I jumped up and rushed over to Jack's corner. Grabbing Gus Wilson, Dempsey's trainer, by the seat of his pants, I yelled, "Hey, Gus! Tell Jack to keep throwing the left hook. Tell him to throw a thousand of 'em. One is bound to land. Don't forget. Tell him to keep throwing left hooks until he's down." Then I beat it back to my seat. Doc had seen and heard what I'd done but he didn't say a word. I could sense that he approved and I was sure that he would have done the same had he not had that damned pride.'

Doc Kearns would later recall, 'By the sixth round it was quite clear that Dempsey was the loser. Tunney, a master boxer, was in faultless physical condition. Dempsey hadn't fought since beating Firpo and obviously wasn't in anything like the shape I had always demanded. "His timing's off and his legs are gone," I told Fowler. "He should have had one tune-up bout, maybe more." "Why don't you get up in his corner and help him?" Kelly asked. "The guys in his corner aren't any good at all to him." I shook my head. "No, let him take it. That's the way he wanted it and that's the way it'll have to be."

'It was raining hard. Kelly looked at me and said, "Why, Doc, you're crying." "I am not," I growled, although maybe I was at that. "It's the rain in my eyes." Kelly grabbed my arm. "You're not kidding me. You're crying, you bum. Go on. Get up in the corner and help him." I wanted to. But Dempsey had called the shot and, without him having asked me, my pride wouldn't let me budge. I sat there and watched him take his licking and, as Kelly said, it wasn't all rain that was running down my cheeks. When it was over, I went out and got drunk.'

Ninth round. Dempsey is anxious to get to grips with his tormentor. He knows time is running out on him and he knows he is trailing on points. He throws a hard right to the head but the punch is short and Tunney hits him with a solid right hook to the jaw. They clinch and Tunney wrestles the Mauler back to the ropes. Dempsey tries a left and right for the jaw but the punches are wild in his desperation. The rain is coming down harder now and Tunney's sodden right glove rips upwards to Dempsey's jaw, and the champion spits blood. Dempsey is wild again, this time with a long right, but he gets everything on a thudding left to the body and Tunney is hurt, and he dances away sucking in air. This guy is still dangerous! Tunney regroups and comes back with the jab, once, twice, then a heavy right to the head and Dempsey staggers. Tunney jumps on him and forces Dempsey back into his own corner, lands two heavy rights to the head, and Dempsey reaches for him and holds until Pop Reilly hauls them apart.

'Tunney closed this round fighting Dempsey in Dempsey's own corner,' wrote Dawson in the *New York Times,* 'and battering the champion severely about the face and head with a fusillade of rights and lefts, while Dempsey tore blindly at the body with his right. The crowd sent up a terrific yell for the fighting marine at the end of the round. It was as though the gathering was practising its shout of acclaim for the victorious Tunney; a sort of rehearsal for the greeting which was to come within the succeeding five minutes. Nobody minded the downpour, which drenched everybody and gave no indication of abating. Here was a new champion on the threshold of being elevated and the thrill overcame the inconvenience and discomforture of unfavourable weather.'

In those final three minutes, Gene Tunney was a West Point commander directing his elite forces against a rag-and-bobtail guerilla army that still had its ideals but no ammunition. The old champion charged in, and missed with his best shot. Tunney spanked him with the left hand, then threw a hard right that split Dempsey's left eye. Another right and Dempsey reeled back across the ring and the crowd roared and the rain came down and Tunney closed the Mauler's left eye with a right cross. Dempsey's brown face was now bright red with his own blood, but it was the red badge of courage and he was still trying to knock Tunney out of the ring when the final bell ended his misery, and his reign.

The decision was a formality, booming out from the giant microphones suspended above the ring. 'The two judges have agreed on Tunney as the winner and new champion.' The vote of the referee was not required, but Pop Reilly said afterwards that in the event of a split vote he would have given the fight to Tunney.

With the rain slanting across his battered, bloody face, Dempsey was helped across the ring by Gene Normile, Philadelphia Jack O'Brien, Gus Wilson and Jerry the Greek, to offer his congratulations to the new champion. He was like some old liner being shepherded upriver by three or four fussy little tugboats to be broken up, as the cheering crowds lined the river banks. In that melancholy moment they remembered the good times when he had steamed majestically forth to rule the world.

'I started back for my corner,' recalled Dempsey in his 1960 autobiography, 'and to leave the ring. And then something happened that had never happened to me before. The people were cheering for me, clapping for me, calling out my name in a way I had never heard before. I never realised how much I had hungered for a sound like that, and now here it was, on the night I blew my title. Losing was the making of me.'

Grantland Rice was ringside that rainy night for the *New York Tribune*. In his autobiography, *The Tumult and the Shouting*, he recalled, 'At the end, Dempsey's face was a bloody, horribly beaten mask that Tunney had torn up like a ploughed field. Speed of foot, a sharp jab and a right cross that ripped Dempsey's face like a can opener were going for Tunney that night against a man who, despite a rocky training period, had been installed a 4 and 5 to one favourite. Tunney, at twenty-nine, had arrived on his toes. Dempsey, at thirty-one, departed flat-footed. Dempsey had never been knocked out, but had the fight gone fifteen rounds, the referee would have had to stop it.

'It's fine to help build a champion. But when his time comes to step down, as it always will, it's unpleasant to tear him down and bury him. I intended to give Tunney a fitting tribute in my overnight story that historical night. And I intended to go as easy on Dempsey as I could. I did neither. Due to the rain it was impossible to use a typewriter. I dictated the description of the fight to my wire man. With me that night were Ring Lardner and Benny Leonard, the former lightweight champion. I'd been fighting a cold all that week with hard deadlines, no sleep and too much Prohibition whiskey. Back at the hotel a raging sore throat and a hangover had me in bad shape. "Take a slug of bourbon and lie down," said Lardner. "I'll file your overnight." Leonard, a Dempsey man, told Lardner that he suspected the fix had been in for Tunney to win. The story appearing next day under my byline blistered the hide off both Tunney and Dempsey. Neither spoke to me for several months. I couldn't blame either, but I couldn't open my mouth. I had a ghost.'

Their predictions torn up in front of their disbelieving eyes, the reporters crowded the dressing rooms under the stands as that great throng drifted away into the wet night. 'How does it feel to be champ, Gene?' they yelled.

'Dempsey fought like the great champion that he was,' Tunney said graciously. 'He had the kick of a mule in his fists and the heart of a lion in his breast. I never fought a harder socker nor do I hope to meet one. Once or twice he may have hit me a little low, but always it was by accident. He never meant it . . . I don't care what they may say about him, he is certainly a man in the ring. The hardest blows I felt were two socks on the Adam's apple. That's why I'm so hoarse. I have no plans for the future, but am content to rest a while with the ambition I have nourished for seven years at last realised. The marines, you know, are always first to fight and last to leave. No matter how heavy the going may be you will always find them there in the end.'

Dempsey said simply, 'I have no alibis to offer. I lost to a good man, an American.'

20

America in Shock

After the last of the reporters had been ushered from the dressing room, the new heavyweight champion of the world, Gene Tunney, was soaking himself in a hot shower when he had a visitor. 'Suddenly the shower curtain was yanked aside,' he recalled, 'and a great bear of a man plunged into the shower with me. It was my friend Bernard Gimbel, fully clothed and bursting with enthusiasm. "You did it!" he exclaimed. Then, oblivious to the drenching, he excitedly recounted the details of the ten-round fight. A few days before the fight, Bernard visited my training camp. He asked if I had a plan of battle. "Yes," I said. "I'm going to try to surprise Dempsey. I'll start feinting and make him think I'm afraid of him. The first opening I get I'll nail him with a right. Even if I'm hurt, I'll keep punching." "That's a good plan," Bernard said. "Promise me you'll stick to it." "I promise," I said, and we shook hands on it. It was a few days later that Bernard, plunging into my shower, shouted, "You kept your promise!"'

Apart from a few close friends like Bernard Gimbel, Gene Tunney's stunning victory over Jack Dempsey that rainy night in Philadelphia was a major shock to the sports world throughout America. Practically every boxing writer and sports columnist had predicted a knockout win for Dempsey, as had fight managers, trainers, and boxers such as Benny Leonard and Tom Gibbons.

'Gene Tunney made only two mistakes in his life,' wrote Dumb Dan Morgan in his 1953 book, *Dumb Dan*. 'Number one, he soundly trounced the most popular heavyweight champion the world has ever known and, number two, he used his head for something more than just holding his ears apart. The public has never quite pardoned him, for either error. For the longest time after he committed the cardinal sin of defeating Jack Dempsey, the populace, particularly that portion of it known as the fight public, regarded Gene as slightly lower in the social scale than the current Public Enemy No 1 in the FBI files.'

'They could not conceive of a man with the frame of an athlete, the face of a priest, and the mind of a scholar as champion heavyweight boxer of the world,' wrote Ed Van Every. 'And after it was all over, did they graciously concede that Gene Tunney had been greatly underestimated and had won on the strength of his masterly effort? Not to any great extent. Many of them began to throw mud at the contest as a means of finding alibis for their poor judgement. Jack Dempsey was as good as ever, according to most of the glowing reports from his training camp at Atlantic City. Of course, with only two fights under his belt in five years he had lost something. That was the truth as I saw it, also, as I wrote, the poorest Dempsey that had yet defended his honours was staking his championship against the best man he had yet fought.'

'You will hear tales of how this fight was not fought on its merits,' wrote James P Dawson in the *New York Times*. 'Such tales were circulated before the fight, but they are groundless and a rank injustice to Tunney, a true fighter who undoubtedly will take his place among the ring's greatest champions.'

'Tunney didn't need any outside help to beat me that night,' recorded Dempsey in his 1960 autobiography. 'It's been written a thousand times that I was doped before the first Tunney fight. Something like that wouldn't have been hard to do. I did feel a little groggy in the hours leading up to the fight. But there's a better chance it was a combination of other things. I had three lawsuits pending. Kearns was after me with writs, court orders and attempts to hold up my money, and even the fight. Normile was a nice guy and the guys around me knew the boxing business, but I felt I had run my own training camps, first in California, then at Luther's place in Saratoga. I couldn't concentrate on training. I hadn't picked up much weight. But I couldn't untrack myself. I had been out of the ring for three years.'

Manager Gene Normile still suspected that his champion had been got at before the fight and held an inquest. 'Every day when Jack is training,' said Jerry the Greek, 'he takes some olive oil. Day before yesterday it seemed to make him sick. In the morning Mike Trent gave it to him.' Trent, a member of the Chicago Police Department, had been Dempsey's bodyguard for a few years and Dempsey wouldn't hear of him being involved in anything untoward. But Normile jumped on Trent as soon as he walked into the room.

'Where the hell were you?' he asked angrily. 'Why weren't you on the train? You're being paid two hundred bucks a week to keep bums away from Dempsey.'

'I missed the train, and took the next one,' said Trent defensively.

Normile wasn't satisfied. 'What kind of crap are you giving me? You weren't at the fight or in the dressing room! What the hell, I'll pay you off now.' Normile wrote out a cheque for $1,000 and handed it to Trent. He took the cheque and walked out of the room without speaking. Dempsey still didn't think Trent had been involved in anything, even after Normile told him that in Chicago on the morning of the fight, gambler Frankie Pope and his pals had bet half a million bucks on Tunney, bringing the odds on Dempsey down from 3–1 to 7–5.

'I didn't know what to think,' recalled Dempsey. 'Normile wouldn't let things rest. He was convinced that he smelled something rotten. Everyone he talked to put his two cents in, including Chicago newspapermen Westbrook Pegler and Gene Fowler. A lot of insinuating questions were asked and too many names were dropped, including Tunney's. That was the last straw. I told the three of them to shut their faces. It was my own goddamn fault I had lost and that was that.'

In another interview the day after the fight, Dempsey told a newsman, 'The title was mine for seven years and I'm not crying now that someone else has it. It was taken from me fair and square by a lot better fighter than he gets credit for being. Maybe my condition wasn't as good as it appeared to most of the boys; I knew there was something missing all the time I worked. But let me tell you I was licked by a darn good fighter and I only wish some of the guys who say Tunney can't hit could sample the first smash I got at the very start of the fight. There was plenty on that sock and I never really got over it through the rest of the fight. There's always a lot of funny talk after a big fight, but some of the boys I have in mind ought to know me well enough to know that I'd give my right arm to keep the championship.'

In hindsight, of course, all the signs were there for an upset. The guys in the know should have known better. Dawson of the *New York Times*, Gallico of the *New York Daily News*, and Rice of the *New York Tribune* were just a few who had helped build the *Superman* myth around the heroic figure of Jack Dempsey, the Manassa Mauler, heavyweight champion of the world. But with the passing years, their Jack the Giant Killer had become Idle Jack. In five years Dempsey had fought only twice, retaining his title with a fifteen-rounds decision over Tom Gibbons and surviving that titanic battle with the Wild Bull of the Pampas, Luis Angel Firpo. It had been three years since that last fight – three long, inactive years. A superb fighting machine had been left to rust.

Why hadn't Tex Rickard, Dempsey's promoter, put his million-dollar meal ticket in the ring at least once a year? One reason could have been the fact that from 1924 to 1926 Dempsey's leading contender was Harry Wills, the menacing Brown Panther. It was Wills who forced the Dempsey–Tunney fight out of New York City to Philadelphia, when he gained the full backing of the New York State Athletic Commission to the extent that they would not recognise Dempsey in a title contest unless Wills was in the other corner. Tex Rickard, who had promoted and refereed the infamous battle between Jack

Johnson and Jim Jeffries back in 1910, had sworn that he would never again promote a mixed battle for the title. He never did.

While the champion was resting on his laurels, loafing his way through exhibition bouts, marrying his movie star, the lovely Miss Estelle Taylor, and honeymooning in Europe, a young contender was punching his way to the front – a fellow named Gene Tunney. In the three years since Dempsey fought Firpo, Tunney had racked up nineteen fights without defeat. Sure, he was a good boxer, the press boys acknowledged, but he couldn't punch his way out of a wet paper bag. Well, he punched hard enough to stop ten of those nineteen opponents, and among those not around for the final bell were Georges Carpentier, Bartley Madden and Tom Gibbons. Dempsey couldn't stop Gibbons! Nobody stopped Gibbons, only Gene Tunney.

Paul Gallico of the *New York Daily News* was one who would ruefully admit that he had misread the signs pointing to a Tunney triumph. 'The night before he broke his camp at Stroudsburg, in the Pocono Mountains, where he trained for the fight with Dempsey, Tunney did a thing that was characteristic,' recalled Gallico. 'And he did it practically in privacy. Only one or two of the boxing writers were there. What was the use of too much coverage? He was going to be knocked out by Dempsey anyway. Tunney in his final workout took on three of his best sparring partners for a round each and never let a punch go the entire time, but contented himself merely with blocking, slipping, and ducking punches.

'I had a little boxing writer on the job down there by the name of Jackie Farrell. Farrell reported to me that it was the most marvellous exhibition he had ever seen anywhere, any time. Tunney boxed the entire nine minutes consecutively and without a rest, one man after the other, each sparmate attacking him for three minutes, and in that time not one solid punch was landed on him. It didn't seem possible, but it happened. I wish I had listened to Farrell. I picked Dempsey.'

★   ★   ★

The new champion slept late that Friday morning after the fight. He dressed and had breakfast, and the talk around the table was relaxed and happy, with Billy Gibson the loudest and happiest of them all because he had what every fight manager dreamed of, a heavyweight champion! Wearing a blue serge suit and a light-brown felt fedora, Tunney left with Gibson and they went over to the Bellevue-Stratford Hotel, where Rickard had his headquarters. Apart from slightly swollen lips and a small sticking plaster over his left eye, Tunney looked none the worse for his ten rounds with Dempsey.

The same could not be said for his opponent. Dempsey's left eye was discoloured and shuttered tight like an empty shop window. The cut over his left eye had taken six stitches and he was stiff and sore all over. The only good news was that his remodelled nose had survived the marine's attack and would be good for a few more movies. The old champ was happier when Estelle arrived at the Adelphi Hotel and rode the elevator to the sixth floor, where they embraced and she sobbed when seeing his face.

'What happened, Jack?' she asked.

'Honey,' he said smiling, though the effort pained him, 'I just forgot to duck.'

Mel Heimer, in his book, *The Long Count*, writes, 'One of the newsmen heard it. When it got into the papers the next day, it was to change abruptly the relationship between Jack Dempsey and the fluctuating public of the United States. Before, the populace had liberally booed him, plagued him, muttered that he had been a war slacker and prayed that the men he had fought, amiable Bill Brennan, skillful Tommy Gibbons, the fierce larger-than-life Luis Angel Firpo, would knock his block off. Now suddenly the old lion had lost his hold on the pride, and the people read what he had said to his wife at the door of the Adelphi room and said, You know, I guess he's really not a bad guy at that.'

The English sportswriter Trevor Wignall had another slant on that oft-repeated anecdote, as he related in his 1949 book, *Almost Yesterday*. 'When Jack Dempsey lost his heavyweight title to Gene Tunney on a wet and filthy night at Philadelphia his press agent sent out a pretty story that was more hungrily read than the millions of words that were composed about the battle. It was to the effect that when the old Manassa Mauler stumbled back to his room, bruised and battered and tearful, he was met by his wife, Estelle Taylor of the films. She was less upset than she might have been, for she badly wanted her husband to quit the ring so that he could transfer his talents to the stage and movies, for both of which, incidentally, he was in no way equipped, as was afterwards shown.

' "What happened, Jack?" she is supposed to have asked. "Honey, I forgot to duck," the dethroned champion is reported to have replied.

'It was a lovely example of the press agent's art and imagination, and it is still going the rounds. Unfortunately, however, it had no more truth than the other story that just before he climbed into the ring Dempsey was slipped a slow-action drug by a gambler who had betted heavily on Tunney. I saw Dempsey, and talked with him, less than twenty-four hours after his descent from the mountains. His features were mashed and discoloured . . . All he said to me about his defeat was this, "The old dogs went back on me." Dogs, in his lingo, meant legs.'

That first day as heavyweight champion of the world, Gene Tunney had lunch with former governor James M Cox of Ohio and Dan Hanna, the Cleveland newspaper owner, and a few hours later visited Dempsey at the Adelphi Hotel to pay his respects to the old champion. 'I found Gene Normile, dishevelled and weeping, in a silk dressing gown,' Tunney recalled in *A Man Must Fight*. 'He was in his bare feet. Before him was a half-empty bottle of Scotch whisky. Tommy Laird, a San Francisco newspaperman, and Jerry the Greek, Dempsey's trainer, were the only others I knew. I was not in the room two minutes before I experienced for the first time the resentment that some of the experts and followers of boxing felt over my defeat of Dempsey.'

Tunney was ushered to a room in Dempsey's suite. 'In about

five minutes Jack came into the room from the hall,' he related. 'He looked the worse for wear. Unless my face after the first Greb match was as bad a looking sight as his, I have never seen its equal. He seemed heart-broken over the loss of his title. Hearing from me that he had hit me some hard blows, he seemed to cheer up a bit. As I was leaving, Jack said wearily, "Gene, your troubles are just beginning, whether you know it or not. Every time you turn around you'll find a process-server." I took my leave with the thought that I had never known a more gracious loser.'

The next day, Saturday, Tunney boarded a train for New York City, and home. His city did not let him down. Thousands crowded into Pennsylvania Station to greet their champion and they lined the route as he rode in a gleaming limousine with a police escort down Seventh Avenue on the way to City Hall for his reception by Mayor Jimmy Walker. A great fight fan, James J Walker was minority leader of the New York Senate in 1920 when he introduced the Walker Law, legalising boxing in the state of New York. He was elected mayor in 1925. In his official speech, he welcomed New York's new champion, saying, 'Those who have known your character and the citizenship you represent and the high principles you learned at your mother's knee, not only look upon you as the champion boxer of the world, but as a champion model American young man.'

Over lunch, Walker made Tunney laugh when he described the Philadelphia fight as, 'the greatest swimming exhibition I have ever witnessed'. Walker also related how, after the fight, having been persuaded by Damon Runyon not to bet on Tunney because he hadn't heard him grunt when sparring, he went looking for the columnist and told him to get himself a hearing aid.

When Tunney emerged from City Hall, a large crowd cheered him. He spoke to them briefly, explaining that one of Dempsey's punches had hit him in the Adam's apple and he was still hoarse from the effects.

A limousine took the new champion to the Biltmore Hotel,

where he was to meet the metropolitan sportswriters. Manager Billy Gibson was already there, berating the journalists who had ridiculed Tunney's chances against the Manassa Mauler and proclaiming that, 'Dempsey, the best day he ever saw, could not lick Gene Tunney!' To which Tunney responded, 'I think Billy is a little too tough on the writers he's talking about. But then, I guess I've always baffled them. They always made me a short-ender, and I'm grateful on behalf of the boys in the Village. They have profited handsomely in the betting.'

Later that afternoon, Gene made his way to his home on Arlington Avenue in the Riverdale section of the city, where his mother anxiously waited to greet her champion son. His father didn't live to see Gene reach the top of his profession, dying in 1923. A posse of pressmen had shadowed Gene all day, from the moment he stepped off the train at Penn Station to the very door of his home. And that was far enough for Gene, though he was already resigned to his new-found status – 'I belong to the public just as much as the stars do to the universe.' Turning at the door, he announced, 'Gentlemen, you have been with me all the day. I have answered all of your questions. Now, you will have to excuse me. My mother is waiting to see me and she wants to see me alone.'

★ ★ ★

'It was the custom for people to try and sue the new heavyweight champion on whatever grounds could be scraped up,' writes Mel Heimer in *The Long Count*, 'the man had ready money, didn't he? But the first suit that was an aftermath of the Philadelphia fight was against Dempsey. A man said that Jack, in making his way to the dressing room after the bout, hit his wife in the side with an elbow, causing her to fall. It could have been the best shot Dempsey landed all night.'

On a more serious note, Doc Kearns finally landed his old champion in court. In the United States District Court in Manhattan, Kearns charged that he still had a valid contract with Dempsey as his manager and as a consequence was owed hundreds of thousands of dollars. The ex-champ, through a New York firm of lawyers, counter-sued on the grounds that the alleged contract didn't exist, and charged that Kearns had forged Dempsey's signature on a contract for one of his fights and had even admitted as much to Dempsey. Jack didn't appear too worried by the case as he and Estelle enjoyed opening day of the baseball World Series at Yankee Stadium, acknowledging a wave of cheering from the crowd. And when reporters asked if he was serious about retiring, Dempsey smiled, shrugged, and said, 'I might fight again, and then again I might not.'

Stories were still circulating in the sports pages as the writers seized on anything that would excuse Dempsey's poor showing that night in the rain. In New York, a Dr Russell announced that shortly before the Tunney fight Dempsey had suffered an attack of boils on his left arm, stating, 'I am inclined to believe that it played a considerable part in the fight. Dempsey was a man intoxicated by poisonous matter in the blood when he entered the ring.'

Later, a signed article in the *Baltimore News* by Police Captain Charles J Mabutt declared that a poisonous substance had been put in Dempsey's coffee on the Saturday morning before the fight. Mabutt stated that he, Dempsey, Jerry the Greek, and Mike Trent had breakfast that morning at the Carney Cottage in Atlantic City. 'Trent took his coffee black, the rest of us all took cream and all suffered afterwards.' Trent, a sergeant with the Chicago police, called the story a load of rubbish. 'I always take cream with my coffee,' he said, 'and furthermore, I don't remember Mabutt taking any meals with the Dempsey party.'

The whole thing was put into context by 'Philadelphia' Jack O'Brien, the old light-heavyweight champion who had been in Dempsey's corner for the fight. 'The only poison Jack got was that first round punch of Tunney's to the jaw,' he said, adding, 'Three minutes before the fight I would have bet five thousand dollars to a thousand on Dempsey, but not one nickel three minutes after it started.'

21

Dempsey Comes Back

Like the rest of America, Tex Rickard was in a state of shock after Tunney's victory. Late that night he sat in his hotel suite in Philadelphia as reporters pestered him for his views on the fight. 'I can hardly believe it,' he said. 'I never thought it could happen to him.' Quizzed about his future plans, Rickard shook his head. 'I dunno. This other feller ain't never been a drawing card. Dempsey was the one who drew them in.'

A few days later Rickard was at work in his office at Madison Square Garden, telling the press boys he would run an elimination tournament to find the next challenger for the new champion. One fighter who wouldn't be invited to compete was Harry Wills, the Brown Panther, who was still tenuously hanging on to his number-one ranking. Rickard was angry with Wills's manager, Paddy Mullins, explaining, 'There's no room for such as him in sport. He tried to say he was offered a bout with Tunney last year only on condition that his fighter lay down.'

Promoter Humbert Fugazy, anxious to push Rickard off his pedestal, promptly announced that he had signed Wills to box leading contender Jack Sharkey at Ebbets Field in Brooklyn on 12 October, adding, 'I don't see how Gene Tunney can avoid meeting the winner of this fight.' Sharkey arrived in New York City from Boston with manager Johnny Buckley and booked into the Astor Hotel. After an impressive workout at Stillman's Gym on 8th Avenue, Sharkey told reporters that after he had

beaten big George Godfrey, Godfrey had told him he would
beat both Wills and Tunney.

On Columbus Day some thirty-five thousand fans sat in
Ebbets Field and watched Sharkey shatter forever the myth of
Harry Wills. When a microphone was shoved in Sharkey's face
as he waited for the bout to start, he said, 'I'm not afraid of
Wills. I'll beat him sure as I'm standing before this microphone.' At 34, Wills had seen better days and Sharkey gave him
one of his worst, outboxing and outpunching Wills all the way.
The Brown Panther had 26 pounds on the Boston Gob as well
as height and reach advantages, but he had nothing else.

Recalling the fight, Nat Fleischer wrote, 'Sharkey gave Wills
as artistic a shellacking for twelve rounds as any heavyweight of
that period had ever taken. Age seemed to have taken its toll
both on Harry's punch and his speed. He couldn't cope with
the faster and younger Sharkey. Jack hit Wills almost at will
with a powerful left to the head and body and poked a right into
the Negro's face so often Harry became bewildered. He soon
had Harry's eye in mourning. Sharkey proved that Wills at that
time was a much over-rated fighter and the defeat substantiated
the opinion of Dempsey's followers that it was a lucky thing for
Harry that he had not faced Dempsey who would have beaten
him without doubt. Wills fouled repeatedly and was frequently
warned by Referee Patsy Haley. Haley in disgust finally pushed
him to his corner in the thirteenth round and awarded the fight
on a foul to Sharkey.'

Harry Wills subsequently drew a thirty-day suspension from
the New York State Athletic Commission, a meaningless slap
on the wrist. Tex Rickard wasn't at the fight. The day before he
was in Lewisburg, West Virginia, where he married Miss
Maxine Hodges, a 24-year-old Broadway actress.

Gene Tunney, in the meantime, had been to City Hall
again, this time to receive a commission as a first lieutenant
in the Marine Corps Reserve. The champion looked
resplendent, if a little uncomfortable, in a new blue officer's
uniform. He had applied for a commission several months
previously and it was granted because of his 'distinguished

service overseas with the 11th Marine Regiment.' A crowd of some five thousand waited in City Hall Park to see Tunney, who was accompanied by Major Anthony J D Biddle of the 8th Regiment, Philadelphia.

The man in the street seemed to be warming to the new heavyweight champion quicker than the fight fans. 'When I walk on the street I am recognised instantly,' Tunney wrote in a magazine article. 'I walk into a haberdasher's to buy a necktie and a crowd will gather outside the door. Many wartime buddies come up and greet me. While driving through Newark, New Jersey, some kids playing baseball spotted me in a traffic jam and surrounded my car. Kids recognise me quicker than grown-ups. It is not surprising people recognise me. My face has been made familiar to the world in hundreds of newspaper photographs and in motion pictures.

'After my victory over Dempsey I received enough letters and telegrams congratulating me to fill two large clothes hampers. I received fifteen hundred letters and telegrams from Legion posts alone. I have writer's cramp from autographing books, photographs, menu cards, fight programmes, boxing gloves and notepaper sent through the mail. I found time to write a personal note to twenty boys and girls in an English class in George Washington Child School in Philadelphia who had sent me letters of congratulation. They asked and received the consent of their teacher to let the work count as part of their lessons. I prize these letters, and I answered all of them. Questions or no questions, it's great to be champion.'

To many boxing fans, however, their champion was still Jack Dempsey. This was again demonstrated on the night of 22 October when Tunney and Dempsey attended Madison Square Garden to be presented with championship belts by the Metropolitan Boxing Writers' Association. Dempsey entered the ring to a standing ovation from almost nineteen thousand fans, whereas Tunney was greeted with sporadic cheers and a lot of boos, bringing a smile to his handsome face. 'That was an outrage,' said Dempsey as he came down out of the ring. 'I felt just as badly as Gene did.'

With mild interest Tunney watched the main event, featuring one of his contenders, Jim Maloney, who knocked out Arthur DeKuh inside two rounds. That night he was more concerned to learn of the tragic death of his old antagonist, Harry Greb. A newsflash from Atlantic City stated that former world middle-weight champion Harry Greb had died in a local hospital through haemmorhages following an operation on the nose a million punches had knocked out of shape. Greb was just 32 years old. When they buried him on Wednesday 27 October 1926 in Pittsburgh's Calvary Cemetery, world heavyweight champion Gene Tunney was one of the pallbearers. After the funeral Tunney talked with columnist Damon Runyon about the fighter Ernest Hemingway called, 'one of our great Americans'.

'He was never in one spot for more than half a second,' said Tunney. 'He'd jump in and out, slamming me with a left and whirling me around with his right, or vice versa. My arms were plastered with leather and although I jabbed, hooked, and crossed, it was like fighting an octupus!'

'I agree,' said Runyon. 'Greb was one in a million. I saw that first fight you had with him and I never thought you'd live to talk about it.'

As they parted, Tunney added, 'If ever an athlete deserved a monument to his greatness, to his endurance, and to his sportsmanship, it was Harry Greb.'

Tunney spent the beginning of November on holiday in Bermuda, sailing back into New York Harbour on Armistice Day. As the ship approached the North River pier, a bugler played taps and Tunney stood at attention. Speaking to reporters on the quayside, he recalled that as a young marine in France eight years before, when the armistice was being signed, he received $60 back pay. 'It looked like a million dollars to me then,' he said.

Billy Gibson had arranged a vaudeville tour for Tunney, through the William Morris agency, giving four shows a day at $7,500 a week. On opening day, at Loew's State Theater in New York, the champion was arrested backstage on a charge of violating the state law by appearing in a boxing match without having a licence from the Commission. The charge was ridiculous. As everyone knew, Tunney was merely performing exhibition bouts of sparring for which no licence was required. The case was kicked out of court by Magistrate Jesse Silberman, who cleared Tunney and six others arrested with him, and berated Commissioner Farley for having caused Tunney's arrest without justification in law or fact.

Tunney was never too keen on the tour. 'After a week I decided that the theatre would have to get along without my Thespian ability,' he wrote in *A Man Must Fight*. 'I had signed a fourteen-week contract which I hoped to buy myself out of to the advantage of all parties. Alas, there was no retreating. It was fourteen weeks or "dishonour" to me and my booking agent. At least that was Mr Morris's story. He persuaded me to continue my "histrionic" career to the end of the contract.'

A month into the contract, Tunney almost did break it, as recorded in Mel Heimer's book, *The Long Count*. 'On Sunday, December 26, the *New York Times* came out with a front-page story to the effect that the world had almost lost its new heavyweight champion. At Rockwood, Maine, Tunney, his host Pert Fowler and two other men were crossing frozen Moosehead Lake, where in spots the water is more than a hundred feet deep, en route to Christmas morning Mass. In trying to leap an ice wrinkle Tunney lost his footing, the *Times* stated, plunged into the water, and was only saved at a point halfway across the lake, by a human chain of the other men with him. "That was the closest call I ever had," Tunney was reported saying in the Rockwood Hotel, where he stayed in bed until his clothes dried. "I'll never forget this Christmas." The party of men then returned to their camp at Tomhegan Point, travelling ten miles by automobile and walking the last four miles rather than try the lake again. Tunney's later version was a bit different. He had gotten soaking wet, he said, but only from the water around the broken ice. "I was never really in danger," he said. It didn't matter. It made a good story.'

A story on the sports pages at that time said that Humbert Fugazy had offered Tunney $585,000 for a summer title defence at the Polo Grounds against Jack Delaney, the former light-heavyweight champion who had just given up his title to campaign among the big boys. A few weeks later, however, Tex Rickard announced that he had signed Tunney to defend his title in the summer. Tunney would receive what Dempsey had received for the Philadelphia fight, a guarantee of $475,000 plus fifty per cent of the gate if it went over $1 million.

'In signing to box for Mr Rickard,' the champion told reporters, 'I tinged business with a little sentiment, or loyalty, if you will,' adding that even if Rickard's offer had been topped, 'I would have stayed with the man who gave me the chance at the title.'

Rickard, of course, was hoping that when Tunney did step into the ring to defend his title, the guy in the other corner would be Jack Dempsey. The former champion was back in Los Angeles, still not committed to making a comeback. He had done some light training in a local gym and said he was only twelve pounds over his fighting weight. Rickard kept bombarding him with telegrams and telephone calls, asking when he was coming back. 'How'd you like to meet Tunney again?' he would ask. 'It'd draw a pretty good gate, just like we like 'em, kid.'

Maybe the push Dempsey needed came from another big hitter in the sports world, baseball's Babe Ruth. The star of the New York Yankees was in Hollywood and called in to see his old pal, Dempsey. 'He and I had met in 1921,' said Dempsey, 'and over the years we'd watched each other reap glory and publicity.'

'Listen, Jack,' said Ruth. 'You lost your crown while still on your feet. Sure, it's tough, but don't you think you owe yourself and your fans one more crack?'

'No, Babe, I know when I'm through,' replied Dempsey.

'Awright then, sit on your ass and feel sorry for yourself,' growled Ruth, anger in his voice. 'You know, pal, it's guys like us who just can't back off from the spotlight. Pals of mine say that letters are pouring in to sports desks all around the country for you. And here you are, walkin' sideways and bumping into yourself, for Chrissakes.'

'Babe,' Dempsey said in that high voice of his, 'I don't know if I've still got it, see?'

'Well, goddamn it,' said Ruth, taking his leave, 'you won't know till you get out there and try!'

Rickard was on the telephone again, ringing long distance from New York City to LA, and Dempsey still wasn't sure what to do. Rickard knew the right buttons to press.

'Well, maybe you're right, kid,' he said. 'Maybe Tunney's too tough for you. No one likes to get licked by the same guy twice.'

'Wait a second, Tex,' Dempsey protested. 'Tunney's not that tough. And I ain't no cream puff, you know. It's just that I'm kinda fat and out of condition.'

'Tell you what, kid,' came back Rickard. 'Why don't you start training and we'll see what happens. Maybe I'll arrange for you to meet someone else before Tunney. That way, you'll have a fight under your belt when you step into the ring. What do you say, Jack?'

Dempsey agreed to start working out. He rounded up Gus Wilson, Jerry the Greek and a couple of sparring partners, and went up into the hills. He chopped trees, did calisthenics, raced against dogs, jumped rope, and climbed the trees he hadn't chopped down. He ran seven miles on the road every day and started punching the light and heavy bags. When he moved camp to Soper's Ranch in the Ventura Mountains, his name started appearing in the sports pages again.

'The only sportswriter I allowed to observe me at close range,' recalled Dempsey, 'was Bob Edgren of the *New York World*. I felt that he had a good eye for boxing, he had been a pretty good amateur fighter himself. After spending three days with me, I could tell he liked what he saw. Returning to New York, he confirmed what I hoped, writing, "Jack Dempsey has come back."'

In May there was a big crowd at Yankee Stadium to see Jack Sharkey fight his Boston neighbour, Jim Maloney, who went into the ring a 7–5 favourite. But the favourite came unstuck as Sharkey decked his man three times before knocking him out in 52 seconds of round five. 'Maloney put up a great fight,' Sharkey said in the dressing room. 'I want Tunney now. He's the next man for me. But if I have to, I'm ready to battle Dempsey.'

One impressed ringsider was heavyweight champion Gene Tunney, telling reporters, 'He [Sharkey] is as good a fighter as I've ever seen. He has everything. I was really astonished at his showing. He's smarter than Dempsey and faster, though he's not as hard a hitter.'

Breaking camp in California, Dempsey growled, 'Sharkey and Tunney look alike to me. I'll fight anyone. I know I have a lot of fight and a lot of hard punches left in me.' Gus Wilson came east, booked Luther's place at Saratoga, and was seen around Stillman's Gym in New York looking for sparring partners.

Tex Rickard had his next big fight: Jack Dempsey versus Jack Sharkey, at the Yankee Stadium, on 21 July 1927, both fighters getting 25 per cent of the gate. Rickard arranged for Leo P Flynn to take over as Dempsey's fight manager, while Gene Normile handled the business end of things.

'Flynn was as tough as a drill sergeant,' said Dempsey. 'He was a master of strategy just as Doc had been. He told me what to do from the moment I got up till my head hit the pillow at night. I didn't mind. I needed it.'

Writer Paul Gallico recalled the veteran Flynn as, 'old, white-haired, leathery-faced, one corner of his mouth exhibiting a small permanent orifice from talking and spitting out of it, calluses on his under forearms from leaning on the ropes and side-talking advice into the cauliflower ears of the fighters he used to call his bums. He was any casting director's vision of the perfect old-time fight manager.'

Dempsey's training did not go smoothly. His weight wasn't coming off as quickly as Flynn would have liked it to and the old guy kept closing the camp, and barring press and public alike. When the reporters were allowed to watch Dempsey work out, they were not impressed by his condition. He was up one day, down the next. With three weeks to go to the fight, he suffered a personal blow when he was informed that his brother, Johnny, had killed himself and his wife at their home in Schenectady, upstate New York. 'He had been on hard drugs for quite a while, unable to kick the habit despite the numerous cures Teddy Hayes and I had arranged for him,' said Dempsey. 'I left the training camp to make arrangements for his body to be returned to Salt Lake City and to break the news to my mother and father.'

Sharkey was training in New York, at the Madison Square Garden rink on the roof, and he drew crowds to see his workouts. The writers were impressed and Sharkey seemed confident that, at 24, he could defeat the 32-year-old former champion and go on to challenge Tunney for the title. In one sharp routine Sharkey knocked out sparmate Johnny Urban, and former champ Jim Corbett remarked that the Boston Gob looked in good shape. However, Corbett was far more impressed when he paid a visit to Saratoga to see Dempsey working.

'I came up here expecting to look at an old broken-down warhorse,' remarked Corbett. 'Instead, I looked at a good fighter. It will take a great fighter to beat him.'

Jack Sharkey was not a great fighter, but for six rounds against Dempsey that July night at New York's Yankee Stadium he was a good enough fighter to beat what was left of Jack Dempsey, and book his place against Gene Tunney later that year. The ex-sailor steamed into Dempsey from the opening bell and not only outboxed the Mauler but outfought him. Tex Rickard had another million-dollar gate – $1,083,530 paid by a crowd of 75,000, according to Fleischer's *Ring Record Book*. But the promoter reckoned he had had 83,000 tickets printed and at 2 p.m. on the day before the fight he had only 900 left. Ticket touts did a roaring trade, getting as high as $125 for tickets with a face value of $27.50 as people fought to see Dempsey make his ring comeback in the battle of the two Jacks.

At ringside for the *New York Times*, James P Dawson wrote, 'The first note of the battle made by this reporter was,

"Dempsey waits for Sharkey to come." It tells more clearly than anything else the extent to which Dempsey has disintegrated. Dempsey never waited for anyone. He was the first to leap in on the attack, the first to land a blow and the first punch invariably was clean and carried a salutary effect. But last night Dempsey stood half-crouched, waiting for Sharkey to lunge at him, instead of whipping out like the Dempsey of old.'

The old champ was at his best when he was able to get inside, where he punched away to the body, but Sharkey whipped lefts and rights to the head and Dempsey was bleeding from the mouth. Sharkey staggered Dempsey with a left to the head then drove him across the ring with lefts and rights to the jaw, and Dempsey looked about to fall at the bell. In the second round it was Sharkey taking the fight to his man, hammering both hands to the head, bringing blood from Dempsey's nose and at the bell he was cut under the right eye. In the third round Dempsey looked more like the old Manassa Mauler as he took the fight to Sharkey, ripping punches into the body and driving a terrific uppercut to the face, and Sharkey slipped in his own corner as Dempsey drove him back.

As Dawson described the fourth round, 'Dempsey was lost until he got to close quarters, where he drove both hands to the body. Sharkey hooked a short right and left to the face and kept repeating the blows as Dempsey came in wide open, leading for the body. Dempsey was groggy on his feet. His right eye was cut and bleeding, his nose was bleeding and his mouth was bleeding. He could hardly come in on his legs and he pawed the air, feeling for Sharkey. But he fought gloriously, coming in against Sharkey's lefts and rights to the face, lashing out with both hands to the body, and just before the bell hooking a left to the jaw which had the crowd on its feet yelling wildly.'

In the corner after the fifth round, Leo Flynn shouted at Dempsey, 'Keep boring in. Keep pounding 'em home until he folds up.' Dempsey recalled later, 'I wondered if he realised what a pounding around I was taking in return. This Jack Sharkey was tough!'

Round seven and all hell was let loose! In his biography of Dempsey, Nat Fleischer wrote, 'Dempsey came out of his corner in a crouching position. He avoided several jabs and then rushed in and landed a left to the body. The pair then stood at close range and exchanged blows. Dempsey drove the right with telling effect into the body. One seemed to hit on the leg and another just below the belt. Sharkey complained to the referee who refused to heed him. Sharkey raised his eyes toward the official and dropped his guard, and while he was in that position, Dempsey, not waiting for the referee to intervene, shot up a short left hook and Sharkey fell on his face in the middle of the ring, apparently in pain. He tried to rise but could not and the fight was over. I felt, up to the knockout, that Dempsey was behind on points and that he could not possibly last through to the limit. His legs were showing signs of weakening and he was slowing up considerably. I was one of those who, sitting in the press box just in front of where the disputed blows were struck, insisted from the start that the blows were fouls and to this day I still think so.

'Referee Jack O'Sullivan admitted after the fight that Dempsey had landed two low punches, but declared they did not merit disqualification. This was his version of what had taken place in that final session. "I saw Dempsey hit Sharkey with a right to the left leg. He did that twice. They were sweeping blows that glanced off the leg and did no damage. They called merely for a warning and not a disqualification. They were followed by a beautiful solar plexus punch that caused Sharkey to grunt. Sharkey was ready to sink when he raised his head and started to complain to me about being hit foul. I was about to step in between the men when Sharkey dropped his right hand and Dempsey shot up a pretty left hook that ended the bout."'

'I was convinced that I had won the fight fair and square,' recalled Dempsey, 'and that Sharkey should never have dropped his hands. My left to the jaw was the blow that ended the fight, not the ones to the stomach. I was riding high again and it was nothing short of glorious.'

22

Chicago

In a March 1932 issue of *Liberty* magazine, William Inglis wrote of the Dempsey–Sharkey fight, 'Tunney analysed this fight as accurately as an engineer would analyse a report of bridge building. The early rounds showed that Jack's footwork, never of the best, had slowed down considerably. But his endurance and terrific hitting power were as good as ever. He was still the Manassa Mauler, if he could land his short-arm punches. The thing to do was to make him keep his distance. But suppose Dempsey should land one of those devastating short-arm blows? How could Gene gain breathing time to recover from its effects? The answer was clear: he must be able to run backward faster than Jack could run in pursuit of him. Tunney practised running backward one mile every day on a path hidden in the deep woods behind his camp at Speculator, in the Adirondack wilderness. He developed speed and sureness of foot never before seen in retreat.'

Many years later this story was confirmed by respected sports columnist Arthur Daley of the *New York Times,* who recalled, 'Although I was the youngest and newest member of the sports department, I was given the assignment of covering the Tunney camp by Colonel Bernard St D Thomson, then the sports editor. I reached Speculator in fear and trembling, totally awed by the magnitude of my first big assignment. To the rescue leaped Gene. He practically adopted me on the spot. He was kind, gracious, and helpful. He had me visit him at his cottage and it was there he filled me in with all the extra information I needed for my daily stories.

'Being Tunney's pet, I was permitted to accompany him on his roadwork. Because I was younger than he and still thought I was an athlete, it was no strain. The first time we hit the trail together a strange thing happened, something I never could forget. He always ran backwards for fixed periods. I asked him about it. "In boxing," he said in his pedantic style, "a man is always moving in and out, frequently retreating. This exercise gives muscular skill and helps him avoid becoming leg-weary. I've made this a practice before all my fights. Some day it may pay off." In the seventh round against Dempsey in Chicago it paid off. Big.'

Tunney later revealed one story that young Daley did not get. 'I established my training quarters at Speculator, New York, where I remained until the first of September. During the early part of my training I had a very curious experience. One day, while boxing with a sparring partner, Frank Muskie, we bumped heads. The part of my skull, which is the thinnest, near the temple, struck the toughest part of his, the top. I was terribly dazed. As I straightened up, a long, hard right swing landed on my jaw. Without going down or staggering, I lost all consciousness of what I was doing, and instinctively proceeded to knock Muskie out.

'Another sparring partner, Eddie Eagan, entered the ring. We boxed three rounds. I have no recollection of this, nor of anything that occurred until the next morning when I awakened, wondering who I was and what I was doing there. As I lay in this state of returning consciousness, I became awfully frightened. Gradually my name came to me. That I was a pugilist soon followed. I rose and asked guarded questions. I wanted to know all about the events of the day before. I had to stop training and did not leave my cabin except to eat or take a short walk. On these occasions all seemed queer. The sensation was as though hot water had been poured through a hole in my skull and flowed down over my brain to my eyes, leaving a hot film. There were three newspapermen at camp, reporting my activities. They had to be deceived. I confided my condition to no one but Eddie Eagan. After returning to normal, I decided that any sport in which such accidents could occur was dangerous. I realised I had a concussion. The possibility of becoming punch-drunk haunted me for weeks.'

Tex Rickard, delighted with Dempsey's knockout victory over Sharkey, announced that Dempsey would challenge Gene Tunney for his old title and orders for fight tickets started pouring in with every post. The biggest order would be for an astonishing $100,000 worth! Rickard's only problem was when and where. It seemed everybody wanted the fight to take place in their own backyard; Massachusetts, Pennsylvania, Illinois, Nevada and, of course, New York all showed interest in staging the next Battle of the Century. Commissioner Jim Farley was pushing for New York but Rickard was not keen on the idea, for two reasons. First, the Commission insisted, rightly or wrongly, on a ceiling price of $27.50 being charged for any boxing contest within their jurisdiction though Rickard knew he could charge $40 for ringside seats in Chicago. Second, he didn't think New York had a stadium big enough for the crowds he anticipated for this fight.

Rickard finally announced that the fight would take place in Chicago at Soldier Field and, since it was a requirement of the Illinois State Athletic Commission that the promoter be a state resident, Rickard appointed coal dealer and millionaire sportsman George Getz as the promoter of record and himself as manager of affairs. Rickard had wanted to hold the fight over until 1928 but Getz, a big-game hunter, already had a long trip to Africa planned for that year and he would have missed the match. So the date was set for 22 September, one day short of a year since the Philadelphia fight.

No sooner had Rickard made the announcement than a strong protest was voiced by the American Legion, which did not think it right that a prizefight be held in a stadium dedicated to the service veterans of the Great War. Even though the champion himself had served in France in the US Marine Corps, the motive behind the protest was the old war-slacker charge that had been levelled at Dempsey.

However, there were more serious charges flying about in the heady atmosphere of Chicago in that summer of 1927, the Chicago of Al Capone. Word reached Tunney that gamblers and crooked politicians were trying to get an edge in the fight for Dempsey. Manager Billy Gibson heard all the rumours circulating in the Windy City when he arrived to arrange a new training camp for Tunney. Dempsey heard them, too.

'Al Capone, to whom I was still The Hero,' recalled Dempsey, 'let the word out that he had enough dough and influence spread around to make sure I would win. Not wanting Scarface to do anything I might regret, I sent him a short handwritten note asking him to lay off and let the fight go on in true sportsmanship. I didn't hear a word in reply, but the next day Estelle received what must have been two hundred dollars worth of flowers, with a card signed simply, "To the Dempseys, in the name of sportsmanship." A story made the rounds that Tunney had sent one of his bodyguards to see Capone. He allegedly told Big Al that Tunney was in tip-top shape and suggested that Capone not lean too much toward me. Capone dismissed him.'

Leo P Flynn, Rickard's former matchmaker, was again in Dempsey's camp as fight manager, and he engaged Bill Duffy to safeguard Dempsey's interests. 'There had been rumours and stories printed after the Philadelphia fight', recalled Tunney, 'intimating that Dempsey had tossed the fight because of a huge betting coup, and the Flynn-Duffy combination caused a little apprehension in our camp.'

'Bill Duffy', observed Paul Gallico, 'dressed up like a tailor's model, had strange eyes and was a dangerous man.' William Duffy, often referred to in the newspapers as Big Bill and Broadway Bill, came out of the Gowanus section of Brooklyn, a tough waterfront district. He was only seventeen when arrested for burglary and sent to Elmira Reformatory, and in 1908 he was sent up the river to Sing Sing for ten years on an armed robbery charge. Back on the streets of New York, Duffy teamed up with a guy he had met in Sing Sing, English-born Owen Madden, a notorious criminal who was known as Owney the Killer, for obvious reasons. Gangsters were making a fortune from bootleg booze in those Prohibition days and Duffy fronted several nightclubs for Madden and mobster Dutch Schulz. In 1926 the cops held Duffy on suspicion of murdering a cabaret singer named Elsie Regan, whose body was found under a pile of snow on East 54th Street. He was released for lack of evidence. By this time Broadway Bill was getting involved in boxing, along with Owney the Killer, who had always been mad on the fight game and they would later mastermind the rise of Primo Carnera to the heavyweight championship of the world. In September of 1927 Bill Duffy was in the camp of Jack Dempsey as he prepared for his rematch with Gene Tunney.

There was great speculation around Chicago as to the referee and judges to be appointed to officiate at the big fight. Many years later, in 1951, sportswriter Ed Sullivan recalled in a *New York News* column, 'For two weeks preceding the fight I lived with Dempsey and his entourage at Lincoln Fields. Behind the scenes the Dempsey camp kept trying to arrange the selection of a referee who would be friendly to the ex-champ. Chicago mobs said it could be done and we drove into a Chicago hotel to listen to their reasons. The mobsters, five of them, came to the rendezvous in the hotel room, all dressed in belted blue topcoats, and all wore soft hats. Their fee would be $50,000. "How do you know that your handpicked referee won't double-cross us?" asked Flynn. "Because," said one of the Chicago hoods, "we will be sitting in working press seats and the minute he steps out of the ring, we will take him by the arms and escort him out of the ballpark. If there is a double-cross, when we get outside the park, you'll hear the backfire of a car, only it won't be no backfire. It will be one of us shooting him very dead indeed."

'The proposed referee, sitting there, wet his lips nervously as he heard what would happen to him. "Billy Gibson, Tunney's manager, isn't a damn fool," said one of the Dempsey group. "What makes you think he'll agree to this referee you've hand-picked?" "That's what makes it perfect," said a Chicago hood.

"This guy used to referee fights for Gibson, when Benny Leonard was champ. At Benton Harbour, in 1920, when Leonard's fighting Charlie White, you remember White left-hooked Leonard out of the ring. The referee, to give Leonard a chance to pull himself together, got into an argument with Charlie White, y'hear, and by the time he finishes arguing, Leonard is back in action. Benny wins by a knockout, but he had some help. So Billy Gibson will OK our referee, because he figures he's on HIS side!"

'Back went the Dempsey entourage to Lincoln Fields, to tell Dempsey what they'd worked out. "You're stark, staring crazy," Dempsey told them. 'I told you once before that I'll carry my own referee into the ring, in my fists. Now you want me to put up $50,000 and I say to hell with it. I want no part of it and that's final. Don't make any deals in your name or my name. Tell the boys I appreciate their interest, but no dice." At that exact moment, you could understand why the big guy had been a rough, tough hombre in the ring. He was giving orders in a tone that indicated his willingness to flatten everybody in the room. He was tougher than professional tough guys, and he didn't need a gun as convincer.'

The Tunney camp was equally concerned as to the choice of referee, as recalled by Tunney in his autobiography. 'One day after a workout, Bronson, Gibson and I sat down to discuss who might prove a competent and square referee, one who would remain fair in the face of any threats from sure-thing gamblers or racketeers. Bronson said he thought Dave Miller would make an honest referee, as Miller was a brother Shriner, and Jimmy felt that Miller would not double-cross a lodge brother. Gibson said he was not so confident of Miller, whereupon Bronson said to me, "Gene, there is no use in your worrying about this thing. There is too much at stake in front of all those people. It would be professional suicide. There is but one Chicago referee that I hope is not appointed to referee this fight." "Who is he?" I asked. "Dave Barry," said Bronson. "Dave is honest but I know he doesn't like me. I would feel more comfortable if he were not the third man."'

Paul Gallico recalled, 'the hullabaloo over the referee. There were three candidates who were supposed to be under consideration. Davey Miller of Chicago, Lou Magnolia of New York, and Walter Eckersall, the All-American football player who had become a sportswriter on the *Chicago Tribune*. Magnolia, a big-nosed, bald-headed fellow, was the best referee in New York, given to extravagant gestures in the ring, but honest and efficient. He was the choice of the Tunney camp. Of course, a New York referee had as much chance of pulling down that plum in Chicago as he would have had a chance of flying there, using his hands for wings. Eckersall's honesty was not doubted, but he was an amateur, that is to say, not a licensed Illinois referee. The *Chicago Tribune* was plugging for his appointment.'

As rumours of a fix persisted, Billy Gibson, Jimmy Bronson, and Bill McCabe, an old friend of the champion, went to see Chicago's mayor, 'Big Bill' Thompson, to voice their fears. Thompson hastily called a meeting of members of the Illinois State Athletic Commission in his office at City Hall. Gibson and McCabe were there for Tunney, while Flynn and Duffy represented Dempsey. The mayor informed all those present that he would not tolerate any development that would cast reflection on the city of Chicago and the state of Illinois. At the meeting, the commission named Sheldon Clark of Chicago, a multi-millionaire oil magnate, and George Lytton, owner of one of Chicago's biggest department stores, as judges for the fight. And to avoid tampering with the third man, the commissioners announced that they would have all of Chicago's referees report to ringside and would name the chosen arbiter when Tunney and Dempsey were in the ring.

The favourite for the third-man spot in the ring seemed to be Davey Miller, who ran a pool hall with a gambling room upstairs, and who was Chicago's leading referee. Miller was also reputed to be Capone's man; in fact one of Scarface Al's lieutenants had put the word about that Miller would get the job. But then it was learned that Miller's brother had placed a $50,000 bet on Dempsey to win. Another story circulating said that Miller had been approached by a few shady characters while in a restaurant in the city's Loop district. After their little talk Davey Miller lost interest in anybody called Tunney or Dempsey.

One thing was certain: whoever the referee was, he would have to be familiar with the knockdown rule, which read, 'When a knockdown occurs, the timekeeper shall immediately arise and announce the seconds audibly as they elapse. The referee shall see first that the opponent retires to the farthest corner and then, turning to the timekeeper, shall pick up the count in unison with him, announcing the seconds to the boxer on the floor. Should the boxer on his feet fail to go, or stay in the corner, the referee and timekeeper shall cease counting until he has so retired.'

At a meeting of the Illinois Commission a few days before the fight, attended by Jimmy Bronson, Billy Gibson and Lou Brix for Tunney, and Leo Flynn, Bill Duffy and Leonard Sacks for Dempsey, both parties claimed to have insisted on the knockdown rule being fully explained to all concerned and to the rule being strictly enforced in the championship contest.

The word around town was that Capone had bet $45,000 on Dempsey. When Doc Kearns arrived in Chicago, he went to see Capone and asked him how he figured Dempsey would do in the fight. 'I got a big bet on him that says he wins,' said Capone. 'Not only that, I've let the word get out that he'd better get a fair shake. Nothing preferential, understand. But a fair shake.'

Dempsey had done his training at Lincoln Fields, a racetrack south of the city, and looked in better shape than he had when losing his title to Tunney. Sportswriter Grantland Rice observed that, 'he'd chipped a lot of rust off his plates two months earlier against Jack Sharkey. His seven-round KO of Sharkey had been Jack's hardest victory. With old-timers, whether it be baseball players or fighters, the ability to hit goes last. And Dempsey could still hit, as proved in the Sharkey debacle.'

Huge crowds had watched Dempsey's training sessions; one day over eight thousand paid admissions were recorded, said to be the biggest gathering ever at a training camp. Some of the newspaper boys were not impressed. James P Dawson wrote in the *New York Times*, 'If he can get any benefit out of these drills, he is a wonder. He is training under conditions never before experienced by a fighter preparing for an important bout.'

Another writer, Joe Williams, of the *New York Telegram*, sensed Dempsey was not happy with Flynn. 'There's a smouldering fire, Dempsey vs Flynn. Flynn says he's the boss and Dempsey thinks he is. Dempsey is drawing the customers and he blames Flynn, Rickard's friend, for Tunney getting twice as much money. The latest word is that Bill Duffy will succeed Flynn as Dempsey's manager if Dempsey wins this fight.'

The champion finished off his training at the Cedar Crest Country Club at Lake Villa, a quiet resort some fifty miles north-west of Chicago. At Speculator he had done miles and miles of roadwork, and now he polished up his boxing with day after day of precision practice; blocking, tying up, countering and jabbing. He looked and felt like the champion and the writers were suitably impressed, although quite a few of them were picking Dempsey to regain the title.

An awful lot of American citizens still refused to accept the result of the first fight, and were solidly in Dempsey's camp. They went along with Estelle Taylor, Dempsey's glamorous movie-star wife, when she said that the thing that bothered her most of all following the Philadelphia fight was reading in the newspapers that, at the end of the tenth and final round, Dempsey had staggered to his corner. 'Who do they think they're kidding?' she exploded. 'Tunney couldn't stagger Jack if he had a lead weight in each glove.'

So the smart money guys were betting on Tunney, making him a 7–5 favourite, and the man in the street, and his wife, was putting money on Dempsey to get his title back. Chicago Health Commissioner Bundesen would later tell friends that two days before the fight, he asked his wife if she would like two $40 seats. Mrs Bundesen said she would rather have the money. Next day she said to the doctor, 'I'll bet you eighty dollars on Dempsey.' 'Where are you going to get the money?' he asked. 'Oh,' she replied, 'that's the money I got by not going to the fight!'

Mrs Bundesen didn't go to the fight, but just about everybody else did. The official attendance was given as 104,943, accounting for a gross gate of $2,658,660, the biggest in sporting annals to that time. Tex Rickard, acting on a report from Captain Thomas Callaghan of the Federal Secret Service in Chicago that 10,000 counterfeit tickets had been sent from New York, arranged for an expert engraver to be stationed at each of the fifty gates into the arena to examine each ticket before the bearer was admitted.

If you didn't have a ticket, counterfeit or otherwise, there was the radio. This was Nat Fleischer's graphic description of the big-fight broadcast. 'Borne on the wings of radio, half of the civilised world went to the ringside of that great fight through a hook-up of sixty-nine broadcasting stations arranged by the *New York Evening Telegram* and twenty-five other Scripps-Howard newspapers. The crisp words of Graham McNamee, of the National Broadcasting Company, dramatically painting a word picture of the heavyweight battle, were flung to untold millions listening on four continents.

'They heard it in London. Legionnaires paused in their merry-making to listen in Paris. Out in the Australian bush they gave up their lunch hour to listen. When dawn leaped across the African veldt, they heard Tunney and Dempsey. South America paused over its coffee to hear the news from Soldier Field. Germany picked up the voice and re-broadcast it through the Stuttgart station so that owners of even the humblest crystal sets might follow the battle. Lights burned late over the prairies while radio sets formed centres of excited groups. Nightclubs in Chicago and New York hushed their strident saxophones for the returns. The West Coast heard every word. The Rockies missed nothing of the fight. There was not a hamlet in the United States or Canada that did not hear the roar of the crowd, the clang of the bell and the finish. It was the greatest radio audience that had ever been gathered together to thrill as a unit to the old drama of a meeting of champions.'

The pre-fight editions of the morning newspapers carried glaring headlines on page one, 'MILLIONS TO LISTEN TO RADIO'. But over one hundred thousand people from all walks of life wanted to be there in person, to sit or stand in that huge horseshoe-shaped stadium on the shores of Lake Michigan, and they poured into the Windy City by boat, car, plane, train and on foot. Railroads set a new record for the number of fight specials that rattled their way across the country from all points of the compass, and the first air fight tour flew from Curtiss Field in New York carrying a dozen passengers, among them Princess Xenia of Greece.

When she reached her seat at the ringside in Soldier Field, hers was just another face in a sea of celebrities. There were the governors of nine states and the mayors of nine cities, newspaper barons William Randolph Hearst and Colonel R R McCormick, and owner of the New York Yankees Colonel Jacob Ruppert. Show business stars shone in the light from 44 bulbs over the ring. They included Norma Talmadge, Al Jolson, Fanny Bryce, Fatty Arbuckle, Will Rogers, Irving Berlin, Flo Ziegfeld, Gloria Swanson, Mary Pickford and Douglas Fairbanks, Charlie Chaplin and Tom Mix.

Boxing's royalty had also turned out for the big one. Three former heavyweight champions in Jim Jeffries, Jack Johnson and Jim Corbett; Benny Leonard, Johnny Kilbane, Willie Ritchie, Battling Nelson, Johnny Coulon, Jack Sharkey, old Tom Sharkey, Johnny Dundee, Packey McFarland and Paulino Uzcudun were just a few spotted around the ringside.

British sportswriter Trevor Wignall would recall, 'There was about an hour to go before the first preliminary bout was due to be staged, and a chilly wind was blowing off the lake that made me glad a chambermaid in my hotel had induced me to take along a blanket from the bed. The temperature had dropped about twenty degrees, after an Indian summer spell, and I was wrapping the blanket about my shoulders when Tex Rickard paused to talk to me. He was jubilant and aglow. "Ever seen anything like it?" he demanded. "This is the biggest crowd in the annals of fighting. By the time the big fight comes up at ten o'clock this stadium will be jammed. The takings already are a record, and the way things are going we will soon have to close the gates. You should go back to the very last row, up there on the terraces. Whether they can see the ring is more than I know, but I'm told that some of them have radio sets to pick up the sounds. Between ourselves, they might as well be in Detroit for all they will be able to see." '

23

Battle of the Long Count

At 9.55 p.m. that Thursday night in September 1927, Jack Dempsey climbed the steps of the ring in Chicago's Soldier Field and, slipping through the ropes, walked briskly to his corner. He wore a white robe and three day's growth of beard on his chin. He was accompanied by Leo P Flynn, Bill Duffy, Gus Wilson and Jerry 'the Greek' Luvadis. At 10 p.m. prompt, Gene Tunney stepped into the ring, wearing a beautiful robe in the colours of the US Marine Corps, blue and red, with the Marine insignia on the back. With the champion were Billy Gibson, Jimmy Bronson, Lou Fink and Lou Brix. Dempsey crossed the ring and greeted Tunney, shaking hands and exchanging a few words.

It was zero hour, time for battle. The worries and niggles of the training camp, the rumours, allegations and gossip, it meant nothing now. All that mattered for champion Gene Tunney and challenger Jack Dempsey were the next 39 minutes. Tunney was very much the self-made man, who had spent seven years steeling himself mentally and physically for that supreme moment in Philadelphia a year ago when he became heavyweight champion of the world. Now it was time to prove that victory was not a fluke; time to prove his championship mettle. Dempsey had been champion for seven years, seven long years, and part of him had stayed in that Philadelphia ring along with his title a year ago when the unthinkable happened, when he lost to the New Yorker.

Prize-winning author Studs Terkel was a fourteen-year-old boy in Chicago at the time and he recalled for William Nack in a *Sports Illustrated* article, 'We were devastated when Tunney won. Devastated! Who was this guy, Tunney? Dempsey was boxing in the 'Twenties. Caruso was the opera, Chaplin was films, Ruth was baseball and Dempsey was boxing. We couldn't believe he had lost.' He had lost, and it hit him harder than Tunney's right hand in that first round, the punch that sealed his fate that rainy night. Could he get it all back?

There was something of a surprise for both fighters as the announcements were made. The referee was Dave Barry, not Capone's man, Davey Miller, whom Dempsey had expected to get the assignment, but the man Jimmy Bronson had warned Tunney about. Too late now. Barry called the two men to the centre of the ring for their final instructions. Gibson and Bronson stood with the champion, while Flynn and Jerry the Greek shadowed Dempsey.

'Both you boys have received a book of the rules of this Boxing Commission,' said Barry. 'They have been discussed by your representatives, I understand, for several days at the Commission. The rabbit and kidney blows are barred, of course. Now, I want to get this one point clear. In the event of a knockdown, the man scoring the knockdown will go to the farthest neutral corner. Is that clear, Jack? Is that clear, Champ?'

They both nodded, 'Yes.'

'Now, in the event of a knockdown,' went on Barry, 'unless the boy scoring it goes to the farthest neutral corner I will not begin the count until he does. Is that clear, Jack? Is that clear, Champ?'

Both fighters again answered, 'Yes.'

'Shake hands now and come out fighting.'

At the bell Dempsey advanced from his corner then lunged with a left that Tunney evaded and Dempsey floundered past him into the ropes. They clinched and wrestled into Tunney's corner and, as they moved back to the centre of the ring, Dempsey tried another left, which was short, and they clinched again. They circled, each looking for an opening, gloves at waist level, Dempsey's body swaying from the hips as he went this way then that, the left hanging low, cocked and ready to fire. Tunney landed a snappy left and right to the head, Dempsey circled around and, as he came forward again, Tunney hit him with a chopping right to the head then tied him up at close quarters. Dempsey was short with a left to the body and Tunney forced him back to the ropes with lefts and rights to the head. Tunney led a left then missed a right as the bell ended the first round.

At ringside for the *New York Times*, James P Dawson wrote of round two, 'Dempsey hooked a left to the head with staggering power as Tunney missed a right to the jaw. Dempsey followed with a left to the body when Tunney left himself open and the punch did Tunney no good at all. But through the rest of the round Tunney outboxed and outgeneralled his rival in an impressive exhibition of boxing skill.'

Nat Fleischer on round three: 'They danced about and Gene led with a right as Dempsey hooked three lefts to the body. Gene started a right hook to Jack's body, but stopped the blow short as they clinched. Tunney rushed Dempsey and landed with short lefts. Jack drove away at Gene's body, the blows being perilously close to the belt line. They got in close quarters and Dempsey again hit low and Judge Lytton shouted "Low" to the referee. Dempsey was short with a left and then Tunney missed a short right and danced away from a short left. Gene missed a left and came in at close quarters to hook at Dempsey's head. Again they clinched, with Jack pummelling away at the champion's body.'

Dawson gave the round to Dempsey, writing, 'Dempsey was getting more vicious as the fight progressed and began hitting low with his leads at long range and his punches in the clinches. He was warned for these offences. But he carried the attack so persistently, tirelessly, restlessly, that he had Tunney in full flight, missing awkwardly as the former champion pounded the body and head with vicious drives of both hands.'

Out for the fourth and Dempsey missed a left to the body, Tunney scored a left to the head, landed more solid jabs and then threw a heavy right to Dempsey's jaw and they clinched in a neutral corner. Dempsey tried a left downstairs but Tunney beat him to it with a jolting left to the face. Tunney was pounding his man with lefts and rights, and a right brought blood from Dempsey's eye. Dempsey had been using the rabbit punch in the third and the referee spoke to him in this round for repeating this illegal blow in the clinches.

'At the end of the fourth round,' recalled Tunney, 'I finally nailed him with one of those wild rights on the temple. He staggered back into a corner. He was considerably dazed, but conscious enough to cover up. The bell rang. He went to his corner in an unsteady stride. Despite repeated warnings from the referee, he continued to use the rabbit blow whenever I failed to tie him up. This rabbit blow is the most dangerous blow in boxing. It brings a deadening headache, which seems to rest in the base of the skull. There is a numbness which reacts on the whole nervous system. My bodyguard, Sergeant Bill Smith of the Chicago Police Department, became wildly excited because the referee was apparently doing nothing to stop these illegal blows. Between rounds he climbed to the outer platform of the neutral corner where the referee was making his notes and yelled, "You blankety-blank-blank, if you don't stop those rabbit punches you'll be carried out of here dead!"'

'From the beginning,' Dempsey wrote in his autobiography, 'Gene Tunney held the advantage, even though I was grimly determined to win back my title. He had me staggering and leaning against the ropes by the second round. By the third and fourth rounds I was in a bad way, weary and bleeding. I felt flat-footed and I found I was having difficulty breathing. But I wouldn't give up for anything.'

Dempsey's handlers worked furiously on him in the interval after round four, with Tunney's seconds yelling that the stimulants they were using were unfair. The bell brought them up for the fifth and whatever they gave Dempsey worked. He charged out to harass and worry Tunney with vicious drives to the body and head, but by the halfway mark the champion slammed two heavy rights to the head, which shook Dempsey to his toenails. Tunney backed off, content to wait and pick his punches, but when they clinched, Dempsey again clubbed him to the back of the neck. Tunney finished the session with two nice lefts into the body.

Out for work in the sixth round, both boxed warily before coming together with a flurry of body punches. The crowd let out a roar as Dempsey's right hand smashed under Tunney's heart. Dempsey was cut on the left ear, there was a swelling under his left eye and he was bleeding from two cuts on his face. But there was nothing wrong with his heart and it drove him forward and he turned Tunney halfway round with a savage right hook to the head. Tunney fought back but Dempsey again struck with venom. Two further left hooks and a thudding right cross shook Tunney, and it was a good round for the former champion.

The seventh round defined this return fight between Gene Tunney and Jack Dempsey, giving it its own special niche in the fistic annals. It is still talked about today. This is what happened, according to Dawson of the *New York Times*. 'In that seventh round, in a masterful exhibition of boxing Tunney was evading the attack of his heavier rival and was countering cleanly, superbly, skillfully, accurately the while for half of the round or so. Then Dempsey, plunging in recklessly, charging bull-like, furiously and with utter contempt for the blows of the champion, suddenly lashed a long, wicked left to the jaw with the power of old. This he followed with a right to the jaw, the old "iron Mike" as deadly as ever, and quickly drove another left hook to the jaw, under which Tunney toppled like a falling tree, hitting the canvas with a solid thud near Dempsey's corner, his hand reaching blindly for a helping rope which somehow or other refused to be within clutching distance.

'Then Dempsey made his mistake, an error which, I believe, cost him the title he values so highly. The knockdown brought the knockdown timekeeper Paul Beeler to his feet automatically, watch in hand, eyes glued to the ticking seconds as he bawled "one" before he looked upon the scene in the ring. There he saw Dempsey in his own corner, directly above the prostrate, brain-numbed Tunney, sitting there looking foolishly serious, his hand finally resting on the middle ring strand. Beeler's count stopped. Referee Barry never started one. Dempsey stood there, arms akimbo on the top ropes of the ring, watching his rival, his expression saying more than words, "Get up and I'll knock you down again, this time for keeps." Dempsey had no eyes for Referee Barry who was waving frantically for the former titleholder to run to a neutral corner, even as he kept an eye on the fallen Tunney.

'Finally Dempsey took notice of the referee's frantic motions. He was galvanised into action and sped hurriedly across the ring to a neutral corner, away from Tunney. But three or four, or possibly five precious seconds had elapsed before Dempsey realised at all what he should do. In that fleeting time of the watch Tunney got the advantage. No count was proceeding over him, and quickly his senses were returning. When referee Barry started counting with Timekeeper Beeler, Tunney was in a state of mental revival where he could keep count with the tolling seconds, and did, as his moving lips revealed. It seemed an eternity between each downward sweep of the arm of Referee Barry and the steady pounding of the fist of Timekeeper Beeler. Seconds are like that in a crisis, and here was one if ever one existed.

'Tunney's senses came back to him. He got to his feet with the assistance of the ring ropes and with visible effort at the count of nine. He was groggy, stung, shaken, his head was whirling, but Dempsey was wild in this crisis, a floundering, plodding man-killer, as Tunney, back pedalling for dear life, took to full flight, beating an orderly, steady retreat with only light counter moves in the face of the plunging, desperate, vicious Dempsey, aroused now for the kill.

'Dempsey plodded on so futilely and ineffectively that he tired from his own exertions. The former champion stopped dead in his tracks in mid-ring and with a smile spreading over his scowling face, motioned disgustedly, daringly, for Tunney to come on and fight. But Tunney was playing his own game and it was a winning game. After motioning Tunney in, Dempsey backed the champion into the ropes again and lunged forward savagely with a left and right to the jaw. But Tunney clinched under the blows and held Dempsey for dear life, and Dempsey never again got the chance that round to follow his advantage. As the bell sounded, Dempsey was warned for striking low with a left for the body.'

This was how Nat Fleischer recorded what happened after Tunney was sent to the canvas: 'Referee Barry raised his hand and was on the verge of starting the count when he noticed that Dempsey was in his own corner, which happened to be almost on top of Tunney. It was then that Barry rushed over to Dempsey, grasped him by the arm and urged him to go to a neutral corner. This order Dempsey failed to obey and the penalty followed. It was a command that could be plainly heard at ringside and was heard by me, for I was sitting in the third row of the press box just in front of where Tunney went down. Referee Barry said to Dempsey, "Go to a neutral corner, Jack." "I stay here," snapped Dempsey, scowling. Tunney was on the floor exactly thirteen seconds, which, with the one second final count as he arose, made the full count fourteen seconds. This was the official announcement of Paul Beeler, the official knockdown timekeeper. I have always felt that Gene Tunney was not in a helpless condition and that he could have arisen any time after the first four seconds and then it is problematical whether Dempsey could have put him away.'

In the *New York World,* Hype Igoe wrote, 'He was outboxing Jack. Dempsey had some tricky little shuffles away from Tunney's lunging left, but when Tunney settled down to finer boxing, Dempsey became a mark. Until the seventh round. Then a thunderbolt came out of the sky. Tunney went into the ropes sideways and seemed stung. Few realised he had been badly hurt. But Dempsey knew.'

In Tunney's corner, Billy Gibson was having fits at the sight of his champion on the deck. Chief second Jimmy Bronson remembered, 'Dempsey caught Tunney at the ropes and nailed him with a left hook. It was a savage punch and it took effect. Jack was probably the first to know it because he immediately followed up with a barrage, eight punches in a row, I counted them. Dempsey delivered the last of these and was standing over Tunney as Gene plumped on to his haunches . . . When Tunney got up he was clear as a bell. And Dempsey couldn't do much with a clear-headed Tunney at any time.'

Grantland Rice was ringside for the *New York Herald.* 'The first six rounds were a repetition of the Philadelphia fight. Tunney boxed beautifully, his straight left jab and combinations jarring Dempsey but not hurting him particularly. I was thinking of my overnight lead in the seventh when, lo and behold, Dempsey landed a right cross over Tunney's left lead. It landed like a bomb on the left side of Tunney's jaw. The lights in Tunney's mind flickered as a second right to the jaw knocked him into the ropes.

'As Tunney came off the ropes, clearly dazed, Jack caught him with a short and crucifying left hook, then a right, a left and a right. Tunney was down on the canvas, his left hand clutching the middle rope near one corner. Dempsey landed six or seven punches. Had Tunney enjoyed anything less than one hundred per cent physical condition, he would have been out at the count of twenty, or thirty. In the space of two seconds, Soldier Field became a braying bedlam. How many seconds elapsed between the time Tunney fell and Dempsey reached that far corner I'll never know. I do know that when Barry started his count and reached seven, Tunney was on one knee, listening attentively, and was up at nine. A tiger flew at Tunney. But Gene, already in almost complete command of his faculties, back-pedalled and circled out of range until his head had completely cleared. That was Dempsey's last chance, the only round of the ten that I could score for him.'

Suddenly in that seventh round, Jack Dempsey was the fighter one hundred thousand people had paid almost $3 million to see in action. He was the fighter sportswriter Trevor Wignall described as, 'the savage, wicked, punishment-loving, vindictive, terrorist Dempsey of the ring and the camps. As a Driscoll he could not keep himself warm. He was a slugger, a trip-hammer hurler of cruel crushing punches, and he would not have won so frequently if also he had not been a sadist. I washed him out as a boxer, but I will take the stand any day to swear that he has never had a superior as a smashing puncher.

'He would have won if he had displayed more intelligence at a critical moment. He had been the champion for seven years, and it was in the seventh round that he crashed in the seven punches that deposited Tunney on his buttocks with one semi-paralysed leg stuck up in the air. I was in the first working press row, next to the timekeeper, and with my elbows on the shelf of the ring, so that I was magnificently placed to see what happened. I am prepared to swear that for seven or eight seconds he was incapable of movement. During those seconds he was either gazing dazedly at the canvas or, apparently, straight into my face. Dempsey had frittered away four seconds by refusing to obey the commands of Dave Barry, the referee. It is the disposition now to blame Barry for the fourteen seconds count. There is no justification for the charges made against him. He knew, and Dempsey and Tunney knew, that in the event of a knockdown, the man on his feet was obliged to retire to a neutral corner.'

Paul Gallico of the *New York Daily News*: 'The night Jack Dempsey had Gene Tunney on the deck I was there. I remember the dazed expression that came into Tunney's face as Dempsey slugged him with both hands over the ropes to the right of where I was sitting, and the film that clouded his eyes as he sank slowly to the ring floor, one leg crumpled beneath him. How could I forget it? We were trying something new that year, something that had never been tried before at a big prize-fight, a direct telephone connection between the working press section at ringside and the composing room of a great metropolitan tabloid newspaper. Cost a pretty penny, too. But, there we were, I at ringside in Chicago, a rewrite man in New York, and our own private telephone line between us.

'It started early in the seventh round with a sweeping left hook that Dempsey threw from the floor, knocking Tunney back into the ropes. It did more than knock him, it befuddled him, and Dempsey knew it. Dempsey was on him like a panther, slugging, hooking, crossing, left-right, left-right, every punch landing on Tunney's unprotected chin, causing his arms to drop and 105,000 souls to scream out of the darkness for the kill. So Dempsey fanned him good, Tunney performing that slow fall to the floor, and Gallico, the boy editor, screamed into his telephone mouthpiece in a voice that had gone considerably falsetto from excitement, "Tunney is down from a series of lefts and rights to the head, for a count of . . ." I stripped an earphone to pick up the count. Barry's arm fell and so help me he was saying "one" again. From there, he counted up to nine, at which point Tunney got off the floor. It did seem to me as though I couldn't have had all that intimate conversation with Nicholas in less than one second.

'When the round was over, someone tapped me on the shoulder and I turned. There was a little man sitting there. He had graying hair, a gnarled ear, and a seamy face. He was holding one of those large, split-second stopwatches with a dial like Big Ben, and he was looking at it with bewilderment. He said, "Hey, whadd'ya know about this? There's somethin' funny. I hit it when he went down and stopped it when he got up." The hand showed that 14.5 seconds had elapsed. The little man and I stared at the watch. It kind of hypnotised us, because, as we both knew very well, if a stricken fighter isn't on his feet inside of ten seconds he is presumed to be out, napoo, finished for the evening. I asked the little man who he was. He told me his name was Battling Nelson. You may take this as the firm belief of this eye-witness: had Dempsey immediately gone to the far corner, permitting the count to proceed as it had started, Gene Tunney would never have gotten up off the floor inside of ten seconds. And if by some miracle Tunney had managed to haul himself aloft by "nine," Dempsey would have pickled him. Tunney won going away. He outpointed Dempsey in the first six rounds. In the eighth he knocked Jack off his pins with a straight right. And in the ninth and tenth, with Dempsey exhausted from the bitter, fruitless chase in that heart-stopping seventh, Tunney gave him a solid thrashing. When the fight was over, and ever after, Jack Dempsey was silent. *He* knew who was to blame for the Long Count.'

In *A Man Must Fight*, Tunney recalled, 'In the seventh round, after some fifty seconds of jabbing, feinting and missing, I led a straight left which Dempsey crossed with a long right. This hit me high. I realised it. So did Dempsey. I danced back a step or two. Dempsey followed. With a long, left swinging hook, he hit me on the right side of the chin. It was a savage punch and shook me up. Suddenly a right followed which I partially rode. My back was to the ropes. I leaned against them quite relaxed. Rebounding with a spring I raised my guard. Dempsey slipped in with another left hook that got inside my guard and hit me as I sprang from the ropes. This blow had the added force of catching me as I hurled myself forward. It landed again on the right side of the chin. It was a terrific blow.

'I began sagging against the ropes. It was the fourth he had landed in quick succession. As I slowly crumpled to the canvas, being partially supported and held up by the ropes, he followed with a hard right, a left, and another right. By the time the last right landed, I was just short of sitting on the canvas. Seven vicious punches in all. I have no recollection of the last three. This was the first time in my life I had ever been knocked down.'

In his autobiography, Dempsey recalled, 'Round seven was the round that made the fight, the round I shall never forget. You don't forget any second of something you waited seventeen rounds for, ten through the first fight and now seven in the second fight. It was my first good shot at Gene. What I remember is that I got to him with a pretty good right, and then I hit him with a real good left hook. He started to go. I hit him seven times while he was going down, hit him with all the punches I had been trying to hit him with in the ring and in my sleep for the past year. I thought he was finished. I forgot the rules. I lost my head and couldn't move as Referee Barry shouted, "Get to a neutral corner." I stayed put. I was the jungle fighter so completely set in my ways I couldn't accept new conditions. I was used to standing over my opponents to make sure that when I pounded them down, they stayed down. The count stopped and started again at one. At nine, Tunney was up.

'He then pedalled around the ring, keeping out of my exhausted reach. In the eighth round Tunney was himself and I was floored. Round nine saw me staggering to the ropes again, a battered, bloody mess. I could taste my warm blood and my eye throbbed with pain. When the bell finally sounded and Gene Tunney was again proclaimed champion, I realised that the time had come to hang up my gloves and leave the ring. I was thirty-two years old, but I felt a hell of a lot older. Many people, for so many years after that, figured I was robbed. I don't think I was. Maybe Gene could have gotten up. Maybe not. Everything happens for the best.'

Although Jimmy Bronson, as Tunney's chief second, would claim years later in a magazine interview that it was he who insisted on the strict interpretation and enforcement of the knockdown rule in the Chicago fight, all accounts of the Battle of the Long Count, as it became known, state that it was Dempsey's man, Leo P Flynn, who raised this point along with Bill Duffy in their meetings with the Boxing Commission. Why would they do that? There was more likelihood of their man knocking Tunney down than of Tunney flooring Dempsey. In most of the Mauler's big fights, and no doubt in a lot of his fights before he won the title, he was a wild man once he decked an opponent, standing over them and belting them again as soon as any part of their body cleared the canvas.

Run a film of Dempsey's title-winning fight with the giant Jess Willard in Toledo in 1919. On at least two occasions after sending Willard to the canvas, Dempsey stood right behind him and as soon as Willard began to straighten up and his gloves left the canvas, Dempsey struck with a savage right to the unseeing head of the champion to send him down again. At one point, Willard hauled himself up by the ropes and was standing there, bent over, both hands holding on to the ropes, when Dempsey attacked again. In his thrilling encounter with Luis Angel Firpo, with the Argentine giant down seven times in the first round, Dempsey was again seen to slug him as soon as his gloves came off the floor. That was Dempsey's style, the way he fought, from the hobo camps to the championship of the world. So why take the trouble to highlight a rule that would work against their man in a fight he had to win?

'Application of such a rule could only hurt Dempsey, who was part tiger, part wildcat and all killer,' wrote *New York Times* columnist Arthur Daley.

'Had not Dempsey's chief of staff, Leo P Flynn, insisted in a pre-fight meeting with the Boxing Commission and Tunney's advisers that the neutral corner rule be strictly enforced, Jack might have regained his crown,' wrote editor Nat Fleischer in a 1957 issue of *The Ring*. 'Due to the fuss made over the farthest corner rule, which at the time was not in the rules of the Illinois Commission, Leo P Flynn and Bill Duffy, Dempsey's advisers, had the boxing board incorporate it in their regulations the day before the Chicago bout.'

Recalling that seventh round, referee Dave Barry said, 'My impression of Tunney after he had been knocked down was that he had regained his senses in three or four seconds, and even had Dempsey immediately retired to a neutral corner, Tunney would have been able to rise in good shape before the final count. I think it was a great fight and there is no doubt about who won it.'

24

Breaking the Rock

The day after the Chicago fight, Eddie Sullivan and Jimmy Eagleton, two of Tunney's friends, were at the station to catch their train for New York City. Al Capone was there, seeing some of his pals off, and he said to Sullivan and Eagleton, 'I lost forty-five grand on the fight, but I don't give a damn because Tunney is from New York. Before the fight I heard Tunney was up in his training camp with a lot of lavender boys in golf clothes and that they did not know what it was all about. So I says this to the guys who told me to go and bet as much as I wanted on Dempsey and that everything was okay.

'One of these guys tells me, "They're all saps. They gotta couple of college guys up there with them running the camp. Tunney's too busy wid his books. He's a mug, I tell yer!" So against me best judgement I bet against Tunney. At five o'clock I had word that the Commission had switched the referee. I did not have time to get off, but what the hell! These mugs in Chicago think New Yorkers are all suckers. Why, I came out here from Brooklyn seven years ago and they ain't made a sucker of me yet.'

Those two fights between Dempsey and Tunney were witnessed by a total of 225,700 people who willingly paid almost four million dollars for the privilege. The live gate receipts for the two fights added up to a staggering $3,848,393. No wonder Tex Rickard wanted to put them back in the ring together. A third fight would break the bank, especially after the

250

Long Count controversy. But it takes two to tango. Tunney was more than willing to give Dempsey a second crack at his old title, provided the contest was scheduled for fifteen rounds. At a meeting in New York, Rickard was authorised to offer Dempsey what would have been the largest purse ever paid to a title challenger up to that time. But the telegram received by Rickard from Dempsey stated simply, 'Count me out, Tex!'

'Tex was eager for a third battle,' recalled Dempsey in his autobiography, 'insisting he could get me a million-dollar guarantee as well, but I wasn't interested. I was afraid for my eye, having been told that if it was damaged again, it would lead to a permanent impairment and maybe blindness.'

The old champion also had a new respect for his conqueror. A few months after the Battle of the Long Count, Dempsey was travelling on a train from Miami to New York and was talking with his companions about that fight. Recalling the seventh round, he said, 'The right-hand punch under the heart that Tunney hit me with when he got off the floor was the hardest blow I have ever received. It was not a question in my mind of being knocked out. I thought I was going to die. I could not get my breath. A second rubbed away the congestion around my heart when I came back to my corner, but for that I would not have been able to come out for the eighth round.'

Tex Rickard had a new champion now, and in Gene Tunney boxing had its first million-dollar fighter. For the Chicago fight, Tunney's purse amounted to $990,445.54. At Tunney's request, Rickard wrote him a cheque for $1 million and Tunney gave the promoter his cheque for the difference of $9,554.46. In retirement, that suitably framed cancelled cheque was one of Tunney's proudest possessions.

With Dempsey out of the picture, Rickard found that his cupboard was somewhat bare of heavyweight contenders good enough to fill Yankee Stadium in a title bout with Tunney for that summer of 1928. On his best form Jack Sharkey was probably the pick of the crop, followed by Tom Heeney of New Zealand, Johnny Risko of Cleveland, and former light-heavyweight champion Jack Delaney. So Rickard staged a series of elimination bouts in Madison Square Garden to find a challenger for his new champion.

In a newspaper interview in January 1928, Rickard declared, 'There is no denying that Tunney is not only a champion, but a great champion. I believe that he is one of the greatest champions the class has seen. Any man who saw Dempsey make the most desperate effort of his entire career and send Tunney down, and then saw Tunney come out of this crisis and fight back until he hurt his man, must admit that in Gene Tunney the American ring has developed another outstanding exponent of science, power, gameness, and sportsmanship.'

A week after Tunney beat Dempsey in Chicago, Rickard had Tom Heeney against Jim Maloney in the Garden, with the winner to go into the elimination series. The Boston Irishman was a favourite going in but Heeney set the ring alight when he forced Maloney to the ropes, smashed a left hook to the body and a right to the jaw, then shoved Maloney out of a clinch. Two more crushing rights to the jaw sent Maloney down and out. Time: 1.17 of round one! A month later the rugged New Zealander was in Detroit to punch Johnny Risko around for ten rounds and rack up a decision.

In January Rickard had Heeney back in the Garden with Jack Sharkey and Rickard let it be known that if Sharkey looked good in this one he would fight Tunney for the title in June. The Boston Gob went into the fight a 3–1 favourite but at the end of twelve rounds the officials came up with a draw. The crowd of almost eighteen thousand gave the verdict a mixed reception, with many thinking Sharkey had won, as did many of the ringside press. Dawson reported for the *New York Times* that, 'Sharkey, despite the decision, beat Heeney in a battle that was savagely and bitterly, if surprisingly disappointingly, fought.'

'Heeney was like a stone wall,' Sharkey would later recall. 'You hit one of these guys flush on the lug and he keeps coming at you and you say to yourself, "How do I get out of this ring, where's the exit, the hell with trying to knock him out, I'm just busting my hands." Heeney could take a punch.'

Rickard gave Sharkey a second chance a couple of months later when he put him in the Garden ring with Johnny Risko, but the erratic ex-sailor blew it when the Cleveland Rubber Man came out with a split decision after fifteen rounds. 'I had beaten Johnny before and I may have been playing the big shot and got beat,' Sharkey said. 'Risko was a terrific body puncher and kept coming at you like a buzz-saw. We had Jimmy Johnston in my corner. We were having a lot of trouble with the New York press and we thought this contact would help. We lost the fight and the press stayed the same.'

Heeney was fighting like a man inspired and a capacity crowd saw him whip the fancied Jack Delaney over fifteen rounds in the Garden. Sharkey bounced back to knock out Delaney inside a round and Rickard had him pencilled in for the Tunney fight. But Tunney had other ideas. He already had a contract guaranteeing him $525,000 for his next fight and he was determined to hold the promoter to it. He was also determined to quit the ring after this next fight.

'There's only Sharkey and Heeney,' lamented Rickard, 'so I guess it'll have to be Jack. He's unreliable, but he's got more colour than the other fella, and the fans like to see Jack licked.'

'I'll take Heeney,' said Tunney. 'At least I'll get a fair fight. With Sharkey anything can happen. He can go berserk, hit me low and get away with it. He could only get a draw with Heeney, so that makes them even. The choice is mine, and I'll take Heeney.'

Against his better judgement, Rickard called manager Charley Harvey to tell him Heeney's dream had come true. 'The fight goes on at the Yankee Stadium on 26 July,' said Rickard, 'and your man is on a guarantee of a hundred grand flat. You got two months to get him ready and play your part in the ballyhoo, because you know as well as I do that this fight will want some selling.'

Sports editor of the *New York Daily News* Paul Gallico highlighted this a few months later in a magazine piece. 'The battlers moved into camp some seven weeks before the scheduled date of the fight,' he wrote 'and the nearest thing to a newspaperman they saw were the local correspondents with buckteeth and the inevitable pencil and pad. Dempsey would have been accompanied to camp by fifteen boxing writers, twelve feature men, two sob sisters, thirty photographers, and six office boys to bring back plates, and his doings would have been recorded at length, daily. It was the first of July before the stately *New York Times* condescended to print dispatches from the two camps, and the *News*, peppiest of the younger journalistic set, waited until eighteen days before the fight to assign regular correspondents to the camp.'

This fight really was a dream come true for Tom Heeney. The thirty-year-old New Zealander had left England after a disappointing stay and sailed to New York merely to pick up enough money to pay his fare back home. Charley Harvey met him at the pier and soon arranged a gym workout at the old St Nick's gym on 66th Street. It was the worst gym trial you ever saw, but Harvey got him a prelim in the Garden, where the matchmaker owed him a favour, and Heeney stopped Charley Anderson in nine rounds to begin his fairy-tale ride to a title shot. Heeney was an unlikely candidate for the champion's role, standing just five feet nine tall, with short arms and a powerful body, but he had a rugged two-fisted style made for close-quarter fighting. It was his great toughness, clean living, and immense reserves of stamina that enabled him to trade punches with the best in the business and that prompted Broadway columnist Damon Runyon to label him 'The Hard Rock From Down Under'.

With just over a week to go, Rickard, desperate for publicity, called on members of what he called his 'Six Hundred Millionaires Club', the stockbrokers and financiers who had bankrolled the building of Madison Square Garden. He loaded a party of these gentlemen on to his yacht, *Maxine*, and, along with several newspapermen, set sail down the coast for Heeney's camp at Fair Haven, New Jersey. The contender was alerted to the impending visit and was loosening up in the training ring, where a young light-heavyweight was shadow-boxing. A few reporters lounged at ringside trying to look interested. They perked up somewhat when Heeney and the kid pulled on the sparring gloves and started moving around.

'Heeney was a rushing fighter,' recalled one of the writers. 'He tore in and slammed away furiously. The stripling stood him off, staying on the defence, blocking and slipping the hardest punches. Once in a while he would clinch and look around, as if expecting Rickard's party to come in, but nobody came. By this time Heeney was getting warmed up and evidently trying to knock the lad out. He would lunge and miss, and come back madder than ever. He let fly terrific swings that the kid barely avoided. You could see the young fellow's ears getting red, too, he didn't feel like taking everything and giving nothing back. Heeney ran in with a wild right swing. The boy stepped inside it with a straight right to the chin. Heeney stumbled and fell forward, glassy-eyed. His sparmate, suddenly realising the importance of his mistake, grabbed Heeney under the arms and waltzed him around until his knees would hold him up. Then the two men separated and exchanged light taps until the end of the round. All of a sudden there was a great bustle at the gate. In poured the guests from the yacht. Rickard hustled up to the first row, and greeted reporters with the question, "Well, what do y' think of him? How does he look?"

'The advance sale had been very light and Tex was anxious for Heeney to make a big impression. Imagine his horror when a loud-voiced gent in row one bawled out, "Hi, ya, Tex! Why din'cha get here in time to see yer man almost get knocked out?" "What d'ya mean?" faltered Tex. "Why, the training is all over. His sparring partner just battered him around the ring." The opponent who had Tom hanging on from a right to the chin was Phil Messurio. The story got around. The fight didn't draw.'

The fight did draw a crowd of 45,890 boxing fans to the Yankee Stadium that July evening to see Tunney's last fight, and his greatest. 'Tunney never had shown himself such a finished fighter as in that match,' wrote Nat Fleischer. 'He possessed everything in the world, speed, accuracy in hitting, splendid blocking, fine countering and perfect calculation in every movement. In addition, he carried that day a harder punch than he had ever before placed on view. There was the master in Tunney. He jabbed when forced in a corner, he hooked with telling effect when Tom tried infighting. He uppercut with frequency when at close range, he smashed with terrific rights to the jaw after forcing Tom into an opening and he let loose some terrible lefts to the heart when Tom worked his way towards him.

'True, he took quite a few telling blows in return in the early rounds, two of which, one in the third and one in the fourth, almost upset Gene, but Tunney was the master throughout. Not even a Jack Dempsey could have given a finer exhibition of the manly art than did Gene. And the Stadium gathering appreciated it. Proof of the fact lies in the wonderful change of attitude of the fans towards Gene. No longer did the fickle ones hiss and boo the Pride of New York. They cheered and cheered, for Gene had vindicated himself at least in the eyes of those whose hero worship goes only to the fighting man.'

The Hard Rock was first to enter the ring, dressed in a Maori robe with the motto, 'Be strong, be active, be brave', which had been sent to him by the widow of Maori parliamentarian Sir James Carroll. That summer night in New York, thousands of miles from his native New Zealand, Tom Heeney was strong, active and brave as he made his bid for the heavyweight championship of the world. In that first round, Heeney landed three heavy rights to Tunney's jaw before Tunney scored left and right to the jaw, then another powerful left, and they were slugging away at the bell. Heeney forced the action in round two; his arms were too short to box Tunney, but the champion jabbed him off and landed a left and right at the bell.

'Absolutely unawed by the power in Tunney's newly found right,' wrote one scribe of round three, 'Heeney plodded into a right-handed exchange with the titleholder. Tom dropped his guard and stood before the champion, hands ready and daring another exchange. Gene accommodated him and they cracked lefts and rights, short vicious pokes that stung jaw and cheek. Gene didn't seem to like that and he bounced back on defence, spearing the challenger with a succession of lefts as Tom stalked after him. Tunney slipped as Heeney swept a right hook to his head and nearly fell, but came back to firmer footing, without having been down and unhurt. Heeney slugged viciously at the champion's head while Tunney met his attack with solid left hooks to the body.'

In the fourth round, the crowd was behind the gritty challenger as he pressed forward and whipped a short left and right to Tunney's chin. But Tunney came back with two heavy rights to Heeney's jaw and rocked his head back with a sizzling left hook. A thudding right to the head made Heeney blink and Tunney, sensing he was getting on top of his man, ripped two crushing rights to the heart. Yet this tough man from Down Under came tearing back into the champion and Tunney was glad to hear the bell.

In the fifth round Heeney was bleeding from a cut under his chin and from his nose, and a smashing right to the heart did him no good at all. Tunney boxed his man wisely now – there was still danger in the rugged challenger if he could break through the champ's defence. The sixth round was a big one for Tunney as he hammered his game rival with lefts and rights, and a heavy right to the jaw brought a roar from the crowd. Tunney was again well on top in the seventh round, avoiding Heeney's rushes, jabbing his head back on his shoulders, smashing rights into the body, under the heart, dealing uppercuts; all going in and not much coming back.

'In the eighth round,' wrote Nat Fleischer, 'the champion drove a right to the challenger's left eye that rendered him partly blind. The blow made a cut in the lid and drove the lashes into the eyeball. Instantly Tom's gloves went up to his face and he staggered away like a blind man groping about in a strange room. Tunney could have followed up his advantage and delivered the telling blow. Instead, as the challenger moved away, helpless for the finishing smash, Gene, standing with right cocked for the delivery, deliberately withheld the blow, stepped back and looked at the referee to see if he would halt proceedings. When ordered to fight on, Gene waited until Tom was in a position to protect himself before letting loose a right. That was the act of a gentleman, a sportsman.

'Throughout the fight the champion kept driving a right to the heart that was as perfect a piece of workmanship as ever was seen in a ring. And it was one of these rights to the heart that almost ended Heeney in the tenth. Tunney put so much power behind it, that when it landed, Heeney was shocked almost dead in his tracks. As he stiffened, and momentarily stood erect, a pretty left hook shot to the point of the chin and the right crashed to the same spot almost in the same motion and down went Tom in a heap. He was flat on his back like a wax dummy. There he lay at full length, inanimate flesh and blood and bone, seemingly lifeless except for the heaving of his hairy chest and an odd quivering of the lips and nostrils. Had the bell not sounded at the count of two, the bout would have ended there and then.'

It was all over in round eleven as referee Eddie Forbes stopped the fight with eight seconds left. In *A Farewell to Sport*, Paul Gallico wrote, 'I remember particularly one kindly old gentleman, a veteran fight manager by the name of Charley Harvey. He was a mild, sweet-looking old soul with innocent blue eyes and a walrus moustache. And I watched this man one night pick his half-conscious fighter up and shove him out to destruction. The fighter was Tom Heeney and his destroyer was Gene Tunney, then heavyweight champion of the world. Harvey had neither the courage nor the decency to stop that fight at the end of the tenth round.'

Damon Runyon reported, 'A knife couldn't slice up a human being's face more than Gene Tunney's left hand slashed poor Tom Heeney's corrugated countenance up at the Yankee Stadium tonight . . . It was all just about as expected, the man from New Zealand wading in bravely to certain destruction. Blood dripping from his nose, blood dripping from cuts along the creases of his strangely old-looking face. One eye partly closed. Woefully outclassed in the boxing. Yes, it was just about as expected. But no one thought a fist could hash up the leathery skin of the tough old fellow from the Antipodes to such an extent that it would be mercy to halt the affair before some of the ladies in the crowd became ill. Heeney's crude, clumsy walk-in style fitted the masterly boxing of the heavyweight champion as neatly as one of the gloves on Tunney's hand. Carefully erect, his thin nostrils compressed, his hands performing Queensberry magic before the bewildered eyes of the hairy-chested Heeney.'

For Gene Tunney, his farewell to the professional ring was an artistic success. For promoter Tex Rickard and his Madison Square Garden backers, the fight was a financial flop. The net receipts amounted to $521,422 with film and radio bringing another $35,000 into the pot for a total of $556,422. But the expenses added up to $712,142, leaving a deficit of $155,719. For the first time since the Dempsey–Willard fight of 1919, Rickard lost money on a major venture, and he promptly issued a statement to the press in which he held the champion responsible for the loss.

'That the Tunney–Heeney fight proved a financial failure', the statement read in part, 'was due to no fault of mine nor of the Garden's promotion forces. I blame Tunney for the flop . . . The trouble with that titular contest was that I was rushed into doing something that I didn't want to do. I never cared to stage a bout of such proportion in July, in the first place, and I urged Tunney not to press the matter . . . Tunney wanted an opponent and he wanted him in a hurry. Conditions were so pressing that Heeney was selected . . . Gene has had his fight and if he fights again, he will defend his title next year under my jurisdiction and I feel that if he enters the ring again, the champion will be as popular as any of his predecessors. It is my opinion that Tunney has come into his own as a fighter and if he retires, as some of the papers intimate, I think he will make a grave mistake.'

However, Rickard's hopes were shattered a few days later when he received a confidential message from Tunney stating that the Heeney contest was his last and that he had decided to retire as the undefeated heavyweight champion of the world.

25

This Was a Man!

'Before the Heeney match,' said Tunney, 'I became engaged to be married. I decided this would be my last ring contest. I had all the money I needed. I had not the slightest desire to continue fighting until my ears began to buzz. I wanted to settle down. I think I could have held my peak for another year or two, but I think I made the right decision. During the training period for this fight, I was completely free from annoyance and worry. The fight with Heeney, I believe, was the most skilful of my career. It was the most satisfactory, personally. Everything clicked in unison.'

Five days after cracking the Hard Rock From Down Under, Gene Tunney gave a luncheon at the Biltmore Hotel in New York, which was attended by sixty newspapermen and newspaper women, members of the New York State Athletic Commission, and friends of the champion, and shocked the assembly by formally announcing that he had fought his last fight. After Commissioner Muldoon had presented Tunney with *The Ring* magazine's Most Valuable Boxer Award, Tunney addressed the gathering, saying, 'This is indeed a great day for me. I have fought my way to the goal of my ambition and on the day of the announcement of my retirement, I am awarded this beautiful bronze by my friend Nat Fleischer, a trophy which, I am told, according to the points on which the winner has been judged, is emblematic of all that is good in the sport that I love. I became a professional fighter because I realised it afforded me the quickest way to earn a fortune. I have earned that fortune and now that I have it, I shall retire.'

In a 1950 article in *Sport* magazine, writer Ed Fitzgerald recalled, 'Gene was in love with the daughter of George Lauder Jnr, a nephew of Andrew Carnegie and a founder of the Carnegie steel empire. The lady, whose friends called her Polly, had not only beauty and high social position but millions of dollars as well. Yet Gene aspired to her, and won her. F E Barbour, the Lauder family secretary, might tell the inquisitive press haughtily that, "the report is too absurd to be dignified by an answer." But it was nonetheless true. Mrs Lauder made an official announcement of the engagement on 8 August 1928.'

A few days after the news broke, Tunney sailed for a vacation in Europe, visiting Ireland and England before joining American author Thornton Wilder for a walking tour of Germany, France and Spain. 'Ireland rolled out a rich, emerald green welcome mat for Gene,' wrote Fitzgerald. 'Ten thousand Celts gathered at the seaport of Kingstown to greet him at the quay and they do say that the state reception they tossed for him marked the first time that Eamonn de Valera and President William T Cosgrave ever drank from the same bottle.'

Tunney stayed in London long enough to visit the Prince of Wales at St James's Palace and ended his hike with Wilder in Rome, where he negotiated his way through a minefield of red tape laid down by church and state dignitaries to complete arrangements for his wedding in the Holy City. Back home in Greenwich, Connecticut, Miss Lauder packed her trousseau and awaited the call from Tunney. When it came, she sailed for Europe on the *Saturnia* and on 3 October Mary Josephine Lauder became the wife of James Joseph Tunney.

Tunney's prickly relationship with the press surfaced again, as related by Fitzgerald. 'At Gene's wedding in Rome, newspapermen and photographers were rigidly excluded from the ceremony. In retaliation the boys staged an ugly scene outside the hotel as Gene and his bride left for their honeymoon. Tunney had refused to allow any pictures to be taken of the ceremony and forbade the boys to photograph his wife as they entered the car. He threatened to break the camera of any photographer who tried to take her picture . . . Back in the States, the stories of the wedding were concerned more with the near-riot than with the clothes the bride wore, the details of the ceremony, or the honeymoon destination. Eventually the newspapers got off Tunney's back. Gene and his wife stayed in Europe for over a year and by the time they came home people had forgotten about the wedding fuss.'

In his insatiable appetite for literature, Tunney had developed a great admiration for George Bernard Shaw, and one of the highlights of the honeymoon was a meeting he and Polly had with Ireland's eccentric playwright. 'Mrs Tunney and I did go back to England in December of that year,' he would recall. 'We had been staying at a lovely resort island in the Adriatic named Brioni and from there I wrote Shaw to say that I planned a trip to Britain to present a trophy to the Royal Marines on behalf of the US Marine Corps. On our arrival in England we found a note from Mrs Shaw advising us of a luncheon she had arranged for us the following day. It was at this luncheon that we met for the first time.'

Out of that meeting grew a friendship that flourished for the next twenty years and the two exchanged letters on a regular basis, discussing everything from books to boxing, of which Shaw was quite a follower. Shaw's novel *Cashel Byron's Profession* was based on the prize ring, although Tunney did not like it and told Shaw as much. They remained friends despite that. In 1951 the editors of *Colliers* magazine asked New York businessman Curtis P Freshel, a friend of Shaw's for forty years, if he could shed some light on how Shaw really felt about the former champion boxer. Freshel produced a letter from Shaw stating, 'I have not been given to close personal friendships, as you know, and Gene Tunney is among the very few for whom I have established a warm affection. I enjoy his company as I have that of few men.'

Sportswriter Trevor Wignall remembered Tunney's visit to England that December. 'Shortly before Christmas of 1928 he journeyed to Portsmouth to present a cup, won in a football competition, to the Royal Marines. Tunney was himself an honorary captain in the US Marine Corps in which he had served during the war, but before he handed over the trophy he made this unexpected statement. "At this time I should like to ask of you the privilege to bow my head in silent prayer for the speedy recovery of your King." Captain James Joseph Tunney thereupon lowered his head, and every officer and man on parade followed his example. There were cynics who averred that Gene had taken advantage of a solemn occasion to be theatrical, but I was of the larger number who preferred to believe that on that bleak Saturday, when a nation was at the bedside of King George the Fifth, he magnificently said what everyone was hoping.' After their year in Europe, the Tunneys returned home to settle in Connecticut, but there were clouds on the horizon. Gene Tunney had reason to recall his visit to Dempsey's hotel the day after he took Dempsey's title. 'Gene,' Dempsey had said, 'your troubles are just beginning, whether you know it or not. Every time you turn around you'll find a process-server.'

'I was soon to learn that Dempsey was right,' recalled Tunney. 'At one time I had four lawsuits against me aggregating 2,150,000 dollars. The first three, two blackmailers and a bootlegger left the jurisdiction of the state after instituting proceedings. The fourth, a bookmaker, went to trial, and after hearing evidence for ten days the jury returned a verdict in my favour in twenty minutes. I am convinced that had the law firm of Chadbourne, Stanchfield, and Levy not taken over my affairs, the parasites would have left me penniless.'

The blackmailers referred to by Tunney were Mrs Katherine King Fogarty, a divorcee who filed a $500,000 breach of promise suit, claiming that Tunney had said he would marry her as soon as she got a divorce, and her former husband who also sued Tunney for allegedly enticing his wife away from him. The charges, which caused the former champion great embarrassment, were eventually dropped.

The bootlegger was Max 'Boo Boo' Hoff, the Philadelphia mob leader who filed a $350,000 lawsuit against Tunney, claiming he was owed twenty per cent of Tunney's earnings in championship fights. John Lardner, in his excellent book, *White Hopes and Other Tigers*, wrote, 'The Hoff story was, and remains a shadowy chapter in boxing history. Hoff's allegation seems to have been that five hours before the fight in Philadelphia, Gibson, Tunney's manager, alarmed by the thought that the fight might be stolen from Tunney, offered Hoff a percentage of the Tunney purse to use whatever mysterious influence he had to protect Tunney's interests. There was a conflicting sports-page rumour that Hoff undertook to send a doctor into the ring to award the fight to Tunney on a foul in case he was knocked down. Hoff said he had give $20,000 to Gibson to bind his end of the deal. The Hoff suit was dropped early in 1930 after Gibson, a material witness, had been declared mentally incompetent following a breakdown caused by the death of his wife.'

It was shortly after Tunney had given up his championship that Billy Gibson's life began to unravel. In 1930, aged 54, after a legal finding that the death of his wife had affected his sanity, Gibson was committed to an institution. Eventually released from the hospital, it was not until 1947 that he regained full control of his affairs. Six months later Gibson was found dead in his room at the Hotel Paris in Manhattan. What became of his considerable fortune remained a mystery that went with him to the grave as he left an estate valued at less than $1,000. Recalling the Hoff business, Paul Gallico would write, 'Scandal fogged Tunney at every turn on his way to the top, because boxing is a scandalous game, but somehow it never managed to hurt him and he always stepped clear of it. Just what protection Hoff was to have given him, or did give him, never developed, because when the bell rang for the first fight with Dempsey to begin, it turned out that it was Dempsey and not Tunney who needed protection . . . As a matter of fact, the only umbrella Tunney needed in Philadelphia that night would have been one to have kept off the rain which pelted down the half hour during which time he was battering Dempsey to a ruin.'

In November 1930 Gene Tunney was fighting again, this time in a Manhattan courtroom, defending himself against

Timothy J 'Big Tim' Mara, described as a sports promoter involved with football and horse racing, and also with gambling as a bookmaker. Mara was claiming half-a-million dollars' back pay, based on 10 per cent of Tunney's purse for fighting Dempsey in 1926 and 25 per cent of his earnings thereafter. He had proof that Tunney offered him the 25 per cent but was vague about what it was for. Tunney claimed that he had hired Mara to use his influence to get the first fight with Dempsey staged in New York. It will be remembered that the New York Commission was trying to force Dempsey to fight Harry Wills in New York, and that Tex Rickard finally took the fight to Philadelphia.

'An important and delicate point arose in the wording of the agreement,' wrote John Lardner. 'Tunney and Gibson wanted to have it stated in writing that Mara must deliver a Dempsey–Tunney match, not just anywhere, but in New York. But Mara got "New York" struck out of the document because, so a stenographer later testified, he felt it might embarrass him if the paper came to the knowledge of the boxing commission . . . The strength of Mara's case lay in the agreement and the personal letter signed by Tunney. The defence suggested, and the judge, in his charge, repeated the possibility that Mara had obtained the agreement by force of threats to kill the fight politically if he wasn't cut in. The jury found for Tunney. However, the Appellate Division reversed that verdict two years later holding that no proof had been offered that Mara used threats. In January 1933, Tunney settled the suit for $30,000, and Mara signed a release of all further claims.' It had taken some time, but Tunney finally escaped from the law courts for good.

In putting together a professional record of 83 contests, of which he won 61, lost one and drew one, with 19 No-Decision bouts and one No Contest, Gene Tunney had amassed over $2 million. Of that sum, $1,942,282 was earned during the two years in which he was heavyweight champion of the world, and he had married an heiress reputed to have been left a fortune close to fifty million dollars! Life was indeed looking sweet for the former shipping clerk from the working-class streets of

Greenwich Village in New York City. Just how sweet that life had become was described by Paul Gallico in a 1931 issue of *Liberty* magazine.

'He lives with Polly Lauder Tunney in a wandering white Colonial farmhouse perched on a glacial ridge in the woods many miles back of Stamford, Connecticut. If you have no one to show you the way you won't find it. It is a temporary residence. Behind it the ridge still rises, thickly wooded, and there, deep, sequestered, and high, the Tunneys will someday build their permanent house. From it they will look over the wood as it falls away to the blue Sound, and the Sound itself, and on clear days to a distant haze that will be Long Island.

'The habits of his lifetime have left him conscious of the care of his body. In the early morning he dons heavy shoes and a sweater and pads over the rough roads for four or five miles. Light and heavy bags hang suspended in the barn, and he works out on them, and I suppose his wife looks on half admiring and half amused. For the first time in his life, I suspect, he is enjoying himself. Fine days are given over to tramping the countryside, the woods and the farm country, with Polly.

'He still boxes for the fun of it with Eddie Eagan and Sam Pryor and Barney Gimbel, and any of his friends who want to put on the heavy gloves for a workout. He likes the sparring with Eagan best because he can let out a bit. A friend recently suggested he return to the ring. Tunney's fortune, wisely invested as it is, has suffered from the depression, as have all fortunes. He could pick up another million fighting the German, Max Schmeling. But he doesn't want it. He has enough. When Tunney quit the ring he said to me, "Paul, if I ever come back, so help me, you can send out the call for the looney wagon."'

Gene Tunney never did make a comeback to the boxing ring. He didn't have to. He went into business the way he went into the fight game, with determination and zeal and a burning desire to succeed in his new life. He was rich, intelligent, and he now moved in the right circles, made the right connections. He would become President of the Stamford Building Co Inc, Director of the First Stamford National Bank and Trust

Company, Director of the Industrial Bank of Commerce, New York City, Director of Eversharp Inc, Chicago, and Chairman of the Board of Denham Tyre and Rubber Company, Warren, Ohio. More and more he was asked to speak at various public functions and he served as chairman on an endless list of worthy causes.

Gene and Polly raised a fine family, three boys and a girl – Gene Lauder, John Varick, Jonathan Rowland and Joan Lauder. Like their father, the kids were big readers – Gene once gave Varick (he was never called John by his family and friends) $100 to memorise a poem – and they would carry on debates around the dinner table. The boys all had a great interest in sports and played tennis and football at prep school. Gene and Varick would go to Yale, while Jonathan, educated at Lawrenceville Prep, went into the Marine Corps, emulating his father. 'There'll be no professional boxing,' Gene was quick to point out in an interview. 'One champion in the family is enough as far as I'm concerned.'

Tunney was back in uniform when America entered the Second World War following the attack on Pearl Harbor. Intensely patriotic, Tunney was given a commission as a Lieutenant Commander in the US Navy and, on the suggestion of his friend, Jim Forrestal, then Undersecretary of the Navy, was placed in charge of a vast physical training programme that took him around half the world before he was honorably discharged in 1945 with the rank of Commander, having earned two citations.

Jack Dempsey had performed a similar task in the US Coastguard, which had been happy to have the ex-champ after the Army told him he was too old. Sworn in as a lieutenant, Jack served as Director of the Physical Training Programme and toured bases in the Far East, going ashore on Japanese-held Okinawa against the wishes of his superior officer. He was honorably discharged in October 1945 and awarded a citation for outstanding performance of duty. 'The applause at this stage of my life, was the most heartwarming I'd ever received,' said Dempsey.

'The Battle of the Long Count gave the two champions the tie that binds and each is appreciative of the effect it had on his future,' wrote *New York Times* columnist Arthur Daley. 'That's why they hold each other in such intense admiration. "Jack Dempsey is the greatest fighter who ever lived," says Gene, with almost Messianic fervour. The old Mauler doesn't have to return the compliment. Inference does it for him. If Dempsey is the greatest, Tunney still is the man who beat him.'

Renowned sportswriter Red Smith was at a sporting dinner attended by Gene and Polly Tunney. 'A guy at the table said to Polly, "Gene tickles me. He always named Dempsey as the greatest fighter of all time. But he never mentions who beat Dempsey twice." "Jack was getting along then," Mrs Tunney said. "He was on his way out." She was a generous lady,' added Smith.

Tunney and Dempsey. Dempsey and Tunney. Their names linked forever in boxing annals, they would become firm friends in the autumn of their lives. Tunney's son, John Varick, threw his hat into the political ring in California in 1964. 'Dempsey is the real champ,' said Tunney. 'When I told him that Varick was running for Congress, he said he'd go out and campaign for him. I said if he would go I would go too. Varick made the decision to run on his own. I advised him to build up his law practice first, and make some money, but he had made up his mind to go into politics.' 'The crowds at my rallies were the largest ever drawn in my district,' said young Tunney. 'Dad would lead off by introducing Jack. Then Dempsey would introduce me. I told the voters that after I finished speaking we would show fight pictures. They had to stay and listen to me to see the movies. They stayed.'

Dempsey recalled, 'Afterward, John thanked me profusely and sent me an album of the campaign and a pair of sterling silver donkey cufflinks. Deanna and I also attended President Johnson's inaugural at the Mayflower Hotel in Washington, where I was buttonholed by a very distinguished gentleman who said, "Mr Tunney, may I congratulate you on your fine son's winning the congressional seat." I thanked him very much.'

When John was elected to Congress, winning his House seat by 9,000 votes despite political opponent George Brown referring to him as 'the lightweight son of a heavyweight champ', his brother Gene was an investment broker in Los Angeles, and Jonathan was making movies for television in Hollywood. Joan Tunney was living in San Francisco with her husband, Lynn Carter Wilkinson, and his two children by a previous marriage.

On 30 March 1970, the idyllic life of the Tunney family was shattered by a tragedy that hit the old champ like a knockout punch. Gene's daughter, Joan, the baby of the family, was charged with the murder of her husband. The Wilkinsons had arrived in England a few months previously on an extended European tour and set up home in Chenies, a village near Amersham, Buckinghamshire. On Sunday 29 March, while Mr Wilkinson was asleep in bed, his wife suddenly attacked him with a chopper, killing him with several blows to the head.

Gene Tunney, then aged 72, was in an Arizona hospital recuperating from spinal surgery. He gave a statement to the press, saying that he and his wife were 'shocked and saddened by the death of their son-in-law. Like all parents, at a moment like this, we have a deep feeling of compassion and sorrow for our daughter, Joan, and a great desire to help her. Our eldest son, Gene, is on his way to London to be with her in her hour of great need, and to assist in whatever way possible.'

At the trial at the Old Bailey in London, Mrs Wilkinson's plea of guilty to manslaughter on the grounds of diminished responsibility was accepted. The court heard from a psychiatrist that she had suffered from schizophrenia for the past nine years and that there was a real danger of her committing further unprovoked homicidal attacks. On 12 June 1970, Mrs Joan Wilkinson, thirty-year-old daughter of former world heavyweight boxing champion Gene Tunney, was ordered to be detained in Broadmoor, the top-security hospital for the criminally insane.

In *When Boxing was a Jewish Sport*, Allen Bodner tells of Charlie Gellman, a former fighter who became president of the

Jewish Memorial Hospital in New York City, where he was able to help a lot of ex-fighters. 'We took care of Gene Tunney,' remembered Charlie. 'Gene Tunney in my opinion was the greatest heavyweight around. This guy had class. Ultimate gentleman, until he took to drinking later on. Which killed him. I used to take him to Jewish Memorial to dry him out. This clean liver. This terrific guy. Later he had a lot of trouble. You know, his daughter killed somebody, I guess her husband or whoever it might be. He himself married a rich woman by the name of Polly Lauder. They lived in Greenwich, Connecticut. It was not unusual for her to call me to tell me he fell, he opened his head. The chauffeur would drive him over to Jewish Memorial. He had started to become an alcoholic.'

Gene Tunney never did get over the heartache of the terrible tragedy that befell his daughter, and he took his sadness with him to the grave. In September 1978 Tunney was rushed into hospital for an operation. He was released in October, only to be readmitted after only two weeks, suffering from blood poisoning. The old champ died in his sleep at Greenwich Hospital on 7 November 1978, aged 81.

Tunney's old rival, Jack Dempsey, then aged 83, was himself gravely ill at the time and when reporters called at his home, his wife said she had not told him of Tunney's death. 'I will break the news to him very slowly,' she said. 'It will be a terrible shock for him. All his friends have already died.'

The old Mauler recovered and when he learned of Tunney's death, he told reporters, 'We were as inseparable as Siamese twins. As long as Gene was alive, I felt we shared a link with that wonderful period of the past. Now I feel all alone.' Dempsey would survive Tunney by five years.

★   ★   ★

Epitaph: Gene Tunney's beloved Shakespeare summed him up well in the final scene from *Julius Caesar*: '. . . the elements/So mix'd in him that Nature might stand up/And say to all the world, "This was a man!"'

Bibliography

Books

Barton, George A. *My Lifetime In Sports*. Minneapolis, Olympic Press, 1957.

Bodner, Allen. *When Boxing was a Jewish Sport*. Westport, CT, Praeger, 1997.

Breslin, Jimmy. *Damon Runyon, A Life*. London, Hodder & Stoughton, 1992.

Bromberg, Lester. *Boxing's Unforgettable Fights*. New York, Ronald Press, 1962.

Brown, Gene, (Editor). *The Complete Book of Boxing*. New York, Arno Press, 1980.

Butler, Hal. *Underdogs of Sport*. New York, Julian Messner, 1969.

Carpenter, Harry. *Masters of Boxing*. London, Heinemann, 1964.

Carpentier, Georges. *Carpentier by Himself*. London, Hutchinson & Co, 1955.

Corbett, Jim. *The Roar of the Crowd*. London/New York, G P Putnam's Sons, 1925.

Dempsey, Jack, with Barbara Piattelli. *Dempsey: The Autobiography*. London, W H Allen, 1977.

Dempsey, Jack, with Bob Considine and Bill Slocum. *Massacre in the Sun*. London, Heinemann, 1960.

Dempsey, Jack, with Myron M Stearns. *Round by Round, An Autobiography*. New York, McGraw-Hill Book Co, 1940.

Evensen, Bruce J. *When Dempsey Fought Tunney*. University of Tennessee Press, 1996.

Fair, James R. *Give Him to the Angels*. New York, Smith & Durrell, 1946.

Fleischer, Nat. *Black Dynamite, Vol V*. New York, The Ring, 1947.

Fleischer, Nat. *Gene Tunney, The Enigma of the Ring*. New York, The Ring, 1931.

Fleischer, Nat. *Jack Dempsey, the Idol of Fistiana*. New York, The Ring, 1936.

Fleischer, Nat. *50 Years at Ringside*. New York, Fleet Publishing, 1958.

Fleischer, Nat. *Nat Fleischer's Ring Record Book 1961*. New York, The Ring, 1961.

Fleischer, Nat. *The Heavyweight Championship*. New York, G P Putnam, 1949.

Fried, Ronald K. *Corner Men*. Four Walls Eight Windows, New York, 1991.

Gallico, Paul. *Farewell to Sport*. New York, Alfred A Knopf Inc, 1936.

Gallico, Paul. *The Golden People*. New York, Doubleday, 1965.

Giller, Norman, & Neil Duncanson. *Crown of Thorns*. London, Boxtree Ltd, 1992.

Heimer, Mel. *The Long Count*. New York, Atheneum, 1969.

Heinz, W C (Editor). *The Fireside Book of Boxing*. New York, Simon & Schuster, 1961.

Heller, Peter. *In This Corner*. London, Robson Books, 1975.

Lardner, John. *White Hopes and Other Tigers*. New York, J B Lippincott, 1947.

Morgan, Dan, with John McCallum. *Dumb Dan*. New York, Tedson Publishing, 1953.

Rice, Grantland. *The Tumult and the Shouting*. New York, A S Barnes, 1954.

Ritter, Lawrence S. *East Side, West Side*. New York, Total Sports, 1998.

Roberts, J B, and Skutt, A G. *The Boxing Register*. London, Robson Books, 1998.

Ross, Barney. *Fundamentals of Boxing*. Chicago, Ziff-Davis, 1942.

Tunney, Gene. *A Man Must Fight*. London, Jonathan Cape Ltd, 1933.

Tunney, Gene. *Arms For Living*. New York, Wilfred Funk Inc, 1941.

Van Every, Edward. *Gene Tunney, The Fighting Marine*. New York, Dell Publishing, 1927.

Van Every, Edward. *Muldoon, The Solid Man of Sport*. New York, Frederick A Stokes, 1929.

Ward, Arch. *Greatest Sport Stories from Chicago Tribune*. New York, A S Barnes, 1953.

Wignall, Trevor. *Almost Yesterday*. London, Hutchinson & Co, 1949.

Wignall, Trevor. *I Knew Them All*. London, Hutchinson & Co, 1938.

Magazines, Newspapers

The Ring, Boxing & Wrestling, Boxing Illustrated, International Boxing Digest, Boxing Pictorial, Popular Science, American Legion Monthly, Liberty, Look Magazine, Sport, Sport Life, Sports Illustrated, Time, Saturday Evening Post, West mag. (LA Times), Chicago American, The Atlantic Monthly, Colliers Magazine, National Police Gazette.

Index